RONALDO

James Mosley was born in Rochdale in 1971 and educated at the Hulme Grammar School in Oldham and the University of Liverpool. After initially setting out in corporate life in London, he decided to take several years off to travel and ultimately research and write this book. He has contributed to skysports.com, *FourFourTwo* magazine and *Golf Monthly* magazine. He currently shares his time between England and Brazil.

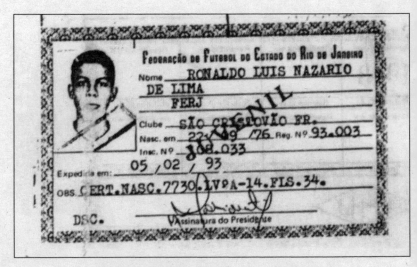

Ronaldo's 'player pass' from São Cristóvão FC.

RONALDO

THE JOURNEY OF A GENIUS

JAMES MOSLEY
Foreword by
Sir Bobby Robson

MAINSTREAM
PUBLISHING

EDINBURGH AND LONDON

This edition published 2008 for Index Books Ltd

This edition, 2007

Copyright © James Mosley, 2005
All rights reserved
The moral right of the author has been asserted

First published in Great Britain in 2005 by
MAINSTREAM PUBLISHING COMPANY
(EDINBURGH) LTD
7 Albany Street
Edinburgh EH1 3UG

ISBN 9781845961145

Reprinted, 2006

A catalogue record for this book is available
from the British Library

Typeset in Din and Times

Printed in Great Britain by
Cox & Wyman Ltd

ACKNOWLEDGEMENTS

There are many people who have helped and encouraged me during the research and writing of this book and I owe them a large debt of gratitude. I would also like to give special thanks to all the people who gave their time to answer my questions and provide valuable insights into Ronaldo's career, as well as providing further inspiration. In no particular order, these people are as follows:

In England: Sir Bobby Robson, Gary Lineker, Carlos Queiroz, Gerry Armstrong, Guillem Ballague, Yumi Ozawa at Nike, Diana Law at Manchester United, Jamie Aitchison, Chris Coyle, Jim King, Todd Littlewood, Daniel Maley, Mark Scorer, Maya Barber, Rachel Dulin at ITV Sport, João Castelo-Branco at ESPN, Sarah Haskey, Michael Henderson, Boris Johnson, Liam and Noel, Grant Best and David Fraser at Sky Sports, Matt Pardoe, all The Sheds, everyone at Swiss Cottage Tuesday FC, Johnny and Victoria Cockcroft, Lenny Webster, all at Midgley United FC and all at The Nelson.

In Scotland: a big thank you goes to my fantastic editor, Kevin O'Brien.

In Brazil: Rodrigo Paiva, Dr Lídio Toledo, Nilton Petrone, José Roberto Wright, Leonardo Ferreira at Cruzeiro Football Club, João Luiz Falcão Meirelles, Carlos Alberto Parreira Peixoto and Renato Alves de Campos at São Cristóvão Football Club, Antônio Carlos Napoleão at CBF, Flamengo Football Club, Raphael Roque at *Lance!*, Livia Faria at Globo TV, Fernando Gaspar, Alex Bellos, Norman Cook, Natalia Rostovska, Isabella Mello, Roberta Wright, everyone at

Botequim Informal, everyone at Jobí, Vanessa Bellamy, Fernanda Henriques, Marcelo Migueres, José Viana, Mauricio Viana, Marcelo Viana, everyone at the Maracanã Stadium, all my brilliant friends in the *cidade maravilhosa* and in particular my brother Richard and his wife, Marta.

In Eindhoven: Eric Lundtz and Roger Buxton.

In Milan: John Moretti and Luigi Fonseca.

In Madrid: Gustavo Gomez, Manuel Dominguez, Craig Frisby and Richard Howarth.

In Barcelona: Noemi Gascons at FC Barcelona, Rafael Delgado, José Dorado and José Gomez.

In Buenos Aires: Belen Pozzo.

Particular thanks go to Brendan Kemp at Getty Images.

I am especially grateful to Cassia Machado, in Rio, whose energy and activity were superb, and also to Jimmy Dowdall in Manchester for his inspiration, encouragement and unmatched sense of realism and advice throughout the compiling of this book.

CONTENTS

FOREWORD

Working with Ronaldo whilst at Barcelona remains one of the highlights of my many years involved in football. The Barcelona board and I took the decision to pursue the signature of Ronaldo from my old club, PSV Eindhoven, and although we had to break the world-record transfer fee to get him, he proved to be worth every penny. Some of the football he played that year for us is perhaps the most breathtakingly brilliant I have ever witnessed. Yes, we had our ups and downs together, which is inevitable, but his overall contribution was immense. Forty-five goals in forty-eight starts tells its own story. He joined a team already full of world superstars – Pep Guardiola, Luis Figo, Gica Popescu, Laurent Blanc – and made that team even better. I feel proud that it was me who put him on the world stage and that my faith in him was vindicated. He was as good a buy as I ever made in my career.

As a player, he had everything. As I've said on several occasions, he's the fastest thing I've ever seen running with the ball and his ability to come deep, turn and then burst forward towards goal, blasting through everything in his path and then scoring, remains one of the most thrilling sights in football. His speed and finishing ability with either foot is as good as you will see in any era. The goals he scored for us that season at Barcelona were of the highest quality. We bought him to put bums on seats and he certainly did that. The fans at Barcelona idolised him. He was sensational.

To work with, he was fantastic: always wanting to stay that extra bit longer in training and always with a smile on his face. I said at the time that if he managed to stay free of serious injury, he had every chance of becoming the best footballer ever. And I stand by that. As we all know, serious injury did visit him for lengthy spells, but to see him return and play again with such verve and passion made me personally very happy indeed. His comeback has been one of football's great stories and his personal redemption at the 2002 World Cup was something that anybody connected to football can only have taken great pleasure from.

Players of his ability come along perhaps once in a generation or so and with the combination of this heaven-sent talent and his wonderful personality, it is no wonder he is so supremely popular and respected in the world of football. He continues to deliver and enthral for Real Madrid and his native Brazil, and he is still very much at the pinnacle of the modern game. What's more, he plays football in the way it should be played: fairly and with a smile. As footballing superstars go, they don't come much better.

James has managed to encapsulate all that is unique about Ronaldo in this outstanding book. I strongly recommend it to you.

Sir Bobby Robson

PREFACE

Ronaldo first came to my attention during the World Cup in 1994. Although he didn't play in any games, the word was that he was a young Brazilian of prodigious gifts, so when a year later as an 18 year old he scored for Brazil at Wembley during the 1995 Umbro Cup, it was apparent he could be something pretty special. From that point, I have followed his career closely and with enthusiasm.

Some time ago, it came as a surprise to me that there were only two English-language books about him available, and from that surprise came my original idea to write this book and provide a thorough review of his career to date.

In writing a biography, one has to be wary of falling into the realms of hagiography, and I hope I have not done so. As big a fan of Ronaldo as I am, I have tried to give an objective view of his career to date, talk to those who've been close to his career, and also add some written colour to the stunning visual aesthetic of his many goals.

The aim of this book is to provide the definitive account of his football career. As well as his native Brazil, he has served four big European clubs with distinction, and from his initial steps into football in Brazil with São Cristóvão, he has remained a prolific goal-scorer of unerring consistency. At times, his play has been so devastating that people have been lost for words, and at Inter Milan they were sufficiently amazed by his play they christened him '*Il Fenomeno*'. Throughout his career, he has always played with a demeanour that betrays the simple fact that he loves football and the pleasure of scoring goals.

RONALDO

He has twice been transferred for the world-record fee and, as Nike's footballing figurehead, has become a globally recognised icon, featuring in many groundbreaking marketing campaigns that are often as memorable as his football. The combination of the Bosman ruling (allowing professional footballers in the EU a free transfer to any other EU club at the end of their contract) and Ronaldo's preternatural talent made the late 1990s a boom period for global football, but despite his vast wealth, adulation and traumatic experiences of injury, he has not become stuck in the carousing quicksand of drugs and booze like so many other superstars. He has visited abyssal depths of injury, which looked set to spell the end of his career in top-flight football, only to return to lift the World Cup and win the Golden Boot in 2002 – an amazing comeback. His achievement in doing this is one of sport's great stories and has become an inspiration for many.

At club level, he has won everything there is to win bar the UEFA Champions League, and, for Brazil, has remained their number-one striker since his debut. He is well on the way to breaking the Brazilian scoring record, the FIFA World Cup scoring record and Ferenc Puskas's international goal-scoring record of 83 goals. Barring further major injury, he should complete all three with ease.

Ronaldo has given me much pleasure over the years as a watching football fan. He remains a ruthlessly efficient machine in front of goal and his unfancied comeback after a horrific and unique knee injury is an example for all.

This is my first book and I sincerely hope you enjoy it.

James Mosley

CHAPTER 1

REDEMPTION – YOKOHAMA 2002

As Ronaldo left the Yokohama pitch just prior to the final whistle of the 2002 World Cup final, he completed a journey that even Hollywood couldn't have scripted. Within a few minutes, he had broken down under a surge of emotion, sobbing like a lost child, as the traumas of the previous four years could be contained no more. Few would begrudge him this moment. These weren't tears of despair, as famously drained by Paul Gascoigne, or those of a surly Diego Maradona during Italia '90, but those of a true sporting champion, a global icon, whose personal and sporting life had been dissected at will over the preceding years and his integrity and resilience questioned. He had visited abyssal depths of personal depression and self-doubt, but had answered all his critics and doubters, plus his own personal demons, in the most poetic way possible: World Cup-winning goals. If you were that Hollywood mogul working on a script for a story of a global footballing superstar, you wouldn't have needed to waste your time with fiction; fact would do just fine.

There have been many good sportsmen and there have been numerous great ones. But there are only a few sportsmen of real genius, who play a game not seen before. Sir Donald Bradman, Pelé, Michael Jordan or Tiger Woods, for example. Each has a gift beyond others, a gift to leave not only their mark on our benchmark tournaments but to leave it in a way that is indelibly etched in history. Each have taken their relevant sport to a new level and in the process have kept the record books busy.

Ronaldo had been quietly wooing the football world during his rise from Brazilian lower leagues to the Dutch First Division with PSV

Eindhoven. But it was his displays at Barcelona that shot him to the world's attention. These preternatural performances would take him to Inter Milan for a world-record fee and would make him top-billing at the World Cup in France '98. But Ronaldo's world had imploded on the afternoon of the final, a mysterious fit reducing him to a passenger. The next four years would prove to be one of acute personal despair as a shattered right knee immobilised his great gifts; but through a combination of courage, determination and expert medical help he returned to the summit of world football, almost four years to the day from that sorry episode in Paris, to take the field at Yokohama for the 2002 FIFA World Cup final versus Germany.

Brazil had arrived at the 2002 finals in the rare position of not being favourites, but despite their low-billing at the start, they were soon regarded as the best side in the tournament and had certainly played the most attractive football. But everybody knows how the Germans love to gatecrash a party and as people took their seats for the final, it was in hope, rather than certainty, that the non-German majority awaited a Brazilian win. With this sense of occasion reserved for the few, Ronaldo was the difference between the teams in a refreshingly open game. Amazingly, for two nations of such sound heritage and success, this was the first time that they had met at any World Cup. The derisive among you may add that this could well explain why Germany's record is so good, as Brazil have proved insurmountable to every other dominant footballing nation at varying times over the years.

One of the sub-plots of the final had been the duel between Ronaldo and Germany's goalkeeper, Oliver Kahn. Kahn had thus far had an outstanding tournament, making world-class saves to defy the Irish and the USA in particular, and achieving that tag of all great keepers in their best form: unbeatable. Kahn embodied the image of the classic German keeper. He was tall, fearless, athletic and fair-haired – not unlike Sepp Maier – and wore similarly huge gloves. A key part of the Bayern Munich side that had been so strong in UEFA's Champions League over recent years, he had justifiably gained a reputation as one of the world's best. He was the leading name, along with the emerging Ballack, in an otherwise dull German side, making up for what they lacked in skill and flair with typically Germanic organisation, fitness and a will to win instilled by their impressive coach and ex-star Rudi Völler.

As the two teams took the field, Ronaldo was again sporting his new-look hairstyle of the diamond-shaped patch. First seen in the semi-final against Turkey, it had attracted many comments of varying candour and also some interesting nicknames: divot-head, tuft-head and wedge-head being some of the less favourable ones. Rumour has it that the haircut was a reaction to his young son mistakenly embracing the TV set every time he saw Roberto Carlos, thinking it was his dad. More importantly, at its conception prior to the Turkey game, coach Felipe Scolari had nailed the relevance of the new hairdo. It meant Ronaldo, reassured of his fitness and his ability, was ready to be in the limelight again. Buoyed by his goals, trusting his fitness, and slowly shedding the dark cloak of France '98, Ronaldo was again enjoying being the best footballer in the world. As the flashbulbs popped to catch the teams as they entered, the purists amongst us were denied the delight of seeing Brazil contest the final in their legendary full home kit – they wore blue socks instead of the traditional white, in accordance with FIFA's bizarre rule that no item of kit should clash so as not to confuse viewers in black and white. Did they really think the watching world couldn't tell the difference between the two nations?!

The first half started well, with enterprising football played from both sides, and it was Kahn who had the better of the early exchanges with Ronaldo. Having slipped through on two occasions, Ronaldo fluffed his big moment with two uncharacteristically snatched finishes, appearing to be fazed by the onrushing presence of the big German, something commentators were not slow to pick up on. Did Kahn have 'the wood' on Ronaldo? At this point, spare a thought for the unheralded Brazilian midfielder, Kleberson. A player from the unfashionable club Atlético Paranaense, he had so far had a good World Cup and had been added to the team in recent rounds to add more steel to the midfield in preference to the slighter Juninho Paulista. Late in the first half, he latched onto the ball in the German half and advanced towards goal, but fate can be a cruel mistress. Jinking past two German defenders, Kleberson unleashed a beautiful, curling shot that arched over the flying Kahn only to hit the bar full-on and spoon out into play. A ball's width is all that stood between poor Kleberson and the best goal in the final for many a long year – perhaps since Marco Tardelli's in 1982. On such thin threads do these things hang. Had it sailed in, his life would have been transformed, with millions added to his value and instant hero-worship back home.

As stoppage time in the first half approached, Ronaldo was again presented with a gilt-edged chance, this time as a Roberto Carlos drilled pass fell at his feet only 12 yards out. Here we had a double demonstration of the wonderful instincts of world-class players. Ronaldo, swivelling on a sixpence, drilled a left-foot drive goalwards, only to be thwarted once more by Kahn, who thrust out a leg to block what seemed a certain goal. Forty–love to Kahn and as the bank of commentators and press gasped, the ref blew for half-time.

As TV stations panned back to their pundit-filled studios, the talk was all about Kahn repelling everything Ronaldo could throw at him. Had Ronaldo's scoring run come to an inevitable halt against the impressive German? Were his earlier goals now diluted as they had been against supposedly inferior keepers? Was he flunking his big examination? Although the first half had not been short of incident, the score was still 0–0 and many people were now casting half an eye to the uncanny ability of Germany to nick games, often against the run of play, and their admirable trait of never lying down. If evidence were needed of this, it was not long in coming as they started the second half the brighter and very nearly went ahead when Oliver Neuville's corner was headed goalwards by Jens Jeremies, only to be blocked by some desperate defending.

Historically, the overall standard of Brazilian keepers has been pretty poor and this weakness has been targeted. Only Taffarel of late has really stood out as a keeper of any sort of class. But Marcos, of São Paulo club Palmeiras, had showed admirable mettle in putting together some fine displays to help Brazil to the final and now he came into his own. Germany won a free kick some 30 yards out and the aforementioned Neuville stood over the ball with intent. He then essayed his attempt, rather like a rugby place-kicker, and from about 10 yards back from the ball he took a good old-fashioned run-up and belted the ball goalwards. It was only a miraculous finger-tip save from Marcos that got the ball onto the post and out to safety. Rather like Kleberson, Neuville was foiled by the narrowest of margins and I doubt a day goes by when he doesn't wonder, what if? But again, some people are just not meant to claim centre-stage, in the same way that others are.

On 67 minutes, the moment came to delight Brazil. Ronaldo, having set off on one of his mazy runs, was caught in possession. He did well to track back and nick the ball back off, of all people, German holding player Dietmar Hamann. Then, looking to play a one–two with Rivaldo, he played the ball and awaited the return, only to see Rivaldo ignore him and unfurl one of his trademark low, swerving drives with his wand-like left foot. Not his greatest effort, but one that needed saving, and, nine times out of ten, Kahn would have fielded the ball easily. But somehow it squirmed free and rolled into the path of Ronaldo, who, showing superb striker's awareness, covered 20 yards or so in case of such an eventuality and stroked the ball in past Kahn's despairing lunge as he desperately tried to atone for the howler. As Ronaldo wheeled away, joy spread over his face and the trademark right index finger was raised to confirm the goal to anyone who doubted what they had just seen.

The sorry, aimless figure, whose somnambulant wander through the final at France '98 had stunned the world, had now scored. Joy turned to ecstasy 12 minutes later when Ronaldo made it 2–0. Kleberson, a strong contender for man of the match, weaved down the right flank and then cut inside to slide the ball through to Rivaldo on the edge of the German area. What happened then was at once a moment of brilliance and ironic symmetry, as Rivaldo, showing marvellous awareness, dummied the ball, knowing that Ronaldo was advancing behind him. Like Ronaldo for the first goal, at this point Rivaldo shaped for a return pass expecting the one–two, but oh no, Ronaldo was having none of it, and passed the ball into the corner past Kahn with sublime ease and grace. A goal made of pure Brazilian DNA.

As the Brazilian bench erupted into pandemonium, Ronaldo meandered towards them, singling out Scolari in particular, who had shown such faith in him. The trademark grin and raised right index finger were in full working order. A special moment for all Brazilians and football lovers, and in particular for Scolari, who had been derided after a poor qualifying campaign and characterised as a dull, negative coach who had betrayed the Brazilian legacy of playing beautiful football. That couldn't be levelled at him now as he'd backed Ronaldo and the other flair players so blessed with this legacy and had without question played the best football of any team at the tournament. He had had the last laugh.

With a great sense of timing and humility, coach Felipão (Big Phil) then substituted Ronaldo, allowing him a standing ovation displaying the affection of all. The unmistakable referee, Italian Pierluigi Collina, soon blew for full-time, and once the tears had dried and he had restored his composure, Ronaldo joined his teammates for the presentation of the great trophy. Milking the moment to the max, FIFA's president Sepp Blatter finally relinquished his grip on the Cup to let Cafu take what was rightfully his, and before long the Brazilian skipper had scaled one of the

CHAPTER 2

THE KID FROM BENTO RIBEIRO

Ronaldo's route to the Yokohama Stadium had been an arduous one. Sport is littered with stories of stars who have made the lengthy journey from humble adversity and Ronaldo's is up there with the best. For many aspiring footballers in South America, the journey is steep and long. Most of you will have seen the scratchy footage of the tiny Maradona as a boy exhibiting wondrous ball skills outside his shanty home in Argentina. Likewise, the *favelas* (slums) of Rio de Janeiro offer little hope of escape to a normal life and the clutches of gun and drug culture are never far away. The *favelas* take several forms but the most prevalent are either the ones in Rio city itself that cling to the hillsides above the apartment blocks of the 'asphalt' below, such as Videgal and Rocinha, or the out of town ones such as Cidade de Deus (City of God), now immortalised in the brilliant film of the same name. Ronaldo was brought up in Bento Ribeiro in the Zona Norte district of Rio. The Rio city borough is divided into two main areas, Zona Norte and Zona Sul, with Zona Sul the more affluent and containing the more well-known places such as Copacabana, Ipanema and Leblon. As a nation, Brazil has an acute polarity of wealth – some economists argue the widest in the world – and Bento Ribeiro, although not as poor as some Rio areas, was certainly in the lower-class bracket.

Bento Ribeiro had long been known as a military area, where young colts went to fulfil their obligatory national service. Since the demise of the dictatorship in the early 1980s, Bento Ribeiro has grown rapidly. Close to the municipal city limits, there was plenty of land into which

RONALDO

the *bairro* (neighbourhood) could expand and Ronaldo's mother, Sônia, took a house on a street called General César Obino. It was simple, of a good size and with basic amenities, and certainly not the hovel that many accounts of Ronaldo's upbringing have suggested. Sônia met Ronaldo's father, Nélio, whilst working at the Rio state telephone company Telerj, now Telemar, and soon fall pregnant with her first child Ione, Ronaldo's sister. Ronaldo's elder brother, Nélio, came along shortly afterwards. When Sônia fell pregnant for a third time, she and Nélio senior decided that this would be their last. Sônia had had to quit her decent job at Telerj and with Nélio's employment record proving to be very up and down, they needed to focus on giving the three children as good an upbringing as possible. It would be a long struggle to make ends meet.

Sônia Barata Nazario De Lima gave birth to Ronaldo on 18 September 1976. Without a name for the newborn child and in the absence of his unreliable and often drunk father Nélio, Sônia was at a loss as to what to call her nascent offspring. Looking up to the delivering doctor, she asked him what he was called. We must be grateful that the doctor on duty at the time had the perfectly respectable name of Ronaldo Valente and we are not now acknowledging the three-time FIFA World Player of the Year with some lamentable Christian name. Had the doc perhaps been a bit more on the ball, he may have got Sônia to sign a copyright agreement which would have netted him a small fortune in merchandising rights about 20 years hence, but not to worry. So, Ronaldo Luiz Nazario De Lima – Ronaldo to you and me – entered the world in good health and was passed into the arms of his mother. She no doubt wondered if the prophecy recently given to her by a local witch doctor would come true. He had assured her that not only would her third child be a boy, but one that would possess wonderful skills that would help Sônia and her family escape from the hardship of Bento Ribeiro for good.

Ironically, Ronaldo actually celebrates two birthdays (an early sign of his regal presence, perhaps?) as at the time, his aforementioned father Nélio was unable to provide the birth registration fee of ten Brazilian Reals (BR$). It took him four days to cobble this amount together and, to avoid a fine for late payment, he declared that Ronaldo had been born on 22 September. As such, Ronaldo celebrates 18 September with his family and 22 September is his 'official' birthday.

Ronaldo's mother now set out on a determined path to secure as good a future as possible for Ronaldo, and with half an eye on the witch doctor's prophecy, grafted every hour she could. Invariably, this involved fairly unglamorous manual cleaning or assistants' jobs, often working 12 hours a day, and sharing out the care of young Ronaldo to the rest of her relatives.

Ronaldo's elder siblings gave him the nickname of Dadado, and by all accounts he was incredibly active and alive with energy. He learned to walk relatively early and was up and about in well under a year. He was also extremely quiet and, according to his mum, hardly said a word. He underwent a fairly traditional Catholic upbringing in Brazil and enjoyed the benefits of being part of a large extended family. Bento Ribeiro provided a pleasant, if unspectacular, place in which to grow up.

Ronaldo received his first proper football when he was four years old, from his father Nélio, and one can imagine it being like a Jedi Knight receiving his first light sabre: a seminal, time-splitting moment. The following years saw Ronaldo playing football at every available opportunity, with his pals out on the patch of wasteground by his home.

Having witnessed first hand a game of football on these dog-eared patches of ground, it is clear to see where the stereotypical skills of Brazilian footballers have their origins. These pitches are makeshift in every respect. The ground is often uneven, and in parts it can be quite dangerous. There will invariably be a mixture of rubbish, debris, abandoned motor parts, perhaps livestock grazing on it and a whole myriad of other things, but nothing seems to deter the kids as they romp around. The goals that the kids play to are often barely two metres wide, which means that any player wanting to score, due to the smallness of the target, is better off going round the keeper than shooting when confronted by him. Inevitably, the kids perfect this striker's skill at a very young age, on a treacherous surface, and with a dodgy football. Move the clock forward to when these guys graduate to playing on the beaches, and the ability to go round a keeper, at speed, on sand, means that when the gifted ones then graduate to playing on truer grass surfaces, their striker's art is complete and they waltz round hapless keepers for fun. Ronaldo is testimony to this, as are the other mercurial Brazilian footballers such as Pelé, Careca, Romário and Zico. Rounding the keeper is second nature, they can do it with their eyes closed.

Combine this with the sureness of touch and balance developed on the rough ground and beaches, and it is easy to see why Brazilian footballers appear so gifted. These traits are developed the hard way, in the streets, on the wasteground, on the beaches and in the backyards. There is a saying in Brazil that God gave Brazil the most gifted footballers, but to balance this up, he then gave them the worst administrators. One wonders just how strong Brazilian football could actually be if they got their administrative house in order, flushed out all the corruption and the shameful leakage of money, negotiated some decent and lasting TV deals and undertook a Taylor Report-style overhaul of their domestic stadiums.

By now, Ronaldo's affection for the beautiful game was growing into an obsession. He was rarely seen without a ball and any time with his amigos was spent playing football or doing keep-ups, something that Ronaldo was soon the best at. Young children – those most heartless of judges – didn't take long to work Ronaldo out. They nicknamed him Monica, in reference to the massively popular kids' cartoon in Brazil where Monica, the lead character, sports a rabbit-like protruding pair of front teeth.

Being a rather ungainly, goofy young boy, Ronaldo fell victim to the natural selection of all kids' football: he was last to be picked. But as his skills became evident he was soon the one kid everybody wanted in their team as his speed, strength and skill set him apart as the best player around. This was something he would have to start getting used to. When they could, Ronaldo and his crew would make their way down to the beaches of Rio, invariably by 'jumping' trains or buses, to go and pit their skills against other such groups of kids who shared the same love of football and the beach. If Hackney Marshes are the spiritual home of grass-roots English football then Rio's beaches are that of Brazil. Copacabana, a long sweep of glorious golden sand, is perhaps the most famous of these, and along with Rio's other beaches such as Ipanema, Leblon and Botafogo, they provide a quite wonderful place to go and play. With a refreshing dip in the sea available and a stage upon which to strut in front of the beautiful Rio women, one can understand why beach culture is so integral to Brazilian life.

The beaches have a mixture of marked pitches and foot-volley nets (volleyball played with your feet and head) providing kids such as Ronaldo with their first glimpse of something remotely resembling an organised set-up. The sand demands that skill is the pre-requisite to shine, and also develops fantastic fitness. Any football fan should visit Rio to witness the kids of all ages playing beach football: their level of skill is quite frightening, their passion for the game a joy to behold and their smiling faces a reminder that football is the beautiful game. Anyone who has played football on sand will know that it is an energy sapping, static game, but the Brazilians waltz across the sand as if playing on AstroTurf or asphalt – their freedom of movement and speed is quite extraordinary.

There is a famous story about two England internationals playing football on Copacabana beach prior to England's friendly against Brazil in June 1984. Some articles had appeared in the local Brazilian press about the visiting England squad being 'unfriendly', and, in rebuttal, the English FA arranged for two of the players, John Barnes and Noel Chamberlain, to stage what would appear to be an impromptu game of foot-volley beach-football, with local news hacks in attendance. The events that unfolded proved to be acutely embarrassing for Barnes, Chamberlain and the FA, as the local kids ran rings around them, putting their ball skills to shame and allowing the Rio press a field day with on-the-morning editions. Barnes would ultimately redeem himself the day after with *that* goal – from which he would reap another 60-odd caps – and, against all expectation, England won 2–0.

As Ronaldo grew older, he struggled to combine the requirements of education with his love of football. By all accounts, he wasn't a difficult or disruptive pupil at school, he just wasn't interested, and his mind continued to wander to thoughts of football. As his mother desperately tried to instil the benefits and conformity of attending school, she soon became aware that she was fighting a losing battle as Ronaldo and his pals were regular truants who spent their time playing football.

Early heroes for Ronaldo included Brazilian legend Zico, nicknamed 'the white Pelé', who was arguably one of the greatest players in the world in the 1980s, and is the last truly great Brazilian player to have played the bulk of his career in Brazil and not Europe, a late move to Udinese in Italy being the only blemish to this statistic. He played his football primarily for Brazil's largest club, Flamengo of Rio de Janeiro. Zico was a dazzling footballer. One of the earlier exponents of the curling free kick, he was a star member of Brazil's vainglorious side that illuminated, but somehow didn't win, the 1982 World Cup.

For poor kids, being able to watch a game at the Maracanã was a rare treat indeed. Ronaldo's first experience of this behemoth of a stadium came when he went to watch his idol play for Flamengo against fellow Rio side Vasco da Gama. Back in the 1980s, these *classicos* attracted crowds of over 100,000 with an electric atmosphere to boot. Not surprisingly, the young Ronaldo was left mesmerised by the majesty of such a fixture at the world's largest stadium, and seeing his hero Zico perform on such an imposing stage inspired him to try to do likewise.

At nine years old, Ronaldo and his mates joined local club the Valqueire Tennis Club, which, intriguingly for a tennis club, did not possess a tennis court. What it did have, though, was a team of *futebol de salão*, which is a version of indoor football played in Brazil, invariably with a heavier football to encourage the players to keep it on the deck. Even more bizarrely for this non-tennis-playing tennis club, Ronaldo began his time with them in the only position they had available in the team: in goal. Thankfully, this didn't persist and he was given his chance to play outfield in the game against the Championship leaders, Vasco da Gama. With Valqueire 2–0 down at half-time, the switch didn't appear to be having any impact, but, in the second half, Ronaldo got tongues wagging by banging in four goals as Valquiere caused a major upset by winning 5–4. He wouldn't be asked to don the gloves again.

Watching the game that day was a man called Fernando dos Santos Carvalho, known to many as Fernando Gordo due to his ample size (*gordo* is the Portuguese for fat). He was renowned in the area for putting together good teams for *futebol de salão* and was clearly impressed with what he'd seen.

Around this time in 1987, Ronaldo's parents separated. This would have several direct practical effects on him, as well as the emotional upset that such a break-up would naturally cause. With Nélio now elsewhere, the burden once more reverted to Sônia to bring income into the household. Taking up a job at the local Madureira snack bar, she was unable to chaperone him to school as she had been doing and ensure he wasn't playing hookey. Ronaldo would take advantage of this to play football whenever he could get away with it, much to his mum's annoyance.

Before long, Fernando Gordo invited him to join his *futebol de salão* team at the nearby Social Ramos club. This would give Ronaldo the opportunity to train and play on a more formal, after-school basis, for a team that had far more potential than our friends at the tennis club. Sônia welcomed the arrival of Gordo as it meant she found she could trust him to act as a kind of surrogate father in Nélio's absence. Fernando Gordo, with the blessing of Sônia, would collect Ronaldo on Tuesdays and Thursdays, take the bus to Madureira to say hello to Sônia and then go on to Social Ramos. This gave Sônia the comfort that Ronaldo was OK. Ronaldo was still a painfully shy and quiet kid, and the opportunity to talk about football with Gordo on the bus to Social Ramos was something he welcomed.

Although quiet and shy off the *salão* pitch, Ronaldo was letting his football do the talking for him and in the *Campeonato Metropolitano*, a tournament for all the best *salão* teams in Rio state, he annihilated all previous records. In his first season, he scored a monumental 166 goals including one memorable game against Municipal when he helped himself to 11 of the team's 12 goals. Not surprisingly, people began to take notice and one of the directors of Social Ramos, Alirio Jose de Carvalho, was impressed as much by the young kid's attitude as by his goal-scoring prowess.

It wasn't long before Flamengo wanted to have a look at this young goal-scoring machine and invited the 13-year-old Ronaldo to a trial. Along with around 400 other young hopefuls, he arrived at Flamengo's Gávea ground with one thing in mind: to impress the scouts and emulate his role model, Zico. Zico had also risen from adversity to become a legend of football and Ronaldo idolised him. Ronaldo woke early and made the long journey from Bento Ribeiro to Gávea alone – a mighty big adventure for a 13 year old. The first trial went well and Ronaldo was invited back for the follow-up trial the next day. There was, however, one slight problem: Ronaldo had no money for the bus fare. He tried to negotiate with the officials at Flamengo for a loan to allow him to make the trip the following day but they declined. In what is now a famed story, Flamengo refused to lend Ronaldo the 30 centavos (20p) or so he needed, and subsequently failed him as a trialist due to non-attendance – a decision that still haunts them to this day. Understandably, this shattered the young Ronaldo, as all he had dreamed of was taken from him for the sake of a bus fare. To compound his misery, later that day he was mugged by two youths who first relieved him of his watch and then beat him up for good measure. It was a miserable day all round.

CHAPTER 3

THE BOY'S A BIT SPECIAL – SÃO CRISTÓVÃO FC 1990-93

After the dreadful disappointment of the Flamengo situation, Ronaldo had to come to terms with the fact that footballing life might not be so straightforward. One doesn't know how he may have progressed with Flamengo had the bus fare been forthcoming; that is something only for conjecture. But Ronaldo now had to set his sights on something far lower, and began the ascent into professional football from a much tougher starting point.

After his magnificent season with Social Ramos, several people, as well as Fernando Gordo and Alirio Jose de Carvalho, were becoming aware of his ability. One of those was Ary Ferreiras de Sá, who was involved with the São Cristóvão football club in the Zona Norte area of Rio, about 5 km out of the centre. He invited Ronaldo, via Alirio Jose de Carvalho, to come along to São Cristóvão as he was looking for extra players to reinforce the squad. For Ronaldo, this was a stroke of luck for several reasons. It meant he could continue his progression under the watch of people he knew and, more importantly, people his mother trusted. Sônia knew the São Cristóvão area so she had a good feeling about the club. Second, São Cristóvão is about half the distance from Bento Ribeiro than Flamengo and was practically at the limit of the bus fare Ronaldo could afford. Had it been any further, he quite simply wouldn't have been able to afford to go.

I met with the staff of São Cristóvão – or the *Clube São Cristóvão de Futebol e Regatas*, to give it its full name – to find out more. It was a

THE BOY'S A BIT SPECIAL . . .

Saturday morning and my translator and I arrived at the ground at 9.30 a.m. We had scheduled to meet the president, Carlos Alberto Parreira Peixoto, João Luiz Falcão Meirelles, whose marvellously overstated title is the 'technical director of football', plus lifelong supporter and *São Cristóvãoista*, Renato Alves de Campos.

As our taxi pulled up (we had been advised not to drive there, as 'gringos' in a decent car would attract attention and possible trouble), the first thing that hit us was the forlorn state of the ground. The club was founded way back in 1898, making it as old as many traditional English League clubs and a year older than the great AC Milan, for example, but unfortunately the passage of time hasn't been kind. At the turn of the century, São Cristóvão were a force to be reckoned with and competed with the best sides in Rio state. In 1926, they won their first – and only – major honour, the *Campeonato Carioca*. The original huge trophy and wonderful, Corinthianesque sepia team photo still reside proudly in the club's trophy room. Since then, they have slipped into lower league obscurity and struggle to get by. As Rio expanded rapidly as a city, the club somehow managed to stave off redevelopment but could do nothing to stop the construction of the vast, elevated *Linha Vermelho* (red line) motorway that imposes itself adjacent to the ground and provides a constant rattle of noise.

This overhanging motorway also obscures the grand old entrance to this once grand club and it was here that we met the three club officials, who, unusually for *Cariocas*, were bang on time. In stark contrast to some modern-day big clubs and their officials who find it oh so burdensome to lend you their time, they were proud, prompt and ready to welcome us to their club. This civility and grace, I would learn, is the essence of São Cristóvão football club. After a welcome beer (on the house), we sat down in the president's office and discussed the club and their most famous alumnus. João Luiz, the charming technical director of football, cuts a sprightly dash for his 77 years and once he had stopped chatting up my female translator he went on to explain his recollections of the young Ronaldo:

'When he first arrived here, it was at the invitation of Ary Ferreiras de Sá, the director general of the club. I remember this awkward-looking kid, very thin and rangy and with the famous buck teeth. We'd heard about his goals for Social Ramos but this was a different thing: 11-a-side, outdoors and on grass.'

Ronaldo joined São Cristóvão with his friend, Alexandre Jesuino Dos

Santos, or Calango as he was nicknamed. At the time, Calango also had a big reputation as an outstanding young player, so João Luiz was happy to welcome the pair. He told me, 'I remember the two of them. They were virtually inseparable. Calango was a good player and we registered them together.' He was kind enough to Xerox me copies of both their registration cards and said, 'Look, here they are, look at the photos. And also look at the back, Calango has signed his player pass, but Ronaldo hasn't because he couldn't.' Calango, although a talented player, could never convert this into a big career and is currently plying his trade in Saudi Arabia.

João Luiz recalls Ronaldo's debut and said, 'Although Ronaldo was a funny-looking kid, he soon started to impress and I remember his debut well: 12 August 1990 in the *Campeonato Estadual*. We beat FC Tomazinho 5–2 and Ronaldo scored a hat-trick, and a good one too. He was quick and for a shy lad was full of confidence, always willing to take the defence on. His dribbling was very impressive.'

Renato Alves remembers this game too. Born and bred in São Cristóvão, the club is in Renato's heart and as a kid he used to wag school and spend all his time there, helping out wherever he could, mowing or watering the pitch, whitewashing the walls or removing litter. Anything that might get him a few *centavos* or a sandwich donated by some of the then officials. Now in his mid-40s, he similarly helps out wherever he can, helping kids as he was once helped himself, and he recalls Ronaldo's debut saying, 'Yes, he played well and any hat-trick on debut is always a good start, but we never had any idea he would go on to be such a star. He was just so shy, quiet and reserved, almost awkward. It was for this he stood out more.'

João Luiz went on, 'After a time, though, it did become evident he was something special. It was his dribbling that caught the eye, so fast and with the ball stuck to his feet.' With an avuncular pride and glint in his eye not dissimilar to that of Sir Bobby Robson, João went on: 'He became a big success here. In three seasons with us, he scored 44 goals in 73 games, most of them very good ones,' and with great emphasis, he said, 'and with no penalties.'

He continued: 'Ary used to give him money for bus fares, or for a sandwich. Ronaldo never had any money. The club helped him when he needed it. Jairzinho – "The Hurricane" – always claims that it was he who discovered Ronaldo, but I'm afraid it wasn't, it was Ary. He was the man who brought Ronaldo here, not Jairzinho. Jairzinho first turned up here [at the club] in 1991, Ronaldo had joined in 1990.'

THE BOY'S A BIT SPECIAL . . .

'Work it out yourself,' he said with a wry smile. 'Jairzinho tries to take credit for "discovering" Ronaldo but I can tell you it wasn't him. On 27 July 1990, I remember it well, then-president Dr Luiz Orlando Cardona invited two of his friends to come and see Ronaldo.' Who were his two friends? Alexandre Martins and Reinaldo Pitta.

And that is how the relationship started. Impressed by what they saw, they came several times thereafter, and asked Jairzinho as a footballing man what he thought of the kid. Jairzinho endorsed everybody's view at São Cristóvão that he was a bit special.

I spoke to incumbent president Carlos Alberto, a charming, refined man who has the job of trying to keep the club going. Carlos Alberto took me on a tour of the club and what struck me was how, even with all the problems, he and the club still retain their dignity. That morning, there must have been over 100 children there for a soccer school, all decked out proudly in their São Cristóvão kits, all listening intently to the coach's instructions and all playing football with a smile on their faces.

'Is the next Ronaldo among these?' I asked.

'We hope so,' answered the president, 'we hope so. A lot of the kids here are very talented, they just need help and assistance. We help them as best we can.'

I asked Carlos Alberto how the club makes money, to which he answered ruefully, 'We don't. Our only revenue creation is from the soccer school, but we can't charge what we ought to because otherwise the kids couldn't afford it; and from the billboards you see.' He pointed out the two billboards that are on the side of the clubhouse facing the *Linha Vermelho* motorway; one was advertising shampoo and the other mobile phones. He also pointed out two other dilapidated ones that he was in negotiation with the local council to use to generate income. 'Apart from that, that's the only income we realise. The rest I pay for myself.'

Carlos Alberto explained how he personally pays for everything, including the cost of the upkeep of the ground, the maintenance of the groundsman's equipment and, interestingly, the bus fares home of most of the senior first team.

'Yes, I pay that too, and I buy them lunch on most match days.'

It struck me that this was exactly what the previous president had had to do for Ronaldo and Calango, to which Carlos Alberto nodded, and said, '*Sim, nada muda.*' ('Yes, nothing changes.') It also echoes the abrupt end that Ronaldo's Flamengo trial had come to.

As Carlos is by no means a wealthy man, I asked him why he did it.

His answer provided a wonderful insight into the generosity of most Brazilian people and their love of the game. He answered, without any sign of looking for recognition or credit for his generosity, 'Because if we didn't help, who else would? How could these kids get a chance to play football? Without football, what hope do they have? And without hope, what have they got? That would be tragic. We hope that one day another Ronaldo will come along out of these guys [looking at the soccer school] and that is what makes us do it; that and our love of football.'

I asked how much money the club has made from Ronaldo. Carlos Alberto answered with a crestfallen raise of the eyebrows, 'The club made $7,000 when we sold his player pass, which at the time paid for four months' electric bills which were badly overdue. Several years ago, Ronaldo did give the club [somewhat naively] a cheque for $200,000, but the then-president ran off with the money. We are trying to get it back but the legal system here is difficult and it is hard to prove. We could have done everything with that money. What we hope is that one day, Ronaldo stages a game here at the ground and we can get TV cameras and all that here. To have Ronaldo back here playing on the pitch where he first appeared would be wonderful for everybody concerned and I'm sure we could raise a lot of money. The club is in big trouble.'

I suggested that they could perhaps factor in a future percentage of subsequent transfer fees, like English clubs do, but Carlos Alberto replied, 'Yes, that is something we would love to do, because as you know, we sold Ronaldo's player pass for $7,000. He then went on to Cruzeiro for $25,000, who then sold him to PSV for $6 million and then to Inter and to Real. The combined fees were well over $50 million. But, because he was a junior with us and left before he was 17, we are not entitled to do that by Brazilian law. It is a shame because we discovered him and gave him his big chance.'

As we came to the end of our meeting, I thanked the three officials and asked Carlos Alberto for his fax number so I could send various documents through to him. He shrugged wistfully, saying, 'Hang on a second, I don't know our fax number; nobody ever sends us one.' And with that he rooted through the manual still sitting atop the redundant fax machine in the corner. 'Ah, here it is,' he said. 'Yes, send us a fax, that would be nice, we're not sure if this machine works!'

We wandered over to the club bar to have a few more beers and a chat and I thanked them for their time. I asked them just how proud they felt of Ronaldo.

THE BOY'S A BIT SPECIAL . . .

'*Bastante, bastante, bastante,*' (a lot, a lot, a lot) the three of them said pretty much in melodic unison. João Luiz added, 'When I see him in that white shirt of Real Madrid, which is white like ours (not the other way round!), it makes me feel very proud that he started at our humble club. Yes, every day we're all very proud of him and what he has achieved.'

Ronaldo's three seasons at São Cristóvão are impressive. In 1990, he scored 8 goals in 12 games; in 1991, 17 in 28 and in 1992, 19 in 33 – 44 goals in 73 games and, as João Luiz stressed, no penalties. This record would catch the attention of many, and with Jairzinho now involved to lend some cachet to the situation, Martins and Pitta felt it was time to start to cash in on their new charge. They signed him up to a contract aligning him to them, a contract covering everything from their commissions from transfer fees to their commissions from image rights, marketing, merchandising, you name it. The contract was watertight. After three excellent seasons at São Cristóvão, Ronaldo said goodbye to his friends and colleagues and headed north to the city of Belo Horizonte, about a four-hour drive out of Rio, bound for their main club, Cruzeiro.

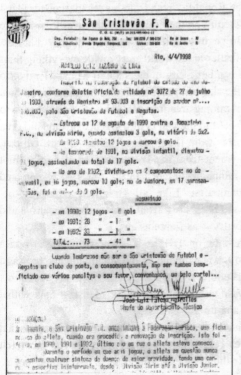

Ronaldo's 'player report' from his time at São Cristóvão, signed by technical director of football João Luiz Falcão Meirelles, showing his 44 goals in 73 games.

CHAPTER 4

MAKING WAVES –
CRUZEIRO FC 1993–94

For any young 16 year old, leaving home for the first time is always a testing experience. However, Ronaldo, fresh from his recent transfer that gave his agent duo a timely return on their initial $7,000 investment, was eager to show that he could begin to fulfil his earlier prophecy that he would become the best footballer in the world and provide everything for his family. Belo Horizonte is a large city in the state of Minas Gerais, a vast sprawling state about the size of France that takes its name from the fact it used to be the general mining area from the colonial days. Rumour has it that a lot of the gold held in the vaults of the Bank of England on Threadneedle Street originates from the mines of Minas Gerais, which the English received in payment from the Portuguese royal family for protecting them from the rampaging French in the times of Napoleon Bonaparte's Peninsular campaign. Like all Brazilian cities, Belo Horizonte is football mad and boasts two front-line teams, Cruzeiro and Atlético Mineiro, whose rivalry is as fierce as any.

On arrival in Belo Horizonte, or 'BH' as it is known, it didn't take Ronaldo long to settle into his new abode as the small suitcase he was carrying probably didn't take long to unpack. But as his goals began to rain in for Cruzeiro he wasn't short of gifts from idolising fans with which to furnish his basic apartment.

However much he may have been missing his family and friends back in Rio, he was able to seek refuge in the place where he felt most at home: the football field. He didn't take long to give his new employers a taste of what they had got their hands on with a stunning debut in the junior *Campeonato Mineiro* (the Mineiro State Championship), banging in four goals as Cruzeiro easily beat Oliveira 7–0. In the next game against Matozinhos, he was on the scoresheet again with a brace. The interest in Ronaldo increased further when, in a reserve-team game against their fiercest rivals, Atlético Mineiro, and in his first *classico* for Cruzeiro, Ronaldo duly obliged with the only goal, sending the place into ecstasy.

Cruzeiro's coach Pinheiro, ex-Fluminense and a veteran defender from the Brazil side of the 1954 World Cup, was understandably delighted with his new charge, but even that didn't free him of dissenters who were concerned that he was playing the new star too often and was in danger of burning him out. This charge was later to resurface after France '98 and the first of Ronaldo's horrific knee injuries. Hindsight is a wonderful thing and one sympathises with a coach who wants to play his star talent and has a crowd to please, and also with the player himself, who lives for the joy of scoring goals. Further concerns were raised about Ronaldo's penchant for hamburgers and fizzy drinks, accusations that would likewise later resurface, in this case ten years on at Real Madrid.

But at Cruzeiro, as would later be the case at Real Madrid, the dissenters about his dietary preferences were left to marvel with the rest of us at his on-pitch wizardry. Similarly, at Cruzeiro, as word spread that they had a player who was something special, the media circus was never far away and Ronaldo became the darling of the locals, especially the females. Footballing nations seem to throw out talent of such class about once every ten years or so, and within a very short time at Cruzeiro, Ronaldo was making headlines. In short, he was a sensation. His heroics for the youth team clearly didn't go unnoticed and at the age of 16 years and 8 months, and having been on Cruzeiro's books for only 83 days, he made his debut as a senior professional. From humble beginnings, Ronaldo's life was about to commence on an upward spiral that would catapult him into the realms of a global icon.

One of Ronaldo's most memorable early games was for the Brazil Under-17s *seleçao* (selection) in a warm-up game at the Maracanã. The game was versus Fluminense Under-17s and was a curtain-raiser for the final of the *Campeonato Carioca* (Rio State Championship) between the two Rio giants Fluminense and Vasco da Gama. The Maracanã was packed and it was Ronaldo's first time in front of the legendary Maracanã crowd: on this occasion well over 100,000 people. With his team trailing 1–0 at half-time, as Ronaldo emerged for the second half he heard a shout from the stands. It was his old coach from Social Ramos, the avuncular Fernando Gordo. Full of words of encouragement for his old charge, the friendly voice lifted Ronaldo and he went on to score the equaliser as the game ended 1–1. Even better news was to follow as Cruzeiro won the *Campeonato Mineiro de Juniores* (Mineiro State Juniors Championship) and, with his nine goals, Ronaldo was yet again making waves as *artilheiro da competicão* (leading scorer), something that was becoming a habit. He was soon to be leading marksman again when on tour to Richmond in the USA with the Brazil Under-17s *seleçao*, as a precursor to the impending World Cup. He scored five of Brazil's eight goals in their victories over Chile, USA and Spain. Ronaldo was beginning to demonstrate a wonderful strike rate, so precious in a centre-forward and one which on his return to Belo Horizonte and Cruzeiro was already beginning to cause one or two ripples.

Things were beginning to hot up. On arrival back at Cruzeiro, Ronaldo found that coach Pinheiro had been relieved of his duties and replaced by the experienced coach Carlos Alberto Silva, and within a week of returning from the USA, Ronaldo was invited to join the Cruzeiro team in a tournament in Portugal that included Benfica, FC Porto, Belenenses and Peñarol of Uruguay. Again, Ronaldo's goals caught the eye, in particular those of certain directors of FC Porto who offered to buy the player there and then for $500,000. Cruzeiro refused this, asking for $750,000, whereupon the conversation stopped, so it was back to Brazil and the ensuing league season with Cruzeiro, under the new guidance of Carlos Alberto Silva.

After a tough start with three straight defeats, Ronaldo scored his first goal in the *Campeonato Brasileiro* in a 3–1 win over Bahia and at first found life in the first-team dressing-room hard to adjust to. The inevitable dressing-room situations were evident: certain cliques, old players and new, established and un-established players. Ronaldo had arrived with a glowing reputation that created envy as well as support. For a young lad just turning 17, a long way from home and, by nature, very shy, these were trying times. Ronaldo spoke little. A combination of this shyness and the limited education he had received meant that he lacked confidence and was happy to remain quiet. Language for him was never a way he would choose to express himself. Ronaldo's release from this came with talking about football, something he was always happy to do. As such, to journalists he came across as a pleasant, agreeable young chap, always polite and with a mummy's-boy shyness that they warmed to. Inadvertently, this worked in Ronaldo's favour. He came across as a humble, down-to-earth and level-headed lad, a son to the elder players and a friend to the younger ones. The journalists, invariably treated with much caution and sometimes contempt by players, had a soft spot for Ronaldo and as such their press was kind. As the goals started to roll in, their fondness grew into adulation and Ronaldo began to enjoy the first encounters of his long-standing popularity with the majority of the world's football press.

I caught up with Leonardo Ferreira, head of Cruzeiro's marketing department, who remembers Ronaldo's time well. I asked him about the impact he remembers Ronaldo making. Leonardo told me, 'He was a long way from the beaches of Rio, but he learnt quickly that he was here to live the life of a professional footballer. He was adapting daily, was always smiling with that soon-to-be-famous smile and was quickly adopted by some of the older players – in particular, full-back Paulo Roberto, who became his friend. The first steps of his career here passed quickly and he was very impressive. The local journalists here were soon in his thrall and I remember them describing him as "the purest of talents".'

As he settled into life with Cruzeiro, Ronaldo soon acquired the trappings of a bright, young, football talent. Although perhaps not yet the baubles of the modern star, they were still unheard of riches to the young Ronaldo, such as the car (albeit only a red VW Gol) and the girlfriend, Luciana, daughter of a wealthy Cruzeiro businessman. But Ronaldo demonstrated that he had the temperament not to get carried away by all this. He maintained frequent correspondence with his family back in Rio, and regularly sent them money to live on, rather than squandering it on the distractions of stardom. As George Best famously said, 'I spent most of my money on wine, women and beer – the rest I just squandered.' Ronaldo showed that he had the resolve to rise above this and keep his talented feet on the ground.

Ronaldo was demonstrating from very early in his professional career the hallmarks of his game with which he would later illuminate the world stage: stunning pace, Velcro control, the ability to weave past opponents on either side, and boxer-like strength. Sir Bobby Robson claimed that Ronaldo was 'the fastest thing I've ever seen with a ball at his feet' and compared his physique with that of a well-tuned middleweight. He was a fearsome proposition to defenders of any class. The above gifts are the things that give defenders sleepless nights. Carlos Alberto Silva wasn't long in realising that he had his hands on something special and was keen to alert people that not only were they in the presence of a player who could scale the very highest heights of the game but that they must also be patient and not overburden Ronaldo at such an early stage in his career.

Ronaldo's career was fast gathering pace and he was soon to make his debut in the Copa Libertadores where yet again he marked a debut game with goals, this time a hat-trick in Cruzeiro's 6–1 demolition of Colo-Colo of Chile. Next game up, this time in the *Campeonato Brasileiro*, Ronaldo notched two more against Rio's Botafogo, and was again to the fore in the return leg against Colo-Colo as he made two of the three goals. With further goals against Nacional of Montevideo, Ronaldo yet again won *artilheiro do torneio* with eight goals in four games – a breathtaking return for somebody only four months into his professional career. Local journalists marvelled at the contrast in Ronaldo. Off the pitch, he was a typical, wide-eyed teenager in every respect, but on the pitch he was a calculating goal machine demonstrating maturity and match savvy beyond his years.

The netbusting showed no sign of slowing down, with a stunning five-goal salvo in the next game versus Bahia, firing them past Rodolfo Rodriguez, for many years the Uruguayan national goalkeeper, who was left dazzled by the ability and power of Ronaldo. He was first to acknowledge that he had witnessed something special and in a strange way, despite the humiliation of shipping five goals, seemed almost privileged to be part of such a master-class, telling pitch-side journalists after the game with marvellous candour, 'Jesus, that boy's good.'

This game was not only famous for the glowing testimony from a player of Rodriguez's stature but it was also perhaps the first time that Ronaldo felt the power of television. Globo TV, one of Brasil's leading national cable channels and famous for its football coverage, showed the goals repeatedly in its news bulletins for all the (football mad) nation to behold, and inevitably the buzz it created glowed like a burning flame. A national star was born. With Ronaldo's ability now exposed to the nation, and the early hype fully illustrated to an expectant nation with TV pictures, Ronaldo was now being talked about in terms of the national team. With USA '94 just around the corner and qualification assured thanks to Romário's brace against neighbouring rivals Uruguay, certain

CBF (Brazil's Football Association) sages began to stroke their chins at the prospect of these two strikers, one already great (Romário) and one soon to be great (Ronaldo), being paired together. Alive to this, Carlos Alberto Parreira included Ronaldo in his *seleçao*.

Leonardo recalls this moment well, saying, 'We all remember this moment here at the club for it was a big honour for us. Ronaldo had always said one of his dreams was to follow his idol, Zico, and play for the *seleçao*. When this came true with Parreira's list of 22, it was a great day for all concerned with Ronaldo and Cruzeiro FC.'

Let's just pause here and look at the context of this selection within the 'old enough–good enough?' argument, as in, should a player ever be precluded from representing his country because he is too young? Ronaldo was 17 years old, had played only 23 senior games for Cruzeiro and had scored 21 goals. He would go to USA '94 but not feature in any games. He would soon demand a place of his own and become fully established – well before he was 21. England has similar parallels in Michael Owen, who caused a stir for Liverpool in the 1997–98 English Premiership season when his form and goals were so irresistible that England coach Glen Hoddle had no option but to include him in his squad for France '98, ironically leaving out one Paul Gascoigne, who eight years earlier had himself been the subject of the time honoured 'old enough–good enough?' debate. Owen would go on to have an excellent tournament and score a Ronaldoesque wonder goal against Argentina to put himself in the world spotlight. Ronaldo and Owen are prime examples that if you are good enough, it doesn't matter how old you are, your class will shine through. Fernando Torres, Wayne Rooney and Lionel Messi are fine current examples of this.

Ronaldo would ultimately only play a spectator's role at USA '94 as he sat from the bench watching Brazil march to their fourth world crown. In a tournament staged in the USA for the first time, again an 'experiment' by FIFA, or, more to the point, a clear attempt to tap the vast dormant potential of the game in such a huge commercial place as the USA, Brazil had proven to be the best team. Inspired by player-of-the-tournament Romário, whose impish finishing won several games, and Bebeto and Dunga, Brazil's football may not have touched the dizzy heights of 1970 or 1982, but they won, and that is what matters to a nation who demand to win every four years. In fairness to FIFA, the tournament proved to be a big success as the Yanks turned out in force to fill their college stadiums, some holding up to 80,000 people, and seemed to take the game to their hearts, fuelling speculation that soccer may at last have taken a meaningful foothold in the land of gridiron and baseball.

The impact of USA '94 had an influence beyond the football field as, by winning the tournament, Brazil, with those famous yellow shirts (provided at the time by UK firm Umbro), left an unknowing but strategic calling card with the US people – something that wouldn't have gone unnoticed by sportswear giants Nike, who had recently taken their first bow into football, and, in line with their corporate strategy, would soon be looking for the key player within the game to build their marketing around.

As he returned from USA '94, it was clear that Ronaldo's life would be changed for good. Although he didn't feature in the tournament on the field of play, journalists ever eager for the 'next big thing' from Brazil were curious as to who the kid was on the bench, who still looked somewhat younger than his years. Several stories surfaced and some of the only collateral available was his record thus far for São Cristóvão and Cruzeiro, and the footage from Globo TV. But inevitably, this was enough to fire peoples' imaginations and, in fairness, prior to Vanderlei Luxemburgo's tenure as coach – he was suspected by local journalists of giving fringe players caps to boost their transfer value – you didn't get into the *seleçao* for nothing. Ronaldo hadn't featured in any games and, as a place in the Brazilian *seleçao* carries a high price, he was clearly being groomed for higher office at a date in the near future.

Cruzeiro FC had also been watching USA '94 with interest and were aware that they had a key asset on their books. Leonardo went on, 'We knew we had somebody very special with us; his speed, his touch, his ability to dribble past people with ease. He just knew what to do with the ball in virtually every situation he was faced with, and with both feet. I simply don't remember any weaknesses in his game; it was impossible to identify any, even at 17!'

On returning from America, Ronaldo was presented with a revised contract from Cruzeiro which now made him the highest paid player at the club – not bad for a teenager. Around the club and in Belo Horizonte, Ronaldo was the talk of the town and a general mood of respect and appreciation came from all corners. Despite this ubiquitous admiration, Ronaldo managed to remain humble and when asked about his prospects of breaking into the national team, replied, 'It would be a dream to shake hands with Bebeto and Romário, idols of the *seleçao*.' However, he further demonstrated growing commercial awareness of his worth when he added, 'My contract with Cruzeiro runs until July, but I do not think I will stay beyond this due to interest from outside. I live in reality and I dream of success.' At this stage, Ronaldo had a lot on his side. Apart from his burgeoning football talent, he combined a boyish charm with a determined commercial desire to succeed and become a genuinely great player and extend his horizons beyond Belo Horizonte and Brazil.

The Cruzeiro in-tray was also beginning to see some lively activity as offers for Ronaldo's services began to stream in. FC Porto of Portugal, who had turned down buying him for $750,000, now significantly upped the ante to $3 million. Inevitably, the big Italian clubs weren't far off the scent either, as AC Milan sent along a couple of dignitaries to evaluate Ronaldo, and various German clubs also sent scouts to check him out, with expectant cheque books tucked in the back pockets of their lederhosen. In response, Cruzeiro hiked the asking price to $10 million, which would have made Ronaldo the then record transfer in Brazilian footballing history – an amazing accolade for one so young. The stakes were high.

Ronaldo further enhanced his worth both as a goal-scorer and commercial icon on a pre-season trip to Japan, where he banged in a hat-trick against Jubilo Iwata, whereupon Cruzeiro's president duly received a further two offers from undisclosed clubs.

Returning to Brazil for the *Campeonato Mineiro*, Cruzeiro blew all before them and romped to the championship (Ronaldo's first as a pro) with Ronaldo being the leading striker of the team with 22 goals in 18 games. His appetite for goals seemed insatiable. It was around this time that Ronaldo scored one of his most famous goals. Against Argentine legends Boca Juniors, receiving the ball on the halfway line, he burst forward at high speed, slalomed past four defenders and then waltzed around the keeper to plant the ball into the empty net. Ronaldo, against the club Maradona holds so dear to his jittery heart, had scored a goal that the pint-sized maestro would have been proud of himself.

By now, the national hysteria and clamour for Ronaldo's inclusion in the *seleçao* was at fever pitch and coach Carlos Alberto Parreira was under mounting pressure to blood the young tiro. The chance came in the *seleçao*'s next game against arch rivals Argentina in Recife, where he came on as substitute, aged seventeen years, six months and one day. Comparisons with Pelé, who had also debuted at seventeen, were inevitable, but Ronaldo just shaded the legend from Santos. On call-up for the national team, Pelé's stats had been as follows: 50 professional games with 41 goals at 0.82 goals per game. Impressive as these undoubtedly are, Ronaldo's stats were even better, and having ironically played the same number of games as Pelé, was just short of the magical 'goal-a-game' mark at 50 games, 49 goals, at 0.96 goals per game. As these figures were digested, the question surfaced: were we in the presence of a player better than Pelé?

Further comparisons with Pelé continued apace as Ronaldo's early career began to take off. Football is a game full of statistics, especially those for goal-scorers and, as outlined above, Ronaldo had already edged the great Pelé in terms of goals scored prior to his first appearance for the *seleçao*. Performances like these were not to go unnoticed by the wider footballing world for too long and soon the larger European clubs began to circle. In 1960, Pelé had been offered $1 million by several Italian clubs – a staggeringly huge sum of money at the time. Money was not the only difference back then as Brazil was also in the grip of a dictatorship which often used the successful *seleçao* as national propaganda. The Italian clubs were politely, but surely, told that Pelé was not for sale and was not leaving Brazil under any circumstances; he was in fact later designated as a National Treasure. It would be interesting to see what Jean-Marc Bosman would have made of such a ruling.

Thankfully for Ronaldo and his eager agents, the dictatorship had been overthrown in 1984 and, furthermore, Europe was seen as an essential destination for any Brazilian player of genuine ambition and ability. In addition, with Brazil due to defend their world crown in France in 1998, the more players they had exposed to the European climate and pace of the game, the better. As you observe the Brazilian leagues both back then in 1994 and today, it is alarming just how many of their best stars are playing overseas and in Europe in particular. Admittedly, the salaries are way beyond what a faltering Brazilian national league can offer and the way of life is free from the day-to-day hassles of, say, a Rio or São Paulo, with its threat of car-jacking and kidnapping. Many locals in Brazil say that it is very kind of the European leagues to act as a finishing school for all their stars and prepare them so well for each World Cup, but my view is that there is still some bitterness and frustration that the Brazilian national league can't retain its stars for itself.

With Ronaldo's superb league season at Cruzeiro under his belt – 54 goals in 54 games – he was now firmly on the shopping list of most of the major European clubs. Talks were held and meetings scheduled with Ronaldo's agents and it seemed likely that one of the Italian giants would seal the coveted signature.

What transpired proved to be of benefit to Ronaldo both then and later in his career. Instead of opting for, say, Milan or Turin, he chose PSV Eindhoven – one of the three main clubs in the Netherlands along with Ajax Amsterdam and Feyenoord, but not one you would class as a European giant. Several factors were key in this move and it is important that they are fully analysed here to understand its real advantages to the then only 17-year-old Ronaldo.

PSV is backed by the Dutch electronics giant Philips. PSV itself stands for *Philips Sport Vereninging* (Philips Sports Association) and PSV's shirts bear the Philips logo. Philips's backing has helped the club remain very stable over the years, and although perhaps not quite as mighty as the Fiat-backed Juventus of Turin, they have helped it to be able to develop in 'the Dutch way' stars such as Ruud Gullit and Ronald Koeman, plus current big stars such as Mark van Bommel and Ruud van Nistelrooy. Prior to Ronaldo's arrival, fellow *Carioca* Romário had spent several outstanding seasons there before moving on to Barcelona. Dutch football, and its larger clubs in particular, is famed for its diligent coaching, where emphasis is placed on ball skills, technique and personal expression – all perfect for a budding star like Ronaldo. PSV's 'system' would also ensure that Ronaldo was well looked after by a local family, where he could be assisted in learning the language and have a period of incubation away from the spotlight of media attention, something he would not have been able to do in the more intrusive environments of Italy, Spain or England.

Ronaldo would have taken particular comfort that Romário had served such a positive term at PSV. Romário had arrived in 1990 from Rio club Flamengo and had worked under former England coach Bobby Robson. This had been a successful period for both Romário and Robson, winning back-to-back Dutch league titles. When I interviewed the now Sir Bobby Robson for this book, I asked him about his time spent at PSV and in particular about working with Romário:

'We had a good team at PSV with the likes of Hans van Breukelen, the legendary Eric Gerets, big Stan Valckx at the back and Barry van Aerle. But the icing on the cake was Romário.'

Sir Bobby continued, 'Romário was a dazzling player, who could turn a game in an instant, but at the same time he could be mightily frustrating, at times not touching the ball or seeming interested in the game at all. He rarely tracked back, resented responsibility and could infuriate his teammates. But with two touches he could transform a game and all his laziness, cockiness and womanising were forgiven. He was a gem. He did pretty much as he pleased and flew home to Brazil more often than I would have liked, but his goals kept coming and all was forgiven.'

Goals were something Ronaldo dealt in with the élan and proficiency of Romário so knowing that this was the preferred currency at PSV gave Ronaldo every encouragement to sign. Ronaldo's agents Martins and Pitta also showed canny awareness by stalling the inevitable 'big' transfer to Italy or Spain and sending their protégé to the Netherlands. This would enable Ronaldo's stock to rise on the European bourse in readiness for a scheduled next transfer perhaps two or three seasons down the line. It would also allow Ronaldo to develop at his own pace in the less intensive arena of Dutch football. He wouldn't be expected to be a one-man show as perhaps in Italy or Spain and could blossom not only as a footballer but as a person – hopefully shedding the chronic shyness exhibited in his earlier years. Sir Bobby's path would later cross with Ronaldo at Barcelona, but more of that later.

Shortly after the World Cup of 1994 in the USA, Ronaldo signed to PSV for $6 million, making him a very expensive teenager. His agents pocketed in the region of $400,000 in commission. Ronaldo acknowledges the role Romário played in his decision by saying, 'Romário told me that PSV is one of the most professional and best organised clubs in Europe. Everything is there: a huge coaching staff, interpreters, professional mangers, a superb stadium, and a perfect blend of youth and experience in the team. He said it would be best to acclimatise in Europe and to learn about European football. I think he is right.'

PSV were understandably chuffed to have nabbed Ronaldo from under the noses of far more powerful suitors in Italy and Spain. Director of football Frank Arnesen was relishing the prospect of working with such a hot property and couldn't wait for the new season to get under way.

Despite his apprehension and teenage nerves, Ronaldo was eager to get started at PSV. He could now sense that all his childhood dreams were within his grasp. He was following in the footsteps of his idols such as Romário, Bebeto and Zico. He was on his way to Europe with a good salary, good advice and a top club. True to his humble self, he played down the mawkish comparisons with Pelé, saying, 'There is only one Pelé. I only hope I can become as good as him, or even nearly as good as him and people will later say there is only one Ronaldo.'

Ronaldo was now being bracketed with stars such as Romário, who, although now at Barcelona, was the star of USA '94 and had heaped further cachet on his previous club PSV. PSV were successful, highly respected, had a history of fine coaches, an impressive hall of fame and a proven system of nurturing young stars of both Dutch and foreign origin. Eindhoven proved to be the right move at the right time. For Leonardo and everyone at Cruzeiro, 'It was a sad day because we all loved him. But we knew he had to go. He will always be remembered here with great affection and warmth. He is a great person, a friend, and the fans simply adore him. We will never forget him.'

CHAPTER 5

GOING DUTCH –
PSV EINDHOVEN 1994-96

Despite the abundance of help laid on by PSV to help Ronaldo acclimatise and settle in the Netherlands, he still found it tough and homesickness was never far away. The initial house provided by PSV was not to his liking, and despite the plethora of electronic goodies laid on by Philips, Ronaldo was soon to move – with the prompting of his mother – to a bigger and better place in Eindhoven. By nature, *Cariocas* are very homey and family-oriented people, so having his mother Sônia around him to cook him his favourite and familiar meals was in many ways inevitable. The addition of his new Brazilian girlfriend, the dishy 19-year-old Nadia Valdez Franca, further added to this home-from-home enclave being created in part of Eindhoven.

The first few months proved particularly tricky as mother, son and girlfriend struggled to settle in together, with Sônia frequently registering scorn at the suggestions of girlfriend, and son invariably caught in the crossfire between the two. On occasion, when he wasn't laid out knackered on the sofa after training, he would be busy playing electronic games or watching a vast array of football videos.

As already discussed, PSV's pedigree is sound, and this is amply reflected in the coaches they hire. The aforementioned Sir Bobby Robson served a successful tenure, Dick Advocaat and Guus Hiddink have managed the Dutch national side, and Hiddink took the unfancied co-hosts, South Korea, to the World Cup semi-final in 2002. As a club, they know what they want from their sides and their players and they recruit the right staff to achieve it. Although not a truly big club, PSV's consistently high standards are a credit to all involved. A world away from the chaotic and haphazard management of Brazilian clubs, Ronaldo was impressed by what he was now part of. When the mind is at ease in the workplace, you often do what you are employed to do well, and Ronaldo proceeded to dazzle the PSV faithful with his burgeoning skills.

Ronaldo's first game was against Vitesse Arnhem, a respectable mid-ranking Dutch team. He duly scored on debut (again) after ten minutes and PSV went on to a comfortable 4–2 win. Any striker will tell you the lustre and value of a debut goal and the time it buys you to settle in at a new club. Not that a player of Ronaldo's evident ability really needed to buy himself time as two weeks later, in a game against Bayer Leverkusen, Ronaldo thumped in a hat-trick but ended up on the losing side in a 5–4 ding-dong encounter. Rudi Völler, ex-Germany boss and opposite number to Ronaldo that night, commented after the game in some disbelief, 'Never in my life have I seen an 18 year old play in this way.' Portentous words indeed from the permed striker who would see a more mature Ronaldo shatter his World Cup dream eight years later in Japan.

Although initially finding the language a challenge, he was helped by full-back Stan Valckx, who had spent a season in Portugal and had learnt basic Portuguese to help him get by. Between them, they were able to communicate with the basics of shoot, pass, man-on and the like, but it wasn't long before the only words Valckx needed were, 'Great goal.'

Inevitably, with acceptance on the pitch came gratification off it. As Ronaldo began to settle, ably assisted by PSV's assigned aid and interpreter Koos Boets, he began to enjoy the relaxed way of life offered by the Dutch. Famed for their tolerance and laid-back nature, they are in many ways similar in outlook to *Cariocas* and Ronaldo warmed to this. Ronaldo further warmed to new coach Dick Advocaat, who had been brought in mid-season to replace Kees Rijvert. Under Advocaat, Ronaldo played probably his best football at PSV and his goal-scoring record reflects this. His first season was a roaring success as he netted 33 times in all competitions from only 35 starts and was leading scorer in the Netherlands. His return was the best for PSV since Coen Dillen in 1960 who scored 31, and also outshone Romário's best return for the club of 25. Not bad for an 18 year old. Ronaldo has spoken highly of the set-up at PSV as a key factor in helping him settle and relax, and cites director of football, Frank Arnesen, as one of the key figures in easing him into European football so smoothly.

RONALDO

In researching this book, I took time to question those most sage of footballing fans, the local cabbies. This proved a productive and most amusing method and, without fail, the cabbies of Eindhoven, Milan, Barcelona, Madrid, Belo Horizonte and Rio were never short of opinions or anecdotes. Eindhoven in particular proved to be fertile ground and the Romário versus Ronaldo debate proved highly inflammatory.

Eric, an affable Eindhoven driver, gave perhaps the most noteworthy response, and in his charming MTV English he explained how, 'Ronaldo was amazing, so fast, so focused. We loved him. Romário, he could play too, but was too busy fucking. Ronaldo came to learn and progress; for Romário, it was just another club and a place to party.'

Around this time, towards the end of 1994, events began to take shape that would bear a heavy influence on Ronaldo's life. These didn't take place in Rio, Eindhoven or Milan, but in Oregon, USA. Oregon, home of sportswear giants Nike, had seen immense changes in the 20 years or so since Ron Bowerman had co-founded a small running-shoe company in 1974. Nike had reinvented the running-shoe industry and along with Reebok in the '80s had reinvented the fitness and sportswear industry, earning huge sums in the process. Since then, they had been focused on earmarking emerging markets for their swoosh logo, and had been highly successful in virtually everything they had attempted. It had helped that their decisions to enter new markets had combined with the emergence of outstanding talents in sports such as basketball and, later, golf.

In basketball, not long after he made his debut for the Chicago Bulls, Michael Jordan was promptly snapped up by Nike to create perhaps the most successful marketing tie-up in sports history. Nike Air Jordan shoe sales were as high and unstoppable as Jordan's prodigious leaps, slam-dunking the competition into submission and forcing many a strategy rethink. In fairness to Nike, they identified Jordan early and set out to build their basketball brand around him. One man, one vision, one goal: market domination. They would later repeat this bullish strategy to enter golf, using the emerging star Tiger Woods as their vehicle, to stunning effect.

As Nike's global might grew, they were conspicuously absent from the truly global game – football. For years, Adidas and Puma had dominated the football-boot market, with any pro worth his salt being seen only in Puma Kings or Adidas World Cups/Copa Mundial. Take a look back through the careers of most big stars and these boots will have graced their feet at some point during their career. Standout marketing deals, such as George Best with Stylo Matchmakers back in the '60s, Kevin Keegan with Patrick in the '80s, and Gary Lineker with Quasar were the odd exception to the rule, but in the late '90s this began to change.

Adidas were also dominant in the kit market, with smaller brands such as Umbro, Le Coq Sportif and Hummel trying to loosen their grip. In short, it was a fairly closed shop but Nike would soon disturb the status quo. To achieve their goal, Nike set out on a carefully planned strategy. This began with the Brazilian national team. Ask most non-Brazilians who their second-favourite national side is and most will say Brazil. Their global appeal and popularity is huge as their interpretation of the beautiful game has consistently proven easiest on the eye over the last 50 years or so. Since the golden shirts glistened to prominence in the Mexico sun in glorious TV colour for the first time in 1970, they have acted as the paragon for all that is good within the game of football: style, flair, grace, passion, beauty . . . and that is just the fans! The contract was signed late in 1994 with the Brazilian CBF and their president, Ricardo Teixera. Exact figures for the terms of the deal vary, but the consensus is that the CBF signed for ten years, worth $200 million.

Quite where this money went when you see the state of Brazil's stadiums is open to debate, but that is not for this book to explore. Included in this contract was the proviso for Brazil to play exhibition games in countries at Nike's behest – inevitably, countries where Nike was looking to expand its footballing brand. For many, this was seen as a sell out by CBF, and it is still a bitter topic in Brazil today.

As with most things they turn their hand to, Nike launched the kit superbly, combining expert marketing with fabric technology to present the new Nike Brazil strip as a breakthrough in kit design. This wasn't just some lairy piece of man-made material that gave you nipple rash, as was the norm with mid-'90s kit design. No, this had new things such as Dri-Fit, Thermo Fit and innovative vented areas. Not only was this the peerless gold of Brazil, but it was brimming with technology and Nike gimmickry. It might even make you play better, was the message coming from Nike. It sold by the truckload and other national teams such as USA and Italy soon signed with Nike too.

Next stop for Nike was to break the domestic kit market. As discussed, the likes of Adidas and Umbro had had this sewn up for years. But again, Nike soon made inroads. In the Netherlands, PSV signed with Nike (arch-rivals Adidas losing out) and it wasn't long before they began to enquire about the rights for Ronaldo himself. He already wore their boots and, although still only 18, could Ronaldo do for Nike in football what Jordan had done for them in basketball? Was he the man to build their strategy around? As his agents Pitta and Martins beavered away behind the scenes negotiating with Nike, Ronaldo continued to do the business on the park.

By now, after his blistering debut season in the Netherlands, there were few in the game who weren't aware that there was potentially something very special about Ronaldo. Next up was the pre-Euro '96 rehearsal at 'The Home of Football', England. Still desperate to shed the image of their notorious football fans, England had done well to clinch the showcase Euro '96 tournament and were desperate to put on a good, violence-free show. As part of the extensive build up, the Umbro Tournament was staged in the summer of 1995 and who better to invite than Brazil? Japan and Sweden made up the other two teams in a thinly veiled attempt by the FA to ensure an England v. Brazil final.

Despite the decaying relic that Wembley was prior to its demolition in 2003, to many overseas players it still retained some mythical charm and playing there was always something foreign stars looked to add to their CV. A goal was always a bonus and Ronaldo obliged, with a sublime piece of finishing which I remember well. Ronaldo was slipped through beyond the offside trap in a one-on-one with England goalkeeper Tim Flowers. Before Flowers could even set himself for the situation, Ronaldo fizzed the ball past him, unerringly into the net. It was genuine blink-of-an-eye stuff and the bemused look on Flower's face told its own story. It was a finish of rare sharpness and sent more than a ripple of approbation around the historic old stadium. It was one of those finishes that makes people sit up and take notice, and the BBC *Match of the Day* pundits were warm in their praise for Ronaldo's performance.

Rather like Scotland and David Narey in Spain '82, England had had the temerity to take the lead with an equally good goal from Graeme Le Saux, but were then given a footballing lesson as Brazil eased through the gears to eventually run out 3–1 winners. Ronaldo and fellow goal-scorer Juninho had taken a great opportunity to massively enhance their value, much to the joy of their agents. Juninho's goal was sufficiently admired by the onlooking England assistant coach and Middlesbrough manager Bryan Robson, who subsequently signed him for a then hefty £8 million.

Ronaldo returned for the new season at PSV with more than a spring in his step. Buoyed by his super goal at Wembley and the subsequent media attention, and as reigning Dutch top-scorer, he faced the new season with eager anticipation, keen to build on his impressive return from last year. Also in tow was a new girlfriend, Viviane Brunieri, an interesting girl of São Paulo extraction who had spent time in Japan with her mother, and as such saw no problem with upping sticks and leaving Rio to join Ronaldo in the Netherlands.

But for Ronaldo, the season got off to a slow start and with a hint of sophomore syndrome, it proved to be anti-climatic. Now receiving much closer and heavier attention from opposing defenders, Ronaldo took his fair share of knocks. Unable to reach the heights of the previous year, the season was punctuated by injury and he completed only 18 games, but, despite all the distractions, still managed to find the net a mightily impressive 18 times.

His services were also increasingly in demand from Brazil, and coach Zagallo, returning for yet another stint at the helm of the *seleçao*, called up Ronaldo for the Uruguay game in Salvador, north eastern Brazil. In the crowd that day was Inter Milan president Massimo Moratti. It's doubtful that Moratti was merely passing through or spending his vacation in northern Brazil, so one must deduce that he was there to see something special. Admittedly, there was some strong talent on show, as there always is during a Brazil v. Uruguay game, but a man of Moratti's stature does not make trips such as this, trips that Inter's scouts are paid to do. For someone of Moratti's standing, a trip like this suggests a big decision is in the offing, and for Moratti, big decisions mean money – his money.

Ronaldo didn't disappoint and notched on 17 and 33 minutes, before some trademark hefty challenges from the Uruguayan back-line alerted Zagallo to the benefit of substituting him at half-time, for which Ronaldo and his Achilles were grateful. The second half petered out and Zagallo admitted in his post-match interview, 'The game was one of two stories, with and without Ronaldo. He showed personality and confidence, and when he departed, nobody could follow his exploits in the area.' Zagallo is the wise old owl of Brazilian football. Twice World Champion as a player, he claims to have invented the (left) wing-back role. He was also the coach during the seminal victory in 1970 and assistant coach to Carlos Alberto Parreira in 1994, and has worked or played with virtually every top Brazilian player of the last 50 years or so. He is no fool and would have been fully aware of the value of Ronaldo not just to that evening's game, but more importantly to the defence of the World Cup in

France 1998. Moratti will have also left the game with plenty to ponder.

On Ronaldo's return to the Netherlands after Christmas for the resumption of New Year training, things took an unplanned turn for the worse. During one training session, Ronaldo began to complain of knee pains. Subsequent lengthy analysis diagnosed the problem as the obscure and relatively unknown Osgood-Schlatter disease. Defined in 1903 by Dr Robert Osgood and Carl Schlatter, it is a cause of knee pain in adolescents, identified by swelling below the knee and over the shin bone (tibia). It is common in teenagers who are experiencing growth spurts and can affect one or both knees. The most common cause of it is the powerful quadricep muscles pulling on the attachment-point of the patella tendon during running activities, and it is common in footballers, athletes and basketball players.

Ronaldo's high-speed slaloming runs made him the perfect candidate for this disease as his young, growing body was struggling to cope. Since arriving at PSV, he had grown four centimetres and added seven kilos to his weight, primarily due to the improved diet and training regime afforded him by the PSV staff and set-up. His muscular ratio was increasing too. The ways of overcoming Osgood-Schlatter disease are fairly limited. Conventional medical wisdom prescribes the most appropriate treatment is to ease off on the exercise and activity and let the growing pains sort themselves out, which can take months – clearly not an option for a footballer of Ronaldo's worth to PSV (or Martins and Pitta). They needed him in action. With this in mind, they decided to operate on the problem. The operation is not without risk and the future impact on a player's career is uncertain. Those around Ronaldo, such as Martins and Pitta, were keen to play down the gravity of the situation, understandably fearing it could dilute the interest and subsequent value of their man. But before long, Inter Milan declared their change of heart in Ronaldo and their reluctance to sign a player unable to prove his full fitness – a bitter blow to Martins and Pitta, who had been manoeuvring Ronaldo towards a Milan switch in the close-season. This put the frighteners on the two agents and they were quickly on to their insurance people to tweak the terms and conditions of their policy. The existing policy cost $20,000 per annum and paid out $3 million should Ronaldo's career be cut short by injury. They now trebled the premiums so that $9 million would be paid out to themselves and Ronaldo in the event of a serious injury.

The operation itself proved a success and now Ronaldo went into physiotherapy. Somewhat controversially, he eschewed the PSV staff and chose to recuperate with Brazilian physio, Nilton Petrone, or 'Filé' as he is known. Filé runs a smart clinic in the modern Barra da Tijuca area to the west of Rio and is noted for his avant-garde techniques. A tai-chi expert and keen student of oriental medicine, and accused by some of being a hippy in the '60s, Filé insists on dealing with each patient as *um todo individual* (a complete individual). He had risen to fame through his work with Romário in the early '90s when Romário suffered knee problems of his own – sidelining him from Italia '90 – and he came with Romário's full stamp of approval, something that wouldn't have gone unnoticed with Ronaldo. The prospect of recuperating back home in Rio would also have been a key factor. Not shy of hard work, Filé put Ronaldo through a rigorous, eight-hours-a-day routine consisting of over 2,000 leg exercises per day plus 640 trampoline jumps, to build up both knees and speed him on his way to recovery.

Ronaldo's return to fitness coincided with the end of the season and as the summer approached, transfer rumours began to multiply. With Inter Milan having gone on the record as saying '*non grazie*', and the Bosman ruling turning the transfer market on its head, Martins and Pitta began working overtime to optimise their asset. With two years left on his PSV contract, PSV officials were understandably irritated by the transfer talk, and took a tough stance. They considered Ronaldo their man and 'not for sale at any price'. In short, if you wanted him, you'd better make the offer good.

Some naive remarks by Ronaldo on one of his many visits to Rio about his wish to play for Barcelona didn't help matters either and it was soon clear that it was they who were being lined up by Martins and Pitta as suitor number one. Should a club like Barcelona begin to flex their muscle and wallet then a club like PSV could not hope to compete. It was a footballing mismatch and credit must go to PSV for handling the situation in a most impressive manner, as befits a club of their reputation. More foolish remarks by Ronaldo calling PSV coach Dick Advocaat 'stupid' fanned the flames, and his further insult to the Dutch club in saying he'd be happy to play for Barcelona for free meant the situation was in danger of turning sour.

Events began to take shape and in another of football's circular tales, newly installed Barça coach Bobby Robson entered the frame. Sir Bobby had identified the prolific Blackburn Rovers striker Alan Shearer as his primary target and had made three attempts to sign him, but each time was rebuffed by Blackburn coach, the late Ray Harford. Sir Bobby, again demonstrating his status as one of football's good guys, said, 'OK, I'll leave it there,' and as confirmation came in that Ronaldo was fit – his five goals for bronze-medallists Brazil at the 1996 Atlanta Olympics testimony to that – Robson quickly identified Ronaldo as the man to complete his Barcelona jigsaw, telling me, 'We needed a striker, someone who could put bums on seats, and with 120,000 of them in the Camp Nou, Ronaldo was the man.' At a club like Barcelona, he had the wherewithal at his disposal to go after someone like Ronaldo, who was bound to be pricey. I spoke to Sir Bobby about the deal and he laughed, saying, 'We knew he'd be expensive . . . but not quite that expensive.'

Sir Bobby had used his extensive contact list from his PSV days to get the low-down on Ronaldo, as spending money of the magnitude expected to sign Ronaldo comes with its caveats. In the pressure-cooker environment of the Camp Nou and with a president like Josep Lluis Nuñez and vice-president Joan Gaspart to satisfy, decisions need to be right. The feedback out of Eindhoven was good. In fact, very good. Old pal Stan Valckx was happy to confirm that Sir Bobby was making a wise purchase. Sir Bobby told me that Eric Gerets had also endorsed the choice, saying, 'Just sign him; he won't disappoint.'

As Sir Bobby explains in his autobiography *An Englishman Abroad*, one of the things he enjoyed about coaching abroad was the way you were left to run team affairs. If you wanted players brought in, you identified them to the board and they did what they could to sign them. Sir Bobby identified Ronaldo to Nuñez and Gaspart as the key to his plans. Barcelona already had a high-quality squad full of outstanding international players but Sir Bobby was insistent that Ronaldo was the key.

Happy to relate the intriguing story, he told me, 'We started at £10 million and PSV said no without a thought; we went to £12 million and they still shook their heads. It went to £13 million, £14 million, £15 million and then we were at £17 million.' Bear in mind this was a lot of money – world-record transfer territory at the time. Sir Bobby continued, 'It was serious money, as Nuñez and Gaspart kept pointing out, but I kept on saying he was worth it and they backed me all the way. Gaspart himself at one stage said that it was no use dying and leaving the money with someone else.' As the temperature rose, Barcelona played a cute move and as Sir Bobby explains, 'We decided that if they turned down £17 million we should ask them what it would take to persuade them while at the same time not committing ourselves. PSV took the bait and came back and told us £20 million. I'm sure that figure was meant to frighten us away. It nearly did, for even Nuñez gasped at that figure. But by now, signing the lad was an obsession. We did nothing for a day or two as we knew we were the only club involved. Having sat on things for a while, we went in with a cheque for £20 million, leaving PSV with little option but to accept and cash in on their prodigy.'

It was clear from the look on Sir Bobby's face that it was a serious and high-octane negotiation, with unprecedented numbers involved for one player. But he looks back with avuncular pride and justification at the faith he placed back then in his judgement of the young Ronaldo, and his tenacity and courage in convincing Nuñez and Gaspart to fund the deal. 'I put him on the world stage,' Sir Bobby told me. 'At PSV, he was popular and playing for a super club, but they don't come much bigger than Barcelona and it was me who brought him there.'

So Ronaldo's time at PSV and in the Netherlands came to a close and he signed for £20 million, no mere bagatelle back then. In footballing terms, he could look back with nothing but satisfaction: 54 goals in 57 games, and thrilling the PSV faithful with some breathtaking play. As a person, he had grown in every sense of the word. He had survived his first overseas stint away from his beloved Rio, had weathered various domestic issues and coped with the language difficulties, and had demonstrated himself to be a level-headed, focused young man. He had also suffered his first serious injury and shown admirable resolve to come back in even time from the operation and prove his fitness.

In the minus column, he had made some daft and naive comments about PSV that he would have been much better off keeping to himself, and which did him no favours. He would have been wiser to let his agents do the talking off the field and himself the talking on it. As he completed the switch in the summer of 1996, he was about to experience a year that would change his life for good, with the quality of his football launching him from teenage prodigy to full-blown global footballing superstar.

CHAPTER 6

YOU'RE IN THE ARMY NOW – FC BARCELONA 1996–97

FC Barcelona is more than just a football club, it is a sporting institution and an international passion for many people. Its spiritual home is the stunning Camp Nou – a stadium that holds 120,000 people and rightly lays claim to being one of, if not the best in the world. The stadium is a hugely impressive edifice and as you step out onto the playing surface, you cannot fail to be inspired by its amphitheatrical majesty. It has three vast tiers providing unrestricted views for every spectator and has an adjacent ground for the reserve and youth teams, which itself holds 25,000 people. The club caters for all sorts of sports from tennis to squash to hockey, and all take pride in wearing the red and dark blue, which, amazingly, take their origins from the colours of the Waterloo Rugby Football Club in England from which two of Barcelona's founders, the English Witty brothers, took inspiration. The club's motto *Som mes que un club* (we are more than a club) reflects succinctly the *raison d'être* of Barcelona as the instrument of Catalan pride, an emblem of the region and the army behind which the six million inhabitants of Catalonia are mobilised.

To understand Barcelona, or Barça as it is known the world over, you need to comprehend the fervour that follows the club's every move. From the signing of players, the refusal to carry a shirt sponsor (because Barça is the national side of Catalonia and national sides don't carry shirt sponsors), to the intense daily press coverage, every machination of the club is scrutinised to the nth degree.

YOU'RE IN THE ARMY NOW . . .

Catalans are very proud people not short on emotion. Spain's former dictator General Franco was particularly severe upon the Catalan region, sanctioning programmes of violence and curfew, and refusing them permission to speak their own language. In many ways the austerity and, some might say, humiliation of Franco's tactics and policies has created a situation in Catalonia where symbolism is so strong that many would prefer complete autonomy from Spain and the creation of a Catalan independent state. To spend time in the wonderful city is a joy in itself and the passion that runs close to the surface of Catalans is plain to see. Red and yellow striped *senyeras* adorn shops, restaurants and street corners, and no evening stroll in Barcelona is complete without the whiff of cordite from the ubiquitous fire crackers. This city has passion in abundance.

In particular, the club has a long tradition of foreign superstar strikers. Ladislao Kubala, Johan Cruyff, Diego Maradona, Gary Lineker, Michael Laudrup, Romário and Hristo Stoichkov are just a few of the mouthwatering international *Who's Who* of strikers who've worn the shirt with distinction. Ronaldo arrived as the latest of these foreign imports, treading the same path as his pal and compatriot Romário from PSV and arriving to a swell of expectation that only superstar strikers of Brazilian origin can arouse. Whereas the above names arrived as established world stars often off the back of an impressive World Cup performance, Ronaldo was only 19 years old, had only a handful of caps under his belt, and had cost a staggering $20 million. The spotlight of world football was now upon him. He didn't have the security blanket and relative obscurity of the PSV finishing school to hide behind, and he had the full glare of the Barcelona leviathan media machine to consider. This was the big time and it was game on.

I spoke to ex-Barcelona and England legend Gary Lineker about the pressure of playing for the Spanish club. Gary joined Barcelona after having won the coveted Golden Boot award at the 1986 Mexico World Cup, so he knows a thing or two about pressure and scoring goals. The deal had been arranged before the World Cup had started, primarily due to his scintillating form for English Champions Everton, for whom he netted an outstanding 40 times; and also due to the admiration for him shown by Barça's then incumbent English coach, Terry Venables. Venables, or '*El Meester*' as the locals christened him, was in desperate need of a tonic after the scheduled 'Historic Dream' of European Cup, Spanish Cup and *La Liga* title had come crashing down around him and the people of Catalonia in the most sickening way imaginable. Not only was the Spanish Cup lost and then *La Liga* surrendered to you know who in Madrid, but the European Cup – incredibly still awaiting its first visit to the Barça trophy cabinet – was lost in a penalty shoot-out to 'dour' Steaua Bucharest, the Catalans netting only once. Barcelona would have to wait until 1992 to lift the wonderful trophy for the first time, fittingly, for a club with historical links with England, at the 'home of football', Wembley. But that would remain their only success in that tournament, an alarming statistic for 'the world's biggest club'.

Lineker came to Spain with the fillip of having his profile dramatically raised by the recent Golden Boot award, but was still fully aware of the expectation on his shoulders as he arrived. Despite his standing as probably England's best footballer of that time, he had not played for an overseas club prior to Barcelona and the day-to-day routine of the then pre-Premiership English First Division was tame in comparison. He might provide the odd interview for the local radio station, Elton Welsby's *Kick Off*, or something more substantial if BBC's *Football Focus* was in town. What Lineker wasn't used to was the daily scrutiny witnessed at Barcelona, even back in 1986–87.

I asked Gary whether he thought Ronaldo would have been able to grasp all that goes with playing for a club like Barcelona, especially wearing the number 9 shirt, to which he replied, 'It would have been tough for a young lad coming to such a big club for the first time, but he seemed to be level-headed, even back then. Obviously, a lot is dependent on your character and your personality, but if you've got bundles of ability this can help alleviate the pressure. Plus people tend to be more uninhibited when they're younger and this I think was evident in his early form at Barcelona.'

As genial as his BBC persona suggests, Gary went on to explain the differences he'd experienced as a player moving from the English league to *La Liga*. 'It was a stark contrast – a gulf almost – to what I'd left behind at Everton and Leicester before that. Firstly, and let's not underestimate this, the size and magnitude of the stadium hits you. It's vast. Then the media and press presence hits you. At Everton, you might get the manager being interviewed on a Friday for local TV, and then every now and again you'd have the excitement of a camera crew when *Match of the Day* was in town; but at Barcelona, every single day there were camera crews there, sometimes ten or twenty, from all around the world. Radio too. You come off the plane and there's madness at the airport. It strikes you pretty quickly of the scale of things, so I'm sure Ronaldo would have been aware that big things were expected of him, especially with the price tag. Plus when you arrive for pre-season, you have what they called Presentation Day which forms a kind of combined training session and unveiling session for that year's squad. The coach says a few words and you do a few ball skills etc., and then you're presented to the crowd. But this crowd isn't merely a handful of season-ticket holders and diehards, it's about 100,000! Expectancy is huge. They are a massive club, don't forget that. You have to live up to it and often the foreign players have an extra burden as they are expected to live up to Cruyffs and Maradonas of days gone by.' Ronaldo may have been less overawed at the stadium with having played on occasion at Rio's monolithic Maracanã, but the daily press intrusion would have left him in no doubt as to what he needed to deliver.

I asked Gary about the pressure on Ronaldo for a player of his age. Gary had first-hand experience of a young overseas striker struggling to adapt to Barcelona with Mark Hughes, who had been another of Terry Venables's signings, for a fee of £1.7 million from Manchester United. Venables had ignored the recommendations of youth-team trainer Jaume Olive, who had implored him to sign the emerging Dutch players Marco van Basten and Ruud Gullit, citing them as not only more gifted than Hughes but also more likely to adapt to the Spanish game. Olive would subsequently pay for his ranting with his job, but history suggests he may have had more than a point. Gary, a good friend of Hughes to this day, described Mark's time there thus: 'Mark didn't get off to a fast start and the supporters were soon on his back. Mark was only 21 and wasn't equipped to deal with that. He got down, felt lonely, struggled with the language and it didn't really work out for him.' At which point, I added that Ronaldo had only just turned 20, had a transfer fee that dwarfed Mark's and was much further away from home. 'Fair point,' conceded Gary and we arrived at the conclusion that Ronaldo's ability, above all else, combined with a sound temperament, was the key to his flying start.

Jimmy Burns in his superb book *Barça: A People's Passion* sheds further light on the misery of Hughes and the isolation of a footballer struggling to be accepted. He writes:

> The Camp Nou had always demanded a good spectacle. Hughes
> played a tougher, rougher game than the Barcelona fans were used
> to or even wanted. They nicknamed him *'El Toro'* – the Bull – not

so much because he was brave but because they saw only physical force, without skill. Lineker by contrast was nicknamed 'The Matador' for his goal-scoring abilities and for the graceful figure he cut both on and off the pitch. In Barcelona, Hughes found the football of the effortless touch difficult to master. As Venables himself later recognised, when it came down to it, it was really quite simple: the football he got away with in English football was frowned upon in Spain.

Burns continues:

It didn't help that Hughes, never the greatest of communicators even back home, found learning the local language difficult. His poor communication extended to the early days of training with Barcelona when he also found it difficult to engage in the *rondas*, the small, highly tactile groupings of players into which the team was divided to test individual dribbling and passing skills at close quarters. Early red cards didn't help Hughes either and he was simply seen as a bad-tempered plodder undeserving of a club with an ego as big as Barcelona's.

Now this isn't meant as a 'let's all get at Mark Hughes' session, as being a Mancunian I can vouch for his superb goal-scoring ability and assure you that he found adoration with at least one of his clubs. He is now in charge at Premiership club Blackburn Rovers, but before that was the highly respected manager of Wales, who, prior to his appointment, had been a laughing stock, then came within an ace of qualification for Euro 2004. Hughes was a particular type of centre-forward: robust, physical, what the English would call 'a real handful'. His second spell at Manchester United would cement him as an Old Trafford legend and his reputation for not scoring tap-ins only hints at some of the blockbusting goals which he would delight the Old Trafford faithful with, often in very big games: none more so than in the sweet strike from a famously tight angle that he wellied home in Rotterdam to defeat Johan Cruyff's Barcelona in the 1991 Cup-Winners' Cup final. They say revenge is a dish best served cold, and the icy *coup de grâce* with which Hughes dispatched a seemingly lost cause against his old employers is something he still savours to this day. Hughes will be the first to admit he had nowhere near Ronaldo's natural ability, but where the comparison is relevant is that Hughes arrived at Barcelona with a burgeoning reputation just like Ronaldo, but simply couldn't adjust. Worse, he was shunned by the players (bar Lineker) and ridiculed by the fans. He cut a sorry figure and his stay was miserable. Moreover, ten years after Hughes, Ronaldo joined an already very strong squad, a star-studded cast containing the likes of Giovanni, Pizzi, Luis Figo, Luis Enrique, Nadal, Laurent Blanc, Gica Popescu, Stoichkov, Guardiola *et al.*, and in the words of Sir Bobby Robson, 'made it better'.

On the pressure of being the imported striker, Gary went on, 'I was lucky enough to score after two minutes of my first game and then another after twenty minutes. That lifted the pressure immeasurably. Then, a few months later, in the big one against Madrid, I scored a hat-trick and we won 3–2 in front of the faithful at the Camp Nou. It was my defining moment as a Barcelona player, and guaranteed lifelong celebrity amongst supporters.'

Ronaldo's *La Liga* debut for Barcelona came on 7 September 1996 in the Camp Nou against local city rivals Espanyol. The Camp Nou's most fanatical section, the *gol nord*, was resplendent with Catalan, Barcelona and Brazil flags – some no doubt dusted down from Romário's days but others bought from the grafters outside doing a roaring trade with all things Brazilian. Partnered with fellow Brazilian and close-season signing from Santos, Giovanni, Ronaldo struggled to make an impact on the treacherous relaid surface – a result of unseasonal weather and a rushed re-seed job that hadn't allowed the new pitch to bed in in time for the start of the season. This wouldn't have bothered Espanyol, who revelled in the uncertainty of the conditions and their fans delighted in Barcelona's expensive all-stars fumbling around on a surface not fit for an Under-14 school game. Espanyol took a shock lead and it looked like they'd steal the game until six minutes from time when Giovanni nipped in for the equaliser. Then, with time running out, Ronaldo stirred to life, collected the ball 30 yards from goal and set off on one of his slaloming runs through the Espanyol defence (which would soon become commonplace), and then belted a powerful shot that the Espanyol keeper could only parry into the path of another new signing, Pizzi, who tapped home for the win. No goal for Ronaldo but an early indication of his pyrotechnics.

The match had actually been nothing short of a farce, with the dreadful surface just contributing to the charade. Michael Robinson, former Liverpool striker and now high-profile Spanish TV pundit, tells a famous tale of this game. He said it reminded him of the games he had played at school when the 'good' team had deliberately let the 'bad' team score the goals until the teacher's whistle announced there were five minutes left, the signal for the 'good' team to start playing properly and go for the win, leading to a mass scramble for the winning goals. He suggested too that the Barcelona team could be a real threat for the season ahead, assuming they didn't let the 'bad' teams play for too long.

Understandably, the fans wanted more and were soon given something to cheer when in Barcelona's next game Ronaldo opened his *La Liga* account with a smart goal away against Santander. This was Sir Bobby Robson's initial first-hand account of what he would later describe to me as Ronaldo's 'unique ability to create goals out of nothing'. He continued, bristling with reverence of the memory of such football, 'When he received the ball from, I think it was Pep Guardiola, there was nothing on, but within a few seconds, he'd skipped past two defenders and bang, the ball was in the back of the net. Brilliant. Fantastic.' However, Sir Bobby's then assistant and current Chelsea coach José Mourinho was less sanguine: 'We've told Ronaldo it's no good scoring a wonder goal and spending the other 89 minutes sleeping.' Brusque words indeed from the maverick Portuguese.

However, Mourinho's stern warning was made to look a little peevish as, before long, Ronaldo was scoring goals on a very regular basis, some of them truly outstanding. Gary Lineker recalls working on BBC's *Football Focus* at the time of Ronaldo's arrival at Barcelona and they were soon receiving footage of his wonder goals and showing them at the end of the popular Saturday lunch-time show. Gary went on: 'I remember these clips coming in, almost on a weekly basis, and we all marvelled at his talent and ability. Such pace and power and with the ball stuck to his foot. He could then show complete composure in front of goal having run 40–50 yards with defenders snapping at him. It was breathtaking.'

We discussed the transfer fee and whether he justified it. 'It's always hard to say at the time,' added Gary, 'because it was such a lot of money, but it was clear he was set to be one of the best players in the game, and a club like Barcelona can take that kind of risk with that money. He had so much power and pace and with the ball at his feet too. If there was a player you could take a chance on at that time, then he was certainly it. As the season progressed, it actually started to look good value!'

This was a view that was beginning to be shared by Martins and Pitta, Ronaldo's insatiable agents, who felt they had marked the wrong price tag on their main asset. Working in tandem with Ronaldo's 'third agent', Milan-based Giovanni Branchini, and with the ink still barely dry on his Barcelona world-record transfer, they began to surreptitiously hawk Ronaldo around a very select number of clubs again. You have to admire their front at doing this. Inter, never ones to shirk a good transfer rumour, were still smarting from their decision to pull out of early discussions and being forced to witness Ronaldomania sweeping Barcelona and not Milan. As we've already seen, Massimo Moratti had been willing to schlep to Salvador to have a look at Ronaldo, and now that he was front-page news and scoring goals for fun, soon began to enquire about the state of play. Like most players in Spain, Ronaldo had a buy-out clause in his contract that was intended to scare off any potential suitors. Rumours began to surface that Inter Milan were willing to cover this and get their man, talking in terms of a transfer of $40 million – double what Barcelona had paid not six months earlier. As Ronaldo's form on the pitch went from amazing to extraordinary, these figures began to look realistic and good value.

By now, Barcelona was in the grip of Ronaldomania. He scored twice in the 3–2 win over Real Sociedad, and twice more against Zaragoza in a ding-dong 5–3 win, one of which was yet another high-speed run with a hapless group of defenders chasing their prey like ageing policemen after a fleet-footed robber. The goals were coming thick and fast and, with Barcelona making their best start to a season in a long time, everything seemed to be perfect.

A reflection of his impact in the Catalan town comes from several men of the cloth, who described to me how, where there used to be paintings and pictures of the Last Supper, there were posters of Ronaldo. Burger bars even sold 'Ronaldoburgers'. Ronaldo added to the harmony by happily telling reporters, 'I wish I could play a football match every day. The part I really like is when I look at the fans and they cheer. I am a hungry player; I want to score when I get the ball. The coach [Robson] has given me total freedom. Barcelona is the best club in the world.' Messianic words indeed, but behind the scenes, Martins and Pitta were hard at work, sweating their asset.

Inevitably, Ronaldo was in big demand. TV shows, talk shows, radio shows, magazines: they all wanted a piece of him. At a restaurant opening in the city centre, he was offered a large sum to pose with another human blessed with heavenly gifts, the delightful Cindy Crawford. But Ronaldo refused, no doubt fortified by his latest dental work, and commented arrogantly, 'They should have asked her to pose with me.'

With his confidence clearly sky high both on and off the pitch, it is no coincidence that what followed was perhaps, in terms of skill, Ronaldo's finest footballing moment. Saturday, 12 October 1996 may not stick in the memory as a key date in world history. John F. Kennedy wasn't shot, Poland wasn't invaded, and the World Trade Center didn't implode. But in footballing terms, it was the day Ronaldo was catapulted into the global spotlight and the impact was seismic.

That day, Barcelona travelled to Santiago to play struggling Compostela in a league game. It wasn't long before Ronaldo was in the action as, within a minute, he had weaved down the right flank and forced compatriot William to concede a soft own goal. After a quarter of an hour, he sped down the opposite flank and served up a tap-in for Giovanni. Then, on half an hour, the moment came, the goal Sir Bobby Robson describes as 'The One'. Collecting the ball from within his own half, Ronaldo set off on a run that resembled an army assault course. Compostela players vainly tried to halt him, employing various means, the majority of which were foul. Ronaldo was initially dragged back by an outrageous shirt-pull but his sheer strength pulled the defender along, hitching a ride with the red and blue blur for a few yards before giving up the chase. Unperturbed, and with the ball seemingly attached to his foot, he swerved, shimmied, wriggled, jinked, hurdled and barged his way towards the Compostela goal, defenders bouncing off him like houses in a hurricane, and as the last bunch of would-be ambushers descended on him, he gave them the slip and somehow slid the ball under the advancing goalkeeper for one of *the* great goals. This was football *in excelsis*. Ronaldo was rampant as Compostela were buried 5–1. He was proving to be a true Jedi of a striker, with the ball at his full mercy and an ability to jettison defenders as if using The Force itself.

On closer inspection, the goal can be dissected as follows: he ran for 14 seconds with the ball (think about that), took 16 touches, took 34 steps, beat 5 opposition players and the keeper, and covered 46 metres of pitch. These bare figures alone don't do the goal justice and for individual brilliance it is up there with Maradona's second against England in Mexico '86, regarded by many as the best of all time.

Robson was incredulous and from the sidelines held his hands to his head and looked to the heavens, then turned to the paltry 12,000 crowd (itself a criminally low number to have witnessed the goal first hand) with his arms outstretched as if to enlist them all as witnesses – an unforgettable image. For a man of Robson's vintage and experience, a man who had seen all the game has to offer, that image of him, shaken with sheer disbelief as if he'd seen something beyond conventional footballing comprehension, said everything about the goal. After the game, still pumped on the adrenalin of that goal, he further enthused, 'You can go anywhere you want in the world and you won't find a player who can score goals like that. Can anybody, anywhere, show me a better player?'

That night, sports newswires were buzzing with the game and 'that goal', showing it time after time to awestruck audiences. The Spanish press were gushing in their praise: 'A genius' (*Marca*); 'Pelé returns' (*AS*); 'The star of the 21st century' (*Sport*); 'An aria of football' (*El Periodico*); 'An extra-terrestrial in Santiago' (*El Pais*); and perhaps the best one, 'He left the whole world behind' (*La Vanguardia*). I knew personally that this was big news when a good friend of mine, at the time working in New York, called to say he'd just seen it on CNN and it was causing a stir in the soccer-shy US.

Soccer legends were quick to add their views: 'He could soon be the best in the world' (Alfredo di Stefano); 'From what I've seen of him, he is up there with the best' (Michel Platini); 'He has nothing more to prove' (Cruyff); 'He's from another planet' (Jorge Valdano); and with typically Brazilian impartiality came 'He's the best in the world' (Pelé); and 'Indisputably, he is the best striker in the world' (Tostao) and 'He's at a level beyond the other players' (Tele Santana). His teammate Pizzi added with some candour, 'I play football; Ronaldo plays something different altogether.'

Also purring with approbation were Martins and Pitta, no doubt reconsidering the size of their next yacht as each goal went in. Inter Milan were again chief suitor, and as Ronaldo continued to print goals it became evident that the rumours of a move were now something to be taken more seriously. Not best chuffed was Sir Bobby Robson who, having been so instrumental in bringing Ronaldo to Barcelona and having him spearhead their title charge, was now bemused at the negative attention surrounding Ronaldo and, by association, the Barcelona squad. 'Why should he go to Milan?' he chippily told a packed press conference. 'It snows in Milan and I know he doesn't like the snow.'

I discussed the situation with Sir Bobby and he explained, 'As far as I was concerned, he was our player. We'd spent a lot of money on him and signed him for eight years. It was as simple as that. Or so I thought.' Looking back, Sir Bobby can see that there was a sub-plot all along. 'Ronaldo's relationship with his agents was different to most I've seen. He never called them his agents, but always his "business associates" and that was how he dealt with them. It was very much a business set-up. He would do the business on the pitch and they would take care of business off it.' Then, ruefully, he added, 'I suppose you can't argue with what they've achieved financially.'

By the beginning of December, barely halfway through his first season, reports were coming in that Manchester United were willing to pay £20 million. United were confident they could land Ronaldo's signature and, as one of the largest clubs in the world, had the financial muscle to pull it off. Ronaldo again proved savvy and told one reporter with perfect ambiguity, 'I have no problem with English clubs.' He would later add, 'I know of the interest from Manchester United. I am proud to be wanted by such a famous club because it is so flattering, but I want to repay Bobby Robson for having confidence to sign me.' Again, all angles covered. What United weren't aware of was that they were being used by Pitta and Martins to raise the stakes.

Despite the manoeuvrings and distractions off the pitch, Ronaldo continued to dazzle on it. Another wonder goal versus Valencia again lit up the sports newswires and cemented his reputation as something very special indeed. This time, Ronaldo collected the ball in the inside-right area just inside the attacking half, while zooming away on a diagonal run towards the penalty area, white shirts in hot pursuit. Then, as two Valencian defenders converged on him in tandem, with stopping him the only thought on their minds, he somehow burst through their blockade, like water breaking through a punctured dam, and then, with a pause reminiscent of the latest *Matrix* film's split-speed technology, he set himself, weighed up the situation and calmly finished under the advancing keeper. 'What a goal,' Sir Bobby later recalled. 'He went between two centre-halfs and they bounced off him. The ball's in the net and those two are lying on the ground. Incredible.' If not perhaps quite as extra-terrestrial as his Compostela goal, it confirmed it as no fluke, and now set expectations on him even higher as the crowd bayed for these wonder goals with every touch.

In the quarter-finals of the Spanish Cup, a game surrounded by the inevitable ranting of Atlético Madrid's colourful president, the late Jesus Gil, Ronaldo was to the fore in what Sir Bobby recalls as the craziest match he's ever been involved in. 'A subway strike had kept the crowd down to a mere 80,000,' he said with some jest, 'and by half-time we were 3–0 down and the crowd were going spare, baying for my blood. I gambled and took off defenders Laurent Blanc and Popescu, throwing on Hristo Stoichkov and Juan Pizzi, telling the team at half-time to take a long look at themselves and the shirt they were wearing and go and win the second half 4–0.' What happened in the next 40 minutes still brings a smile to Robson's face today. 'I'd barely taken my seat and Ronaldo had scored twice, one of them another marvellous effort. He beat the same player twice – twice! Then rounded the keeper and rolled it in. Then Figo scored, Ronaldo scored again and then I think Pizzi finished things off for 5–3. It was amazing.'

By now, the writing was on the wall. Since Christmas, Ronaldo's relationship with Barcelona, its coaching staff, back-room personnel and fans had become more and more strained. He had acted naively on several occasions and, although clearly a footballer of genius on the field, he still had a lot to learn in terms of tact and diplomacy off it. As the Rio trips threatened to get out of hand, Ronaldo made Robson's position as coach even more tenuous and each request for leave to visit Rio put Sir Bobby in an invidious situation. Robson obviously had the team's best interests at heart and that meant points. Points came from winning and even in a side as strong as Barcelona's, Ronaldo was clearly his trump card when it came to scoring goals. But Sir Bobby was becoming more and more frustrated with Ronaldo's ambivalence towards team harmony and also his ignorance of the damage constant jet lag was doing to his fitness.

As he became besotted with then-girlfriend Suzana Werner, he was always looking for half a chance to jet into Rio to catch some time with her and catch up with his *Carioca* friends. He'd also drop in on physio Filé, who'd helped him back to fitness after the knee operation whilst at PSV. In Spain, there was growing belief that Ronaldo was overdoing the high life of night-clubbing, launches, late nights and travel and, in doing so, thumbing his nose to his teammates. Rumours of split-camps within the Barcelona dressing-room also arose as the Catalan press, always eager for some good Camp Nou gossip, claimed that there were several factions critical of Robson's tactics. Ronaldo was reported as saying, somewhat crassly, 'Robson needs to change his tactics, not just for my sake but for the whole team. His system might have worked at first, but as soon as we faced stronger sides we've had difficulties. I prefer

Zagallo's [Brazil's coach] formation. The team is more compact and I receive the ball more often.' Ronaldo hardly seemed concerned about tactics for the team but more about tactics to get more of the ball to him. Robson, for once riled by all the negative talk, responded, 'I can't believe it sometimes, everybody's at it: the board, the players. It's like the papers today with Ronaldo criticising my tactics again. The boy's 20 years old, for Christ's sake . . . it's diabolical. He wasn't complaining when we were winning 6–0 and 8–0.'

As the rumpus continued, the Barcelona faithful soon began to get restless too. With anything and everything Ronaldo did plastered all over the Catalan press on a daily basis, they were never short of information as to what he was up to, and as the news became more and more negative, they began to turn on him, in a way that would have been unimaginable earlier in the season. But come January, and with four goalless games coinciding with more air travel than Alan Whicker in his safari-suited pomp, they began to boo and hiss him with each failed dribble. Robson diplomatically stepped in to divert some attention away from his young charge and ask the fans for some consistency. Robson was also acutely aware that Ronaldo's knee was still potentially dodgy and dreaded the possibility that it might buckle under the pressure and frequency of games. Those fans aggrieved at Ronaldo's attitude took the chance to vent their discontent by overwhelmingly voting Catalan local favourite Luis Enrique as their Player of the Year, way ahead of Ronaldo, who had recently been crowned FIFA World Player of the Year in Lisbon. Ronaldo took this affront personally and advised Martins and Pitta to keep negotiating.

Ironically, in the maelstrom of all this hoo-hah came 'the world's biggest game', the Barcelona v. Real Madrid clash at the Camp Nou. A thrilling 3–2 victory was lapped up by the home fans but then Ronaldo again displayed acute naivety, and further wound-up the *Cules* (hardcore Barcelona fans) by swapping shirts with Madrid's Roberto Carlos. Admittedly, Roberto Carlos is his friend and compatriot but this action is perhaps the most contemptible thing imaginable for any Barcelona fan.

With patience starting to wear a bit thin, Ronaldo then somehow managed to swing another trip to Rio, this time for the world-famous Carnaval, an event that taxes even seasoned carousers, never mind pro footballers. With the Catalan press lapping up anything Ronaldo related, he gave them a quarry of fodder as he incredibly chose to join a Carnaval float, dressed up in full Carnaval garb. His outfit was a rather fetching gold number, with large, glittering shoulder pads, a star-spangled headband and finished with a flurry of blue feathers to complete his head dress. The trip could best be described as ill advised, and the Spanish press were happy to tuck into him. With a mixture of contempt and disbelief, they harangued Ronaldo for the irresponsibility of the trip and rounded on Robson for the favouritism they felt it reflected. Fellow Brazilian Giovanni, perhaps somewhat miffed he couldn't swing the trip back to his beloved Carnaval himself, added, 'I love Carnaval too, but as a professional my duty is to be here. A return journey to Brazil for the sake of two days – and with hard partying thrown in – is hard work. Even if I had the time off, I would have stayed here.'

Sir Bobby had actually personally OK'd the last Rio trip, but unaware of the fact it was Carnaval week had advised Ronaldo to get some rest, see his family and keep a low profile. A forlorn hope at Carnaval time. Ronaldo had duped him and when Sir Bobby saw the Carnaval photos he was livid, but again found himself caught between a rock and a hard place. Keen to discipline 'the boy' and also under immense pressure to keep the star in the team, he struggled to find satisfactory middle ground. He was pressured from behind the scenes to keep Ronaldo happy as Barcelona felt they could then conclude the contractual situation with Martins and Pitta at the end of the season. Ronaldo got back to scoring ways with a thumping hat-trick against Zaragoza on 23 February, and then at the end of February, the long awaited 'Ro-Ro' (Ronaldo and Romário) combination was due to debut for Brazil against Norway. Neither shone in the game and by now Martins and Pitta were turning up the negotiating heat with some strong stuff for Barcelona to contemplate: 'We've given the board [of Barcelona] plenty of time to finance the new deal; we can't wait much longer. The train was at Barcelona's station and they let it pass by. We only have to pay his buy-out clause and he can walk.'

The three-way war of words between Ronaldo and Martins and Pitta and the Barcelona board began to intensify and get ugly. Claim followed counterclaim and as the men in suits slugged it out, Ronaldo was invariably left to throw in what he felt were the right words – often merely confusing the whole situation.

Around this time, at the end of March 1997, a Nike spokesman inadvertently blabbed that the fact that Barcelona's current kit supplier was Kappa presented a potential problem in any deal. With Ronaldo now signed up with Nike for a reported $1.5 million per year for ten years, and plans for a Ronaldo sub-brand 'R9' well and truly under way, anything non-Nike was a fly in the ointment. The spokesman cut to the crux of their problem, saying, 'We can't wait three years until Barcelona's deal with Kappa expires. That's three years of Ronaldo's photos in another kit.'

Martins and Pitta were skilled at making Barcelona look like the villains, and as Barcelona began to get stand-offish and criticise the professional behaviour of the two agents, Ronaldo jumped to their defence, saying, 'I'm furious with them [Barcelona]. Martins and Pitta are like parents to me and Barcelona should show them more respect. They've been looking after me since I was 14 and my life has changed for the better thanks to them.' The situation see-sawed all the way to the end of the season with statements from each camp serving only to confuse, and 'Will he stay, won't he stay?' stories running almost daily in the Spanish press. Undeterred by the fuss, Ronaldo was still able to continue his lethal goal-scoring record, netting three more in the 5–2 defeat of Atlético Madrid, but again showing scant diplomacy by celebrating his first two goals by holding his index finger to his mouth in a 'shush' gesture to his detractors.

After the breathless 5–3 roller-coaster versus Atlético Madrid in the quarter-final of the Spanish Cup, two more goals from Ronaldo in the semi-final versus Las Palmas saw them through to the final against Real Betis – a game that Ronaldo would ultimately miss due to international duty. Barcelona prevailed 3–2 in extra time in a ding-dong final at Madrid's Bernabéu stadium, Figo netting the winner in extra time, and Robson lifting yet another national cup competition.

More silverware was to come with the European Cup-Winners' trophy. A subdued Ronaldo scored the only goal in the pretty ordinary final, from the penalty spot in the first half as Barcelona beat Paris St Germain in the final in Rotterdam. Barcelona won a tournament sadly not with us any more, and the calibre of the sides they had to beat, such as AIK Stockholm, Fiorentina and Red Star Belgrade reflects the prestige of this lamented trophy.

By the time of this final in mid-May, it was evident that Ronaldo would be on his way out of Barcelona, most likely to Inter Milan. Jimmy Burns, despite Barcelona's victory, laments the overall performance of the team in a display he describes as surreal in *Barça: A People's Passion*:

I remember being struck by the air of surrealism that hung about the Barcelona camp that day . . . what struck me most was the lack of passion in Ronaldo. Soon after his arrival in Spain, Jorge Valdano had said the player seemed to him like someone who had landed from another planet. In Rotterdam, his whole demeanour was that of a man apart and beyond the club he was playing for and what it represented.

On 26 April, just when all seemed well and Ronaldo would sign a new improved contract with Barcelona, Martins and Pitta upped the ante once again by demanding a staggering $5 million per year, plus, they wanted Barcelona to pay all his tax too. Ronaldo further added to the confusion, stating, 'I still haven't agreed anything with Barcelona. I've not even reached a concrete proposal with the club. The board are saying they've reached an agreement with several sportswear manufacturers but that's impossible. In the first place, I'm not going to get involved with more than one company and more to the point, I've got a contract with Nike.' Off the back of their deal with the CBF, Nike built a new Brazil headquarters in Rio de Janeiro. The conference rooms were given the names '1958', '1962', '1970' and '1994' after the years in which Brazil had won the World Cup. The fifth room remained nameless, but was earmarked to be called '1998' in the assumption that the trophy would again be lifted in France. Ronaldo saw no reason why not, and added, 'If Brazil win and I score more than 13 goals [Frenchman Juste Fontaine's record] then they can name the room after me.'

On 26 May 1997, expectation was high at the Camp Nou as representatives from all sides met to discuss Ronaldo's future. On Barcelona's side were president Nuñez, his son Joe and deputy president Joan Gaspart. For Ronaldo, Martins and Pitta were there along with their Italian 'third agent' Giovanni Branchini. After lengthy negotiations, Nuñez emerged smiling, saying, 'He's ours for life,' adding, 'His contract will be extended to 2006 with a rising wage scale that will net him $2.3 million per year.' All seemed well from Barcelona's side. They had their man.

Ronaldo, away in Norway with Brazil at the time, was happy to add after speaking to his agents, 'I've spoken to Nuñez to thank him for the club's efforts. If I'm World Player of the Year [which he was] then it's thanks to Barcelona; when I was with PSV, I scored just as many goals but nobody noticed. But at Barcelona it's different and that is why I'm desperate to stay.' He then added frivolously, 'As I'm getting more money, I'll have to score more goals! This year, I've scored 35 [it was actually 34] but next year I want to do even better. My aim is to smash the Spanish record.'

But the next day, as the parties returned to dot 'i's and cross 't's, all hell broke loose and the deal was off. Reinaldo Pitta told waiting reporters, 'As soon as we began to draw up the definitive contract, the problems started all over again.' Then Nuñez emerged saying, 'It's all over, Ronaldo is going.' Why this dramatic turnaround happened is difficult to pin down, as exact details are not available, but it is thought Barcelona tried one trick too many, and Martins and Pitta, perhaps with Inter Milan up their sleeve, toughed them out and it all fell down. Ronaldo joined in the rancour by saying, 'It's all over. They [Barcelona] have spent seven months deceiving me. I'm off and that's that. We'll never sit down to negotiate with Barcelona again. The only thing that matters now is our dignity. It's not an economic problem.' Fully warmed up, he then turned on Nuñez: 'Nuñez can say whatever he likes but my managers were working for me and I know exactly what happened. He's a liar and he'll carry on lying. We've tried everything to reach a deal but we can't trust the board any more; they're not men of their word. They blame my representatives but I trust them far more than I trust Nuñez.'

Nuñez's response was curt. 'I'm sure they'd already made a deal with Inter. Their actions and behaviour tell me they wanted talks to break down. We even agreed to pay everything in dollars. Then they refused to accept that Televisio de Catalunya could pay 15 per cent of Ronaldo's contract or my word as a guarantee.' For the first time, Ronaldo appeared stressed and careworn by all the wrangling over his future. His usually ubiquitous smile was gone and he looked tired and fed-up. Many believe that he wanted to stay at Barcelona but forces more powerful than him alone had contrived to take him elsewhere. It was perhaps evident to him that he was no longer his own man. Joan Gaspart, himself gutted to have lost Ronaldo, added weight to this school of thought, saying, 'We now have to forget about Ronaldo. His representatives have got too much power over him.'

But Nuñez wasn't finished and wasn't willing to let Ronaldo go, or let his agents have their way without a fight, insisting that buy-out clauses in Spanish players' contracts could only be exercised by Spanish clubs. Enter Real Madrid. Having watched the royal pickle their arch rivals had got themselves into over their prized asset, Real Madrid then swaggered into town saying that they would happily consider signing Ronaldo, should it be that he could only sign for another Spanish club. Club president Lorenzo Sanz admitted with wonderful Machiavellian candour, 'As president of Real Madrid football club, it's my obligation to try and weaken Barcelona, and doing so seduces me. It's not our war, but if we can take advantage of it . . .'

As it transpired, this was all bluster on Nuñez's part, as Ronaldo's original Barcelona contract had stated that the buy-out clause could be activated by any club who had the wherewithal, not solely a Spanish one. On 20 June 1997, Ronaldo's lawyers, having received payment from Inter, deposited a cheque at Spanish League HQ in Madrid and Ronaldo was a free agent. Inter president Massimo Moratti was purring with satisfaction, saying, 'Ronaldo is mine. I've given myself a present.'

The scale of the deal read as follows. In essence, the transfer fee required to activate Ronaldo's buy-out clause from Barcelona was £32 million – itself another world-record fee and, in fairness to the vanquished Barcelona, some consolation and a tidy return on their initial £20 million investment less than a year earlier. Ronaldo himself reportedly received a £14 million signing-on fee, and in turn £4.7 million a year until 2005 in salary – stratospheric numbers for the day and easily making him the highest paid footballer in world football.

Ronaldo's departure culminated a terrific season in *La Liga* for the neutral observer. The real business had been Barcelona's year-long duel with Fabio Capello's Real Madrid for *La Liga* title. In a fascinating sub-plot to the career of Ronaldo, and another of football's intriguing tales, Capello had arrived in Madrid having shaped AC Milan into one of the best club sides in history. Arrigo Sacchi had built (or rather bought) an outstanding team in the late '80s, bringing the famed Dutch trio of Frank Rijkaard, Ruud Gullit and Marco van Basten together and dominating Italian and European football, its apogee being the 1989 European Cup final when, after having humiliated Real Madrid 6–1 on aggregate in the semi-final, they thumped Steaua Bucharest 4–0 in a symphony of football, causing the dewy-eyed BBC commentator John Motson to provide one of his all-time gems. As Ruud Gullit hammered home the last goal, he eulogised, 'Ohhhh, it's so easy – to fall in love with football played like this.'

Thereafter, Capello had maintained this tradition and rebuilt the team with the likes of Europe's finest – George Weah, Jean-Pierre Papin and Marcel Desailly – their finest hour coming with some irony in 1994 as they buried Cruyff's Barcelona 'dream team' 4–0. These were connoisseurs' teams, playing gilt-edged football that charmed everybody bar the success-starved supporters of Internazionale: the *Nerazzurri*. In many ways, it was this Milan dominance of *Serie A* and Europe that had led Inter Milan to push so hard for Ronaldo's services as they strove to outdo their co-tenants at the San Siro. Capello's reputation as a no-nonsense winning coach who got results was further embellished in his one-year stay at the Bernabéu, where he assembled a quality side, one that would in turn lift the European Cup the season after, ending a 22-year barren spell. The sublimely named and talented Fernando Redondo, Croatian hitman Davor Suker and Capello's pet right-back Christian Panucci were just some of the big names to play under him.

The season developed into a battle of wills between Capello and Sir Bobby Robson, two of the game's most successful coaches. The battle went right down to the wire, with Real just edging it and again I discussed this with Sir Bobby. 'The game that did us was the Hercules game, where we lost 2–1. Had we had Ronaldo [who was away with Brazil for the last few games of the season] we'd have won, and won the league. Real pipped us by two points in the end, and we won one more game than them and scored seventeen more goals, seventeen!' Clearly still smarting from the one title that eluded him that year and would ultimately cost him his job, Sir Bobby went on wistfully: 'We played fourteen more games than Real, FOURTEEN! Can you believe it? And by the end, we just ran out of steam. Real were a good side, a very good side, but I felt we were better.' Despite Ronaldo's 34 league goals and 45 in all competitions, Barcelona had come up short in *La Liga*, and short to their most hated of rivals Real Madrid. Sir Bobby would make way for Dutch coach and Joan Gaspart favourite Luis van Gaal, making himself 'the highest paid scout in world football'.

Looking back, I asked Sir Bobby about his time at Barcelona with Ronaldo. He described to me how he counts working with Ronaldo as one of the great joys of his tenure there and of his career as a whole. He was adamant that Ronaldo was the best player in the world at the time. 'There was no doubt about the role he played in our success. He made a good side better. I enjoyed working with him immensely. He wanted to learn, he worked hard, always called me Sir or '*Meester*', and you could never get him off the training pitch. Most of all, he wanted to be the best. We had our run-ins, yes, such as his numerous trips to Brazil and times when I felt his agents were meddling in his affairs too much, but on the whole he was a joy. His play was absolutely magic, scintillating. He did things I've never seen before. His great strength was the ability to come deep, 40 or 50 yards even, and get the ball, then turn, and anybody who was in his way he could go through. Romário did it over 10–15 yards in and around the penalty area, but Ronaldo could do it over much wider areas, which made him such a bigger danger and harder to mark, virtually impossible. The big shame was that he left.' Clearly still a bit miffed about the situation, he went on: 'I have nothing but respect for the lad, but how was it possible that having bought the finest goal-scorer in the world at a cost of £20 million and on an eight-year contract, we let him go one year later? How could that be let to happen?'

Again, I spoke with various cab drivers in Barcelona, who, as always, were more than forthcoming in their views. Several were vitriolic in the extreme. '*Filho de puta*' (son of a bitch) was a common response, and 'traitor' not far behind. It was evident the sense of loss and betrayal was still strong. Alonso, a chirpy cabbie from the Las Ramblas area, went on: 'I loved him, we all loved him, but you can't do what he did and just leave Barcelona. He was our player. And then he was gone.'

Bear in mind that, since Ronaldo's departure, Barcelona's fortunes have slipped alarmingly, their slide matched only by Real Madrid's ascent. I made various visits to Barcelona during 2003 researching this book, a time when Barcelona had had one of their worse seasons on record, with old boy Luis van Gaal's second spell as coach ending in shame and acute humiliation for the dour Dutchman. After an abysmal campaign where relegation had for a time seemed an outside threat, they had rallied well to scrape a lame UEFA Cup place thanks mainly to Radomir Antic's caretaker skills in the latter stage of the season. It was an inflammatory time to be asking *Cules* about headier days gone by.

But my most revealing and insightful gem came not from the aforementioned fecund outlet of cab drivers but from my knowledgeable hotel concierge and lifelong *Cule*, Gustavo. With English embarrassingly superior to my Spanish he told me over a coffee, 'What we wouldn't give for Ronaldo now. That season was wonderful; the city was alive. He brought an electricity, an expectation to every game that I had never known prior or since. It was like a magic. We went to each [home] game as if it was a celebration. We had a great team but it was all thanks to him. OK, we lost the league to Madrid, and that hurt bad, but man, he was amazing.'

I asked him the difference between Barcelona then and now. 'Jesus, what a change. That team had flair, now we have nothing. Nothing. This season has been over a long time. Look at the team we had then: Ronaldo, Figo, Giovanni, Blanc. What have we now? Van Gaal's Dutchmen. They don't care. Madrid are laughing at us. OK, we have Ronaldinho [Gaucho] coming but I don't think he is a Ronaldo, and we have Rijkaard coming,' to which he added with raised eyebrows, 'another Dutchman.'

I asked him if he'd have Ronaldo back and he told me, 'Me, yes, I would. A lot of people wouldn't because they still feel betrayed, like with Figo. But me, yes. *Claro*! Without a doubt!'

The single season Ronaldo spent at Barcelona was in itself a fascinating study of cause and effect. Looking back, people have argued he was unfocused and easily distracted from his game; Barcelona were lax in letting him travel back and forth to Brazil so often; his agents were accused of callous and mercenary behaviour in blatantly ignoring his contract; the list goes on. But if you examine the whole picture, all of this was largely inevitable with the unique ingredients involved in the mixture. The bottom line was that you had football's most valuable commodity: a marketable striker scoring stunning goals with incredible regularity. That in itself attracts the attention of cash-rich clubs hungry for success which in turn lures agents to the table to discuss numbers and of course commissions, no matter what the existing contract in place says. Barcelona's alleged laxity is also largely inevitable. During the season, Ronaldo was frequently back and forth to Brazil. Admittedly, some of this travel was on international duty with the *seleçao*, but an unusually high percentage was for pleasure. In December and January alone, he racked up nine transatlantic trips with over one-hundred hours' airtime. What would you do if you were Barcelona? Drop him? A tough call when you're fighting for every piece of silverware and your bitter rivals Madrid are chasing you all the way. Sir Bobby was in a no-win situation. If he took the strong line and punished Ronaldo, he could be accused of cutting off his nose to spite his face. Whereas if, as he did, he turned a blind (although annoyed) eye to the proceedings and picked his prize asset, he still felt the wrath from some corners for not being stronger. Not easy.

Can you blame Pitta and Martins? Not really. Their commissions on the transfers in question were huge, life-changing sums. Fiscal moralism is one thing: fiscal reality is quite another. What about Ronaldo himself? Young, famous, very wealthy and riding the crest of a wave. Everybody wanted a piece of him and who could blame him for living every minute of it? His returns on the field couldn't be argued with and certainly, in his own mind, he would have thought 'I can't be accused of not scoring goals', which, let's face it, is what the number 9 is there for. As for the Barcelona fans, they also, inevitably, showed the legendary fickleness of the football fan. Ronaldo was praised as a messiah on arrival and then as the reincarnation Himself after Compostela, but, as the season drew to a close and it was apparent the *Cules* would lose him to Inter Milan, their religious affection wavered, the memories of the magic became hazy, the loss of the title to Madrid cut like a knife, and Luis Enrique romped home in the Fans' Player of the Year poll, taking over two-thirds of the vote. Ronaldo, the recently crowned FIFA World Player of the Year, trailed way behind. Catalan *Cules* are not ones to be spurned, as Luis Figo would later witness in his acrimonious move from Barcelona directly to Madrid. As the *Cules* learned to live without their former hero, Inter's *Nerazzurri* rubbed their hands in anticipation.

CHAPTER 7

INTER MISSION – INTER MILAN 1997–98

The deal that took Ronaldo to Inter Milan was stunning in every aspect of its conception. It was audacious in that it lured him away after just one year from a lucrative eight-year contract with the 'the biggest club in the world', from fans who had adored him, from a city that had adopted him, and from a way of life that would be the envy of most. For Inter to be able to cherry-pick the jewel in Barcelona's crown was a huge fistful of sand in the eye of all personnel at the Camp Nou. For Inter, it demonstrated ambition and desperation in similar measure. By the end of the 1997 season, few would argue that Ronaldo wasn't the hottest property in world football and to go and poach him from a club like Barcelona showed great daring and skill on Inter's behalf.

But this raid reeked of desperation. As discussed, Inter had squirmed in the shadow of AC Milan's imperious dominance of European football in the late '80s and '90s, and had to look as far back as 1989 and the Teutonic vintage of Jürgen Klinsmann, Lothar Matthäus and Andreas Brehme for their last *scudetto* (Italian League title). This unease had been made all the more unbearable in that Inter had spent similar, if not greater sums than AC during the '90s. They were not mere poor relations such as Manchester City to Manchester United, or Atlético Madrid to Real Madrid, for example. They had a proud European history and trophy cabinet, and had made it their business to sign the world's best each year, but of late each seemed a misfit rather than a maestro, and a flurry of players and a succession of highly rated coaches couldn't work the oracle. They had mediocre success in Europe and at home, but the prize swag of *lo scudetto* and the European Cup proved elusive. As AC Milan steamrollered all before them and each signing settled and shone with almost carefree ease, the green-eyed stares across the San Siro became more envious as the seasons went by.

Massimo Moratti of Inter was a young president in a hurry. Keen to emulate his father Angelo, who was club president when Inter bestrode Europe in the 1960s, with the side containing legends such as Facchetti, Mazzola and Suarez, he was happy to use his oil money to – excuse the pun – fuel Inter's relentless quest to climb the summit of Europe once more. He saw Ronaldo as the alchemy to finally supersede AC and scale the heights.

Ronaldo's arrival got the blue and black half of Milan buzzing in excitement and anticipation. It also caused some concerned looks on the faces of the AC faithful who had savoured with the rest of us his form at Barcelona and were now wondering if Moratti's prediction of *lo scudetto* was more than mere bravado.

Bringing Ronaldo to Internazionale was made possible by several factors. We have discussed the ambition and desperation of Inter themselves; Inter's wealth as a G14 club (i.e. belonging to the group of the 14 largest and wealthiest clubs in Europe); the business flamboyance and tenacity of Martins and Pitta; and the behind-the-scenes manoeuvrings of Branchini. However, there are two other key factors that helped underwrite the massive numbers involved, both of which reflected the marketability of Ronaldo. These factors were Pirelli and Nike.

Let's look at Pirelli first. They are a multinational Italian concern who manufacture and sell tyres, cables and systems, and have widespread real-estate interests. With their 2001 acquisition of a large stake in Olivetti, which since merged with Telecom Italia, they now hold a large stake in Telecom Italia itself, whose mobile arm TIM would later use Ronaldo for its expansion into the Brazilian market. They first joined Inter as a sponsor in 1995 and have since become a major shareholder in the club.

At the time of Ronaldo's signature, they were Inter's incumbent shirt sponsors and had recently become sponsors of Ronaldo himself. A product of this was the excellent billboard advert showing Ronaldo as a deity, in lieu of Jesus Christ atop Corcovado, overlooking his home town of Rio de Janeiro in full Inter Milan kit, arms outstretched, and with his right foot lifted to reveal a tread-like sole, with the legend 'Power is nothing without control'. Combining the majesty of the classic Rio bay area with Ronaldo, it formed a strong ad to promote their new 'green' tyre, the P3000 Energy. It was perfect not only for Pirelli's well-established European markets, but more importantly for their plans to expand further into the South American and Brazilian markets, where the growth in car ownership lags behind only that of cell phones. The initial ads showed Ronaldo in a number 10 shirt, but this would soon be altered to a 9 for later runs of the campaign. A Ronaldo shod in Pirelli tyres was the perfect vehicle to promote their brand. The tie-in with him, and their historical relationship with Inter, was an excellent fit and one they were happy to pay for. As such, they contributed handsomely to the Ronaldo deal by paying a substantial portion of his wages.

As we have already seen in Chapter 5, Nike's quantum leap in the football world came when they signed up the Brazilian national team for a reported $200 million over 10 years, the then largest deal for a national side in footballing history. Since that deal, they had not rested on their laurels and had snapped up several other national and domestic teams, plus some notable individual contracts. Ronaldo had actually been a Nike contracted player (boots) since 1994, signing on the dotted line back then for $150,000 per annum, an average deal for the day. Clearly by now, this was looking paltry in comparison with his ability and global standing and soon Nike were brought back to the negotiating table by Martins and Pitta.

They emerged in mid-1997 with Ronaldo signed to Nike for a reported 10-year deal worth $15 million – effectively spanning his whole career as a footballer and putting him into the realms of Nike's Michael Jordan and Tiger Woods. Not only would Ronaldo wear Nike's boots, but Nike would also create a sub-brand 'R9' of all things Ronaldo. This sub-branding was another of Nike's master innovations, to go with 'Air' Jordan, and 'TW' Tiger Woods amongst others. Nike would also then create 'NikeFootball' and the new 'Scorpion' range. Details of this deal are difficult to confirm but one caveat within it was that Ronaldo must play for a club wearing Nike kits. At the time, Barcelona wore Kappa and, as seen in Chapter 6, this was another, albeit smaller, factor in moving him on to Inter.

As part of Nike's aforementioned rapid expansion into the kit market, Inter had been one of the first major domestic clubs they had secured, signing them for a reported $125 million over 10 years – another huge figure for the day. Nike, with their financial might, were easily able to outbid their rivals who, being predominantly kit-only manufacturers, had less financial clout due to their narrower markets, and who were only able to talk in terms of much shorter deals. With clubs salivating for money to sign the best players, and a company like Nike who could guarantee such large sums in return for lengthy deals, it was simply no contest. As with the Brazil deal, it was Umbro who ceded the shirt at Inter. Although Nike would have to wait a season to see Ronaldo in their Inter shirt (the Umbro deal still had a year to run), it wouldn't be long before they'd squared the circle and any action photograph of Ronaldo would show him wearing only Nike equipment. It was a marketing tour de force.

In many ways, Ronaldo's emergence and subsequent blockbusting transfer to Inter was akin to the arrival and prevalence of Tiger Woods in golf. Woods's supreme marketability and no little skill with a golf club meant that the whole sport was elevated into never-before-seen levels of sponsorship and prize money. Ronaldo was the catalyst for this in football and heralded an era where footballers, some of negligible ability, could earn fabulous wealth as TV, sponsorship and endorsement money rolled in from companies eager to be associated with the game's seemingly endless appeal. Ronaldo himself now had lucrative personal endorsement contracts with Nike, Pirelli, Parmalat, Carrefour and Brahma (a Brazilian beer), which combined outweighed his playing salary from Inter. He was a very wealthy young man. Few people on the planet now didn't know who he was and with his face emblazoned on billboards all over the world, the inevitable question asked was how he would cope with all this adulation, fame and wealth. Would his game suffer, or even become a distraction?

The brouhaha surrounding Ronaldo's arrival in Milan caused a level of anticipation not seen before amongst Inter's fans. The previous season, 1996–97, season-ticket sales at Inter had been 16,000 – a paltry figure for a club of Inter's stature and one with the Giuseppe Meazza San Siro to fill, which, with a capacity of 80,000, is one of football's biggest and best stadiums. However, Ronaldomania Inter-style whipped up the latent *Nerazzurri* into a frenzy and the stampede for season tickets in the close-season meant that, come opening day of season 1997–98, before Ronaldo had even kicked a ball in anger, Inter had sold 51,000 season tickets, a staggering 318 per cent uplift. The week of his arrival they sold over 35,000 Ronaldo shirts and averaged a cool 5,000 per week for the rest of the season. Furthermore, Inter signed up various new sponsorships worth $66 million on the strength of their new asset. The bean counters at Inter were purring with satisfaction. At 20 years old, this simple lad from a tough upbringing in Rio was causing quite a stir in the world of football. Some people have accused Ronaldo of being lucky, but it's what the fortunate do with their serendipity that matters most. Ronaldo had seized the chances his God-given talent had afforded him and had proven himself in one of the world's toughest leagues, *La Liga* in Spain. The spotlight was now upon him as to whether he could do likewise in the defence-oriented *Serie A* of Italy.

Inter, under coach Luigi Simoni and the lavish patronage of Massimo Moratti, had assembled yet another star-studded team of world talent. Ronaldo joined players such as Frenchman Youri Djorkaeff, Italian no. 1 Gianluca Pagluca, Dutchman Aron Winter, Argentine spoiler Diego Simeone, and was partnered up front by Chilean outlaw Ivan Zamorano. As at Barcelona, expectation was high, if not assumptive, that spending + players = trophies, and coach Simoni was under no illusion about what Moratti would be expecting. Now, with the addition of Ronaldo to an already classy squad, the generous Inter benefactor gave him all the ammunition he needed to secure the *scudetto*.

The competition would be hot, with AC and Juventus, a Gabriel Batistuta-inspired Fiorentina, plus the improving Lazio in the hunt too. During this boom period of *calcio* (Italian football), money was sloshing around *Serie A* like vintage Barolo, with high-profile tycoons and businessmen happy to pursue their egotistical dreams of success. Amongst these, at AC Milan, was Silvio Berlusconi, the media mogul and future prime minister. At Lazio, there was Sergio Cragnotti, whose Cirio food business funded some huge transfer activity. Parmalat did likewise at Parma, and Juventus were not shy in spending Fiat's lira either. Their side boasted stars such as Zinedine Zidane, Didier Deschamps, Alessandro Del Piero, and a fine selection of no-nonsense Italian regulars such as Ciro Ferrara and Antonio Conte. But despite the competition, Moratti was confident he had the key, and that key was Ronaldo. He had bought him to transform the team from nearly-men to champions, and that was what he expected. At only 20 years old, this was a massive burden for Ronaldo to shoulder.

Serie A was regarded at the time as the best league in the world, and with some justification. Its teams were consistently strong in Europe and the league boasted the cream of the world's best players. But despite this glossy brochure, the football therein was often dull and negative, with the emphasis on defending and a 'we keep what we have' mentality – the 'what we have' invariably being a one-goal lead. Ronaldo had managed to illuminate *La Liga* with his dazzling runs and solo goals but the *catanaccio* (door bolt) style of Italian defending would be a different proposition. There is an old saying in Italian football about their style of defending: a defender will let a striker go past him, or he will let the ball go past him, but never both at the same time – a code typified over the years by the likes of Franco Baresi, Giuseppe Bergomi, Claudio (not so) Gentile, and Paolo Maldini.

From game one, Ronaldo was marked heavily in *Serie A* and struggled to find the rhythm he had shown to such devastating effect in Spain. Admittedly, he got under way early again, this time in game two away at Bologna, but the early response from the avid Italian sports press was gloomily negative, and somewhat disappointed. Despite the slow start and the negative press, though, Inter were ahead in the league and looking down on *Serie A* for the first time in a long time. All seemed well and as Ronaldo's confidence grew and the wolfish press eased off him for a time, he began to show the magic that everyone knew he was capable of. Two cracking goals in the 5–1 mauling of Foggia got the San Siro faithful roaring in approval. Next up, in the Coppa Italia, he followed with a stunning hat-trick versus Piacenza, the second being a trademark high-speed slalom during which he beat five Piacenza players, rounded the goalkeeper and slotted home. Delirium reigned at the San Siro and the *Nerazzurri* crowned their darling Brazilian '*Il Fenomeno*': a mighty sobriquet indeed. As the calendar year closed, the game's coaches also liked what they saw as they voted, by a landslide, for Ronaldo as FIFA World Player of the Year 1997. Not only was he the first player to win this coveted gong for a second time, he was also surprisingly the first Inter player ever to receive it.

If we pause for a moment to run a half-term review, it is evident that Ronaldo was finding things a lot tougher in Italy than he had in Spain. Italian opposition had shown no qualms in stopping Ronaldo play wherever possible and their suffocating and oft illegal tactics had forced Ronaldo to examine his game for perhaps the first time in his career. There was also the regular concern about his fitness and the strength of the knee that had caused problems in the past. Although on the surface there didn't appear to be anything wrong, only Ronaldo himself could know what impact this might be having on his game. Off the field, things did appear more settled than at Barcelona. For once, his agents seemed happy and were content to leave him be at Inter, and his personal life appeared steady with Suzana Werner. Nor were there the constant back and forth trips to Rio which had caused Sir Bobby Robson and Co. so much angst at Barcelona.

Resuming after the *Serie A* winter break, Inter's first game of the New Year was against fellow pace-setters Juventus. Inter prevailed 1–0 to go top, Ronaldo making the game's only goal, drifting past two defenders to square the ball for Youri Djorkaeff to score. Spring saw the title race hot up even more as Inter and Juventus slugged it out at the top of *Serie A*. Defeat at home, ironically to Juventus's age-old foes Torino, let Juventus take first place, and the bloodthirsty Italian press sharpened their knives once more. *Corriere dello Sport* ran a piece claiming Ronaldo was not a team player and his game was too self-centred, inferring that Inter had to run too much of their play through him. If Ronaldo was having a bad day then this meant Inter would have a bad day, and they backed it up with statistics from the *capocanoneri* (goal-scoring charts) showing Ronaldo way back on 10, behind the likes of German Oliver Bierhoff at Udinese with 16 and Gabriel Batistuta with 14. Suitably chastened by this criticism, Ronaldo went out next game and banged in a hat-trick against Lecce, and then scored again versus German side Schalke 04 as Inter progressed in the UEFA Cup. As the chase for *lo scudetto* warmed up, so did Ronaldo, and by the end of April he was leading the Italian scoring charts on 22 goals, including a crucial brace away at Roma to keep up the pressure on Juventus. He had also scored freely in the UEFA Cup run, with the performance during the two-legged semi-final against Spartak Moscow in April in particular widely regarded as his best game for Inter. He mesmerised the Russians with a display of stunning football, scoring twice in the away leg to reverse the deficit and take Inter through to the final in Paris against Lazio. Those present still revere that performance to this day. Throughout the game, Ronaldo terrorised the Spartak defence with blistering runs and technical brilliance, making a mockery of the hard, corrugated surface.

Prior to the final, though, was the run-in for *lo scudetto* with Juventus and Inter as the leading protagonists on 66 and 65 points respectively. In a piece of footballing theatre and in the type of game that typifies *calcio*, both sides met with only four games left. A true titanic clash for the league. Juventus, serial winners of *lo scudetto* an incredible 27 times, were well versed in negotiating the final furlongs. Inter were less so, and their nerve would be put to the test in this crucible of pressure and tension. It was a typically feisty *Serie A* game with 55 fouls in total – a spoiler's paradise and one in which the likes of Simeone, Montero, Zanetti and Conte revelled, at the expense of the artists on show such as Del Piero, Zidane and Ronaldo. Del Piero gave Juve the lead on 21 minutes but then in the second half came the incident that is still talked about by Inter fans to this day. Ronaldo jinked into the area and was clearly brought down. A nailed-on penalty for all to see, and one which even the Juve players seemed resigned to. However, the man in black that mattered saw nothing and waved play on, and with Inter players remonstrating profusely, Juventus went down the other end and scored past a defenceless Pagluca. All hell broke loose with Inter's staff and players alike incensed at the referee's apparent mistake. Even Ronaldo, not known for his temper or brushes with authority, squared up to the referee in frustration and disbelief. Inevitably, conspiracy theories about referees favouring the Turin club, perhaps with the assistance of bribes, were soon doing the rounds, but this defeat effectively killed Inter's title hopes and, despite thumping Empoli 4–1 on the last day with two more from Ronaldo, they finished second. Bridesmaids again and the agony was tangible.

In the league, Ronaldo finished with 25 goals from 34 starts. A fine haul, but insufficient as for the first time in three seasons he didn't win the Golden Boot, that accolade going to Udinese's Oliver Bierhoff. In total, Ronaldo netted 34 times in 44 games, and shone brightly in the UEFA Cup. Following his masterclass against Spartak Moscow in the semi, he lit up the final in Paris as Inter comfortably beat Lazio 3–0. Ronaldo, rampant all game, signed off with a signature goal for Inter's third, weaving through three defenders and then executing a double stepover to leave Lazio keeper Marchegiani flat on the seat of his pants, humiliated and beaten. It was a consummate finish. Soon after, Almeyda, whom Ronaldo had left for dead en route to goal, had seen enough and with a hack straight from the Argentine guide book on rash tackles attempted to fell Ronaldo in retribution for the embarrassment he had placed upon an internationally renowned defender. Fortunately, he missed, but the intent was clear and he quite rightly got his marching orders. Playing for Lazio that night was Alessandro Nesta. Widely regarded as one of the world's most accomplished defenders and almost as handsome as he is cool, he recalls the evening with a shudder. Having been led a merry dance by Ronaldo all evening, he was candid enough

CHAPTER 8

FRANCE '98 – HUBRIS AND DESPAIR

Rarely has a national side entered a World Cup finals as such strong favourites as Brazil did at France '98. To find parallels, one has to look back perhaps as far as Ferenc Puskas's 'Marvellous Magyars' in Switzerland 1954. But whereas the Hungarians had been unbeaten in three years and had tipped the footballing world upside down by humiliating England 6–3 at Wembley in 1953, and then for good measure stuffing them again 7–1 in Budapest just a few months later, Brazil couldn't lay claim to anywhere near such form. That Hungary would ultimately lose the final in 1954 to West Germany 3–2 having been 2–0 up after eight minutes and cruising, remains one of football's greatest conundrums. Even more when you consider Hungary had routinely buried the Germans 8–3 in a group game less than two weeks earlier. There would be similarities in Brazil's campaign in France.

As Brazil arrived at France '98, their billing as favourites was somewhat contrived and based largely upon two things: 1) Ronaldo, and 2) the lack of viable alternatives. Let's look at these in order.

Ronaldo was without question the best footballer in the world at the time. With his two consecutive FIFA World Player of the Year gongs, he had easily wooed the world's coaches and had brought back to the game some of the colour not seen since the Brazil side of 1970. Second, at France '98, there were no other real 'stand-out' teams who demanded attention. There were the usual suspects, of course, such as Argentina, Holland, Italy and Germany, but although each were good, none was outstanding. Also, France had looked ill-equipped to take advantage of their host status and, in fairness, no one gave them a realistic chance, especially having failed to qualify for USA '94.

Another factor was also prevalent in catapulting the *seleçao* to the forefront of everybody's thinking, and that was who else, but Nike. By now, Nike's leviathan football marketing machine was in full cry, and what an impressive beast it was. With 'best player in the world' Ronaldo at the helm and his seemingly dependable ability to win games single-handedly, it was Nike more than the world's press who had made Brazil the hot favourites. It was an assumptive-close of immense proportions and daring. They spent huge amounts of money on two campaigns in particular. One was the ad where giant billboards featuring Nike-contracted stars came to life and players volleyed the ball to each other, around the world, reflecting the global nature of the World Cup. But the real winner, and the one few will forget, is the TV advert they released ahead of and during the finals which sold an impression of Brazil as an unbeatable dream team.

In Nick Hornby's seminal book *Fever Pitch*, he commends the 1970 Brazilian World Champions for 'the way they regarded ingenious and outrageous embellishment as though it were as functional and necessary as a corner-kick or throw-in'. This, for me, is the essence of Brazilian football and nobody has encapsulated it better than Hornby. It was this very thing that Nike had paid a king's ransom for and were now desperate to thread through their ad campaigns like golden silk.

In the ad, the whole Brazil squad, somewhat bored whilst killing time at Rio's International Airport, decide upon an impromptu kickabout. To Sergio Mendes's famous samba tune to really get you in the mood, the likes of Roberto Carlos, Leonardo, Denilson, *et al.* set off on a series of mazy, trick-laden dribbles with the airport staff chasing after them in a Keystone Kops fashion, unable to do anything to catch them as their Nike-inspired skill proves elusive. Then, in the denouement of the lengthy (and costly) ad, who else but Ronaldo pops up, weaves around a few barriers and security guards, plays a lovely see-you-later nutmeg through the metal detector, only to strike his shot against a railing post acting as the makeshift goal. The rueful smile added to the general bonhomie and charm of the ad, but it proved portentous indeed. For all its brilliance, Nike's campaign broke one of the basic rules of advertising: don't make promises your product can't keep.

There was something actually quite suspicious about the ad campaigns prior to France '98, both from Nike and Adidas, in that all of their featured stars, bar Zidane of France and Adidas, had tournaments they would care to forget. For example, David Beckham, whose name, according to Adidas, should be spelt B.E.C.K.H.A.M., was famously sent off after kicking Diego Simeone. Italy's Alessandro Del Piero also disappointed for Adidas, as did Denilson for Nike, and Marcel Desailly saw red in the final. It was as if the ads had jinxed those featured.

The advertising war between Nike and Adidas meant that France '98 was probably the most hyped and anticipated World Cup yet, but on the whole, the tournament was pretty tame and struggled to spring to life. There were few games of note, with the tumultuous, absorbing, riveting, brow-mopping England v. Argentina clash being easily the best game. This game had everything: Beckham's petulant expulsion, Michael Owen's wonder goal and arrival on the world stage, a four-goal first half, extra time, a disallowed 'Golden Goal' and then a nail-biting penalty shootout. Heady stuff indeed. England's titanic battle against Argentina had infused the tournament with some much needed vigour. It was now hoped that Brazil could be stirred by this themselves and kick-start their own potentially wonderful football – the thing that FIFA craved.

But FIFA themselves can be blamed for the disappointing quality of so many of the games. With the much-maligned Brazilian João Havelange having finally stepped down after a glacial 24 years in charge, many had hoped for a fresh face to bring some new and positive ideas to the world game and rid FIFA of its bureaucracy. Instead, the tinkering Swiss, Sepp Blatter, assumed control and outdid even Havelange for stupid proposals. One of his gems, that *any* tackle from behind be punished with a red card, threatened to reduce the tournament to an eight-a-side farce. Thankfully, most referees applied a sensible layer of common sense to this rule, thus allowing more players to stay on the field of play and entertain the watching millions, but the unfortunate result of Blatter's ukase was that the rule was inevitably applied inconsistently.

With the tournament expanded from 24 to 32 teams – another Havelangean decree – this meant the quality of the entrants was seriously diluted, and there was the added burden of more games to play. Brazil's every move was scrutinised with intense media coverage. Brazil's samba following was a stark contrast to England's tiresome band of thugs and casuals who were causing mayhem, anguish and destruction wherever they went. Brazil's fans, as always, were a joy to behold, adding colour, verve and passion, which blended wonderfully well with their French surroundings. Rather than the prospect of running in sheer terror from the English yobs wrecking all in their path, people wanted to be around Brazil and their retinue of effervescent support. They gave off warmth, friendliness and acceptance, and wanted everybody to join in the Carnaval. This lent to a heady mix in Brazil's opening game against Scotland, who again had exceeded the sum of their parts under Craig Brown's astute, calm and methodical leadership, reaching yet another finals. Their fans, the generally semi-inebriated 'Tartan Army', were a charming and equally menace-free complement to the Brazilian supporters, the kilts, tammies and red hair of Govan and Leith providing an eye-catching blend with the gold and green, tanned, drum-beating beauties from Copacabana. Several Brazilian friends of mine who attended the finals in France were under the impression the Scots had all come in bizarre fancy dress, and were blissfully unaware that such clobber was the national dress north of the border.

Scotland and Brazil opened up the jamboree in the stunning, newly built Stade de France in the St Denis area of northern Paris. The game was billed as the Ronaldo show, as he was expected to score at will against the cumbersome Caledonian defensive pairing of Colin Calderwood and Colin 'Braveheart' Hendry. But these two brave sons of Wallace played out of their skin, stifling the nimble-footed Ronaldo at every turn, who only had one run of merit to remember the whole game. There were rumours that Ronaldo's nerves before the game had got the better of him and as he had tried to take a siesta, he instead couldn't sleep due to hypertension and had broken down in tears. Teammates had just put this down to pre-match nerves and chose to overlook it, but it does shed light on a fragile young man with an overbearing level of expectation on his shoulders. Ronaldo, after the game, admitted to feeling a new level of pressure. Each time he touched the ball, the whole ground fell silent, as if all were expecting him to set off on a Compostela-style dribble and score. Pressure indeed.

The Scots, after falling behind to a soft opening goal as early as the fourth minute, were unlucky to ultimately lose 2–1 after a John Collins penalty had got them back in the game. It was an inauspicious start for Ronaldo and Brazil, but the rather fortuitous three points would prove invaluable. In this game, Brazil had proved toothless against a very ordinary Scottish side. Sceptics were quick to point the finger at the absence of Romário, the pint-sized genius whose impish finishing had done so much to win Brazil the cup in USA '94. Again, João Havelange was implicated as it was during his pointless new creation, the FIFA Confederations Cup, that Romário picked up the injury which ruled him out of France. The mouthwatering prospect of a Ronaldo–Romário strike pairing was thus denied us.

As it transpired, not only was Ronaldo feeling the pressure on the pitch, girlfriend Suzana Werner was also turning up the heat off it. A notorious attention seeker, she had been miffed by Ronaldo's recent, well-publicised meeting with glamorous tennis starlet Anna Kournikova at the Roland Garros tournament in Paris, where the inevitable kiss-for-the-cameras had taken place. Suzana had flown off the handle and given Ronaldo all sorts of aggravation because this encroachment on her own status had left her seething with emerald female envy.

Next up in Nantes, Brazil easily beat Morocco 3–0, with Ronaldo opening the scoring, and his account for the tournament, on nine minutes, and Rivaldo and Bebeto adding the rest. Ronaldo's goal was his first in World Cup competition and undoubtedly a huge relief to him. He added, 'That was the most important goal of my life as it was my first World Cup goal. I was mad with joy, like a prisoner being set free. We enjoyed ourselves against Morocco, we regained our old confidence. When things are going well, it is as if we are on fire. We did not want that game to end. That's when I really started to enjoy playing alongside Rivaldo. I thought we made a great double act.' A great double act they may have been, but Ronaldo wasn't laughing about the special attention he had received from Morocco's uncompromising defenders. He had been clattered through the back early on and picked up quite a severe knock to his thigh, which had required lengthy attention. This, on top of his ongoing knee problems which he was desperately trying to overcome – by whatever means – added to the pressure on his shoulders. With girlfriend Suzana not helping the overall situation, the distractions away from purely playing football grew and grew. As newspapers, especially in Brazil, lapped it all up, Zagallo furiously insisted that all his players observe his directions and keep away from wives and girlfriends during the tournament.

Rumours also began to surface that Ronaldo was receiving regular injections to his problem knee to assist him through the tournament. In a case of 'he doth protest too much', Ronaldo himself called an impromptu press conference to dispel these rumours – a curious move indeed. He claimed, 'I'm doing training along with everyone else and in addition I've had massage and am using lots of ice. The ultrasound equipment in the hotel has also helped.' At a stroke, he had admitted that he did have a knee problem, and whether or not he was receiving injections to curb the pain, he had alerted the world, and opposition defences, that the knee was weak. Furthermore, it also confirmed what many had felt for a long time: the knee was worse than Ronaldo and his medical staff were letting on.

With six points and sitting comfortably atop the group, Brazil's passage into the next round was safe, but they came unstuck badly in their third game against the resolute Norwegians. Without fear, having beaten Brazil comfortably 4–2 a year earlier in a friendly in Oslo, the Norwegians attacked their illustrious opponents with gusto. Their team, like Denmark, was bursting with English Premiership players and with the elegant Tore André Flo enjoying a fine tournament up front, caused the first surprise of the tournament as they came from behind to beat the full-strength favourites 2–1. The message was clear: this Brazil team wasn't invincible; it wasn't the Golden Team of 1970 reincarnated with Ronaldo in lieu of Pelé; they were mortal, they were beatable, and what's more, they were now under a lot of pressure. More crucially, that pressure, like the sun's rays through a magnifying glass, was focusing on Ronaldo, who gruffly rounded on reporters, saying, 'Brazil are not only Ronaldo. I have to help the team but the team must also help me. With Brazil I have to play in a different manner to which I play at Inter [a swipe at Zagallo?], where I am used to receiving the ball differently. With Brazil, I accept I must sacrifice for the team, running and moving around a great deal. But just as I do that for the team so the rest of the team must do that for me.'

Ronaldo's conceited boast whilst collecting his FIFA World Player of the Year award in January, that he fancied breaking Juste Fontaine's World Cup record of 13 goals, was now looking very much like youthful naivety. Nor were the beaks at Nike that impressed either. Brazil and Ronaldo had thus far failed to impress. Nike's self-appointed favourites were looking anything but and in a group containing comparative lightweights such as Scotland, Morocco and Norway, they had not showed anything like the resolve that would be needed as the big nations waited down the line.

But again, Brazil got lucky. Who should they meet in their next knockout game but Chile, who had staggered through their group stage with a mere three points. As a first knockout game, it couldn't have been much easier, and provided Brazil with a much needed tonic; more importantly, it got the insatiable press off their backs for a while. Chile were murdered 4–1, Ronaldo finally coming to life with two much-needed goals, and also hitting the woodwork twice. César Sampaio also netted a brace. The mood within the Brazilian camp was lifted and the samba drums could beat a little more melodically. Ronaldo, having seemed broody all tournament, was now smiling again, with his globally recognisable buck-toothed grin yet again smeared across the world's press as he was back to doing what he enjoyed most.

Yet again, the draw was kind to Zagallo. With the prospect of facing either Denmark, Italy, hosts France, Holland, arch-rivals Argentina, World Cup experts Germany or the in-form Croatia, Brazil bagged Denmark in Nantes: again, easily the softest draw of the round. It looked like 'Lucky' Zagallo had all his rabbit feet and horseshoes safely on his person. However, the unfancied Danes gave Brazil a serious run for their money. Teams had got wise to Brazil's defensive frailties and with Cafu and Roberto Carlos, their two attacking full-backs, showing only scant regard for their defensive duties and exposing the two centre-backs, Aldair and Junior Baiano, the Brazilians were under severe bombardment from a Danish team not averse to playing it ugly when needed. Like Norway, Denmark had their fair share of English Premiership players who had no time for the *jogadores bonitos* from Brazil. For a while, Brazil found the uncompromising nature of the tie much to their disliking. In a ding-dong game, Denmark took the lead through Martin Jørgensen after good work by the outstanding Brian Laudrup. Bebeto had replied to ease Brazilian nerves and then Rivaldo put Brazil ahead after some good work by Ronaldo. But then Brian Laudrup – seizing on a rash mistake by Roberto Carlos who had tried an unnecessary and showy overhead kick too close to his own area – restored parity on 50 minutes, and the tie was set up. The Danes came forward in wave after wave looking for the winner and their place in World Cup folklore but were cruelly robbed when, overstretched in attack, Dunga slipped in Rivaldo, who lashed home from 25 yards for his second of the game. Rieper headed agonisingly onto the bar for the Danes in the dying seconds, but Brazil's, and Ronaldo's, passage was assured. Although Ronaldo had failed to score, he had played well, consistently running at the Danish defenders and causing them all sorts of problems. Forced to suffer him, they resorted to kicking and hacking him and, as would follow in the semi against Holland, this was the only way to stop him. Some of the tackles were shameful and, again, weak refereeing failed to protect him. He was adrift in the Golden Boot scorers' chart he had coveted so much, but Brazil were through and anything could happen.

So to the semi-finals and Brazil now had no choice but to play some decent sides. They drew Holland, who had beaten, breathlessly, the impressive Argentines with a late goal of sublime technical genius from their Ajax-schooled virtuoso Dennis Bergkamp. Argentina, who were probably the best team on paper in the tournament, had seen their dreams shattered again, the Herculean encounter against England perhaps having taken too much out of them both emotionally and physically. Again, Brazil were on the receiving end of some good fortune. Holland's motorised left-winger Marc Overmars was ruled out after limping off against Argentina and it is a fair bet he would have given Brazil's stand-in right-back Ze Carlos a rough old game. Furthermore, Dennis Bergkamp, who had been in such creamy form throughout the tournament, chose this game to have an off-day and without his promptings and string-pulling, Holland never scaled the heights their classy side was capable of. A deadlocked first half was alleviated early in the second when Ronaldo, showing some of his fêted predatory magic, sprang like a jack-rabbit to get on the end of Rivaldo's expertly served in-swinging cross, snuck between the two Dutch centre-halfs and prodded home past Edwin van der Sar. As if energised by this, Ronaldo then went on to have his best spell of the finals, and was at last showing the watching world the magic he was capable of, with his rampant, surging runs causing all sorts of problems for the opposition defence, who struggled to contain him within the laws of the game. Somehow, he didn't score as the lanky van der Sar made a string of world-class saves. But then, with just four minutes left, Patrick Kluivert, the highly rated but temperamental striker, got on the end of an inviting Ronald de Boer cross to head home and send the game into extra time, giving the Dutch a lifeline that had long seemed beyond them.

Ronaldo was again dreadfully unlucky not to score in added time, seeing shots cleared off the line and van der Sar again thwarting him when a goal seemed the only outcome. It remained 1–1 and so to penalties, something the Dutch appear to have a national allergy to on a par with England's. Almost inevitably, Brazil went through 4–2 after the Dutch stars froze, providing the ageing Taffarel with some easy saves.

So Brazil had made it to yet another World Cup final. To most people's surprise, they would meet hosts France there. France had grown in stature throughout the tournament and had slowly but surely crept up on the blind side of most respected observers, who hadn't given them the time of day at the outset. Despite having carried the hapless 'striker' Stéphane Guivarc'h throughout the tournament, surprisingly preferred to the swashbuckling Christophe Dugarry, they had been able to find goals from every angle, most notably when the resolute Lilian Thuram, such an accomplished defender of AC Parma and now Juventus, had amazingly popped up to score two cracking goals in the semi-final against Croatia, one with his swinger of a left peg. The Force was with the French and these Thuram goals offered no better evidence. His goals are rare, very rare. Imagine, for example, Gary Neville netting a brace for England in a World Cup semi-final and you have an idea of the magnitude of Thuram's achievement.

As it would transpire, this French team was one just setting out on a fantastic journey, and one containing talents that would dominate European football for years to come. In Zinedine Zidane, they had a playmaker of near genius talent, able to cast a spell over the ball, and who, despite his shortish fuse, which got him into unnecessary bother from time to time, would illuminate the final. In goal was Fabien Barthez, who combined goalkeepers' eccentricity and Gallic flair in equal measure. But he was no clown, had the gymnastic range of an acrobat and when called upon made some truly outstanding saves. His near telepathic understanding with the equally Gallic veteran Laurent Blanc was a feature of the tournament, as was their ritual head-kissing prior to each game, although Blanc would be robbed of a final berth by the disgraceful play-acting of Croat Slaven Bilic, who got him sent off. The midfield was expertly marshalled by the outstanding Didier Deschamps, whom the exiled Eric Cantona had once peevishly tagged 'the water-carrier'. That he may have been, but his jugs flowed with fine champagne, not mere Evian, and his tactical awareness and ability to transmit coach Aimé Jaquet's wishes to the rest of the team proved peerless. France would be a tough nut for the Brazilians to crack.

All was set for the final few had envisaged, but most were happy with. FIFA were purring with delight. They had everybody's second team, Brazil, they had Ronaldo, and they had their ebullient samba fans lining the picture-perfect streets of Paris. And, of course, they had the host nation, who by now had whipped the whole of France into a frenzy. For Ronaldo, his personal record in cup finals up to this point had been exemplary. In his first big final, for Barcelona against Paris St Germain in the 1997 Cup-Winners' Cup final, he'd scored the penalty that saw Barcelona prevail 1–0. The following year, he had scored the third as Inter Milan comfortably beat Lazio in the final of the UEFA Cup, winning the man of the match award in the process. In the final of the Copa America against Bolivia, he had scored in Brazil's 3–1 win, and in the recent Confederations Cup, he had bagged a hat-trick in the final against Australia. Four finals, four wins, and decisive goals in each. It seemed a natural progression that he would carry on this roll in Paris. All set? Away we go. Or not quite. What happened on that balmy Parisian evening of 12 July will not be forgotten in a hurry by anybody who was either there or watching at home on TV, and remains one of the most sensational sequence of events in world sport.

There has been so much written and proffered on what actually happened on that day in Paris that it is often difficult to sift between the facts and the sensationalism. No one has yet explained satisfactorily what actually happened and my investigations into what went on only revealed a Secret Service-style, pre-rehearsed wall of silence and set answers. In truth, I'm not sure we will ever know what actually happened, as only Ronaldo himself truly knows, and the altered state of mind he was in may never reveal the full chain of events. For all bar the Brazilian camp, first news of the drama unfolding came just ahead of kick-off when both trainers are required to submit detailed squad sheets to FIFA's officials, outlining their starting XI, plus substitutes. When Zagallo submitted his initial sheet, Ronaldo's name was absent, and in his place in attack was Edmundo, the notorious 'Animal' whose talent was only outstripped by his appetite for controversy, on-field violence and outright petulance. (A red-mist merchant of the highest order, Edmundo had punched out an opponent from Bolivia during a Copa America game the year before but, as with most of his misdemeanours, had earned a pardon from the CBF.) As newswires went banzai with this incredible development, TV stations around the world were faced with the prospect of bemused pundits sitting in plush temporary studios quite literally lost for words. All this was unfolding in real-time too and as pitch-side journalists strove to get accurate updates back to their respective studios, nothing short of minor mayhem was breaking out. The Stade de France's brand new, state-of-the-art media facilities were being given a thorough workout.

As studios and the world's media came to terms with the fact that Ronaldo was not starting, and were in the process of trying to second-guess why, news then broke that he *was* in fact starting, that it had all been a big mistake, and Zagallo had written the wrong name down. By now, nobody really knew what was going on and with kick-off time rapidly approaching, one thing had become crystal clear: the Brazil camp was in disarray, and the pre-match billing as favourites they had been given was now firmly handed over, *merci beaucoup*, to the French. As conjecture mixed with hearsay and Chinese whispers to form a murky cassoulet of uncertainty, the fanfare began for the teams to emerge from the dressing-rooms. I doubt that even the President of France watched the French team emerge, as all eyes, plus billions of global TV viewers, were fixed in bemusement and astonishment on the Brazilians, who emerged arm in arm in a (false) display of unity. Unconsciously adding to the suspense unfolding around him, Ronaldo emerged last. So there he was. The world's best was going to play in the final. What had all the fuss been about?

But as the game unfolded, it was clear that there was something seriously wrong with Ronaldo's demeanour. In short, his contribution during the game was nil. The one half-chance he had, he shot tamely at Barthez, who saved without fuss. Ronaldo had appeared vacant, distant, disinterested, almost confused as to why he was even on a football pitch in France. The list of adjectives could go on, and all would describe a young man who had suffered a serious mental jolt. It was immensely sad that a player of such gifts, such colour and joy, was not able to illuminate the ultimate footballing stage. As France cruised to an easy 3–0 victory over a disoriented and sidetracked Brazil, Zidane cemented his place in the record books with a headed brace, and Manu Petit of Arsenal capped a fine game with a well-taken goal in the dying seconds.

As the ceremony and celebrations got under way and Didier Deschamps swapped his tray of water cups for the golden trophy, Brazil were left shell-shocked. They had believed their own hype as tournament favourites, they had expected to return home with the trophy and they had snobbishly underestimated the French whom they deemed not fit to lace their boots as four-times winners. What's more, they had not only lost, but had lost badly, in an abject fashion, and now had the full glare of the world's media attention upon them. Out in the middle of the park, Zagallo, a curiously superstitious man for whom the number 13 is very much part of his life but now finally shorn of his lucky tag, did his best to console Ronaldo. The player, looking confused by all that was going on around him, still had the good grace to drape his unique Nike

Mercurial boots around his neck and afford Nike yet more priceless global exposure. With flashbulbs humming and beaming his image all around the world, Nike were still in the spotlight, however negative the publicity may ultimately have proven to be. In truth, the boots hung heavily. The final, despite the Gallic joy it ignited, will still be remembered as the one surrounded in the mystery of Ronaldo.

In trying to understand what events unfolded, we must come back to earlier in the day. Ronaldo had taken a typically Brazilian lunch of beef, potatoes, rice and salad and retired to room 290 of the Château de Grande Romaine hotel for a rest. Back at the room, Roberto Carlos helped Ronaldo shave his head into the trademark style, and all seemed well.

At around two o'clock, roommate Roberto Carlos was listening to his Walkman when he claims he was disturbed by the muffled sound of Ronaldo having some kind of convulsion. Roberto Carlos, looking on in horror, had raised the alarm immediately and dashed next door to alert, ironically, Edmundo. Edmundo would later claim that he was sure Ronaldo had been hitting himself during the fit as there were bruise marks about his body. As several other players heard the commotion and rushed to the scene, César Sampaio prised open Ronaldo's mouth to ensure he didn't swallow his tongue. At this point, Ronaldo was rigid and foaming at the mouth. The manager of the swish converted French château, Paul Chevalier, had no doubts Ronaldo had suffered a genuine fit of some kind. He told newsmen, 'There was general alarm, with yells and shouts which woke up all the players who were at the time in the middle of their siesta. For a time, we heard people saying, "He's dead, he's dead, he's dead." It created a terrible atmosphere around the team which was clearly seen later on the pitch.' After about a minute and three-quarters, he came round with a start, and then fell into a deep sleep. One can imagine the consternation of his fellow squad members on such an important day.

The players, in a mild state of panic and confusion, called CBF head medic Dr Lídio Toledo, an orthopaedic specialist, who first cleared the room and then summoned his colleague Dr Joaquim da Matta. Zico, assistant manager, ex-star and paternal influence on Ronaldo, heard what was going on and also joined the scene. Zagallo, resting elsewhere in the hotel, was oblivious, and Toledo, no doubt still unsure what the hell was going on at this stage, didn't want to disturb him. At around five o'clock, Ronaldo stirred and came round, whereupon he was whisked to the Lilas

Clinic for extensive tests, lasting over an hour and a half. The tests threw up nothing adverse, almost adding to, rather than alleviating the mystery, and Brazil's medical staff were stumped. Paul Chevalier described the rest of the squad leaving for the Stade de France: 'When the Brazilians usually left for a match, there was a great party atmosphere with singing and music, but this time the mood was very different. When they left, there was complete silence on the bus and we who had got to know them personally knew at that moment there was no cohesion and the Cup was already lost.'

With three hours to go before kick-off, frantic activity now took over the Brazil camp. 'Do we tell him?' asked some of the other players. Leonardo, the level-headed and respected star of the team, was incensed that the medical staff favoured not telling Ronaldo and insisted that he be told, for his own sake, as it appeared that Ronaldo was unaware as to what had unfolded. Medical staff succumbed and Ronaldo was informed of events. With kick-off looming, and the biggest night of his life ahead, Ronaldo insisted he was OK, and backed by the all-clear from the Lilas Clinic pleaded that he was OK to play.

Spare a thought here for coach Zagallo. As required by FIFA, he'd already submitted the team sheet ahead of kick-off, with Edmundo down to start in place of the clearly distracted Ronaldo. This was the correct thing to do. However, he was then faced with a classic no-win situation. Ronaldo has been passed OK by the Lilas Clinic, the Brazilian medical staff can shed no further light on the situation, and he also has the player himself insistent that he is 100 per cent ready. Unconfirmed reports also claim that it was about this time that Ricardo Teixera, all-powerful head of the CBF, breezed into the dressing-room and enquired if all was OK and that he 'assumed' Ronaldo would be starting. What would the reaction be back home in Brazil from 160 million soccer-mad fans? However legendary Zagallo's career may have been within Brazilian football, he no doubt saw it all flash before him as he pondered this conundrum. As beads of sweat rolled down the veteran's forehead, he chose to reinstate Ronaldo and go for broke. Cue an Edmundo red mist. Some suggest that Ronaldo was given a 'blue pill', probably Valium to calm him down – again, if true, a very dodgy medical action. That Ronaldo was in pain and mental torment was evidently clear, and to declare that there was 'nothing' wrong with him was ludicrous.

Nike were conveniently made one of the scapegoats for Ronaldo's hasty reinstatement and while true that their contract with CBF was heavily pro-Ronaldo and demanded he play in a certain number of games, the negative publicity that would ensue from a further fit or convulsion suggests that, as much as they would have preferred their prize asset to feature in the final, they didn't actually insist that he play. What many now believe happened is that the combination of these pressures upon Zagallo, of Ronaldo himself, Teixera, CBF, Nike, the fans, his wish to believe that Ronaldo could spark some magic and lift the Cup for him and Brazil, all led him to reverse his decision on Edmundo and reinstate a palpably unready Ronaldo. It was a decision he wasn't to hear the last of.

After the tournament, Prof. Acary Souza Bulle Oliveira, a neurologist from the São Paulo School of Medicine, would later state that he was certain Ronaldo had had a convulsion which should have been easy to diagnose. This was vehemently denied by Inter's own doctor Piero Volpi. Several other senior physicians added their views that it was a serious misjudgement to allow Ronaldo to play so soon after such a mysterious ailment and that the 24 hours afterwards are when a recurrence is most likely to happen.

So what did happen? To try to get to the bottom of the mystery, I met Dr Lídio Toledo at his Barra de Tijuca clinic in Rio. As head medic of the CBF, Lídio had been the first medic on the scene after Ronaldo's fit. He cuts a smart figure for his 72 years, is an orthopaedic specialist by trade and has been involved in football for over 40 years. He started out in the 1960s as chief medic for Rio team Botafogo in their halcyon period with Nilton Santos and Garrincha. After rising to prominence with them, he was invited by then head of CBF, João Havelange, to join the *seleçao*, where he enjoyed a record six World Cup campaigns until retiring from national team duties after France '98. As well as his two Rio clinics, he still acts in an advisory capacity for FIFA and his beloved Botafogo.

When I met him to discuss the infamous events of France '98, I was not quite sure what to expect, as the episode is still notorious in Brazil. He relayed the sequence as follows: 'Everything had been going fine. We had lunched well at the hotel – as we always did – with a traditional Brazilian meal, and then the players went to their rooms to kill the few hours before we got ready to head for the stadium. Everybody was focused on the match ahead and we were confident of winning. I was then called to Roberto Carlos's room and on arrival found Ronaldo lying motionless on his bed. He had already had his convulsion. We were not sure what had happened to him so we sent him off to the Lilas Clinic for some tests. It was a tense few hours because nobody really knew what had happened. My colleague Joaquim da Matta went with him, and I stayed with the rest of the squad.'

I asked him how concerned he was at the condition of Ronaldo and with a furrowed brow he answered, 'A lot. The worrying thing was that it was such a shock. I had never seen and couldn't recall anything like it. We tried to get Roberto [Carlos] and Edmundo to explain what had happened but none of it really added up. We decided to wait for the results of the tests before we made any decision.'

Lídio went on to describe what happened when Ronaldo came back from the clinic. 'The tests had thrown up nothing. He'd had tests from a neurologist, a cardiologist, and taken a full electrogram. Many, many tests, but none of them presented anything. Ronaldo really wanted to play, but we told him to hang on while we [the CBF medical staff] went off to discuss the situation. He pleaded with us, saying, "Lídio, I'm OK. Brazilians need me and I need to play this game, it's important to me, it's important to everyone. I have to play." Ronaldo then turned round to Zagallo and said, "Coach, I'm going to play, even if we have to play with 12, I'm going to play. I'm going on that field no matter what." He seemed fine. He was coherent, forthright and he seemed fine. We decided to let him play and that's when he was reinstated on the team sheet.'

I asked Lídio what he felt had caused the fit, and if it was the multiple injections to his knee. He answered, admittedly somewhat guardedly, 'No, it wasn't this. In my opinion, it was an emotional problem, brought on by nerves and pressure. Don't forget he was only 21 years old or so. He was the best player in the world and so much was expected of him. In my opinion, it was emotional. Fate decided he would have a fit. These things can happen.'

We then discussed the impact this had on the mood of the camp and Lídio conceded, 'It affected things very badly. Clearly, it wasn't the best pre-match preparation. But credit to France. They won because they were the better team. Soccer can be that simple sometimes. Maybe, as it was Ronaldo's fate to have the fit, it was France's fate to win. They were hungrier than we were.'

I asked him about his overall experience of Ronaldo and he explained as follows, 'He is one of, if not *the* best athlete I have worked with. A fantastic specimen. He was an outstanding athlete and a joy to work with.

RONALDO

He worked very hard and was never problematical. He always looked after himself in the right way. In my opinion, he is as much a phenomenon off the pitch as on it. Look at how he recovered from the patella. Incredible. I am very happy he is now back to being the best in the world again.'

Although Lídio was very open and candid, part of me felt he was hiding something, as if a code of silence had been agreed post-France by those involved first hand. Perhaps the state of Ronaldo's knee and the number of injections he had been given was the key factor – many outsiders believe this to be the case. He would not be drawn on this and pointed the finger of blame at fate for the convulsion. He also flatly denied that Nike played a role, saying, 'No. Nike were not involved. This is one thing that needs to be put straight. Yes, CBF had a big contract with them but Nike are not stupid. They would not and did not influence selection on that night. As I said, Ronaldo came back with the all clear, he was adamant he was OK, and between us all we agreed that he was OK to play. That's it.'

Joaquim da Matta was unavailable for interview so Lídio's evaluation is the best and closest we have to the truth. Lídio's career suffered shortly after the tournament as Brazil went into national introspection over the day's events and the subsequent defeat. Many people went looking for answers. Lídio explained: 'After the World Cup, my career suffered due to the inquiry from the medical board *Conselio Regional do Medicina*, who had opened a case into what happened on the day of the final. We [the CBF medical staff] were asked a lot of things about what caused the fit. Was it epilepsy? Was it a wrong injection? Was it a deeper mental problem? Was it food poisoning, etc.? We told the truth as I have just explained to you. That's what happened. We were declared not guilty. The vote went 36–0 unanimously in our favour because they had no evidence, but of course my career was injured in the process. We did the right thing on the day and I tell you again, it was fate that caused the fit.'

In addition to Lídio's account, there are several theories that exist, some verging on conspiracy. One considered likely is that the painkilling injection of the anaesthetic, xylocaine, administered to Ronaldo for his problem knee on the day of the final, had entered a vein accidentally due to a wayward administration. This is known to sometimes cause this convulsive reaction. Respected Brazilian sports daily *Lance!* claimed he had been given eight xylocaine injections during the finals alone. Conventional medical wisdom advises that over a course of a player's career, you should have no more than four or five painkilling injections. It was evident that Ronaldo had already breezed past this milestone in the preceding couple of years with Inter and Brazil. Any footballer will tell you that when they are carrying an injury, as much as they push it to play, they are never fully sure how strong the injured component is. With a component as precious and potent as Ronaldo's right knee, he must have been going through some acute personal anguish as to whether or not it would last the tournament and not fail him in the final. This, plus a combination of the immense pressure he was under to perform from the CBF, from Nike, the Brazilian people, mixed in with the emotional turmoil he was going through as his relationship with Suzana Werner was failing, makes it easier to understand why it all came on top at the very wrong time for the world's best footballer. We may never know the true reasons for the infamous events.

CHAPTER 9

FRANCE FALLOUT – HYSTERIA AND SOUL-SEARCHING

One can only guess what must have been going through Ronaldo's mind on the long flight back from France to Brasilia. As he sat on the Varig MD-11 alongside all his other teammates, a mood of sombre disappointment and reflection filled the cabin as they contemplated the fact that they were the first Brazilian squad to lose a World Cup final since the pilloried group of 1950 who lost to Uruguay – a defeat that still makes some Brazilians of a certain age nauseous and need to sit down. For Ronaldo, the brouhaha was only just beginning. Though unwillingly, he had provided the world's sports press with one of its biggest stories in a long time, and the Brazilian media themselves were not about to give him any sympathy either.

Awaiting them at Brazil's capital, Brasilia, was the full welcoming committee of CBF dignitaries, politicians eager to make some political capital even out of a losing team, and the President himself, Fernando Henrique Cardoso. The whole country was miffed about the defeat and wanted to know what had happened. Having negotiated the media in Brasilia, Ronaldo made his way home to Rio but despite his best efforts, dodging to-and-fro from his various apartments, he was unable to avoid the predatory media packs who now seemed to be singling him out, quite unfairly, in Brazil's failure to return with the trophy.

What few failed to consider was the possibility that Brazil had actually been rather lucky to get to the final, had played some average football, had had a comfortable draw through the semis and ultimately lost to the better team. Before the final itself, Dutch legend Johan Cruyff had been vocal in his criticism of Brazil, saying, 'I said at the start of the tournament that I did not like this Brazilian team, and I still say that. It would be really bad for football if Brazil won with such poor play, because this team is imitated throughout the world. I am not going to say that France will win, because Brazil are a strong team, but my hope is for the sake of football, because the play produced by Zagallo's team is really poor.'

Cruyff would get his wish, and for once world football was confronted with the rare scenario of the Brazilian national side in disarray. Ronaldo was being made a convenient scapegoat for all this. When I interviewed Sir Bobby Robson in early 2003, I asked him for his thoughts on the whole France '98 imbroglio. Pausing for a moment to gather his thoughts and encapsulate something that was still a sad issue for him, he told me, 'They killed him. They flogged him like a pit horse. He played 80-odd matches in less than a year and it was no wonder his knee packed in. I felt for the boy, I really did. The pressure he was under was crazy. I've never seen anybody, however famous or important, be hounded like he was. It was a tragedy and one he's done well to come back from. He was the best specimen I'd seen as a player, the fastest thing I've ever seen running with a ball, but even he couldn't take the punishment he was asked to endure. He looked dead beat in the final.'

As the media intensity heightened as press-packs were congregating outside each of his and his family's Rio apartments, Ronaldo, with a view to quelling the thronging mass, gave an impromptu press conference, saying, 'I think there's been a big exaggeration in all this. I want more respect. I'm not a fugitive and I don't want to be chased every time I go to my mother's house. I'm trying to lead a normal life as far as possible. I don't want to be chased any more.' This language reflects exactly how Ronaldo was feeling at the time: 'fugitive', 'being chased', 'I want respect' all suggest a tortured, cornered soul who still needed time, a lot of time, to get over the desperate personal events of Paris. To do this he did the only thing he could to escape it all and set off for the swish resort of Angra dos Reis near Rio, where he would spend a month trying to get his head back together. With him went Suzana Werner. After that, remembering his anonymity in the USA, they took off to Las Vegas for a break but back home, and in the rest of the football-loving world, speculation was still buzzing as to what actually happened to Ronaldo and whether or not he had some deep-seated mental illness which could in turn provoke future convulsions and fits. He was becoming like a caged circus animal, being prodded by the world's media, eager to see if he would react or show any signs of abnormality.

Whilst supposedly keeping a low profile in Rio, Ronaldo still found time to open that essential bauble of all high-profile footballers: the nightclub and restaurant. Located in Rio's smart Leblon district, the venue was named R-9 to tie in with the new Nike sub-brand about to be launched globally. A rather over-the-top establishment, and one which never really knew what its role was, be it nightclub or restaurant, it soon bombed, and meant Ronaldo could join the ranks of George Best, Frank Worthington, Terry Venables, Romário and countless other footballers who, on the basis of dreadful advice, think they can make a go of something they know little about. Certainly, in the case of Best and Worthington, their skills and contribution lay in front of the bar, not behind it. Quite why footballers get involved in these ventures remains a mystery.

The Suzana Werner situation would prove to be more contentious than first appeared on the surface. In Brazil, and especially Rio, young women can be quite shameless in their pursuit of fame and wealth. A certain clique of these groupies who chase footballers are known as *'Maria Chuteiras'* (*chuteiras* literally meaning football boots). They are often seen hanging around Rio's bars and clubs chasing the likes of Flamengo or Fluminense players, for example. Clearly a prime catch such as Ronaldo is a different matter altogether, and Suzana Werner was no mug in this respect. She was smart, very attractive, and knew her fledgling acting career would benefit from the tonic of Ronaldo's publicity – but anybody who calls their chihuahua puppy 'Sharon Stone', as she did, must have some pretty serious insecurity problems upstairs.

The off-field bust-ups between the two of them during France '98 were clearly detrimental to Ronaldo's mental state, and accepted opinion in Rio is that Ronaldo loved her far more than she loved him. In Wensley Clarkson's book, *Ronaldo! King of the World*, Rio radio presenter Sergio Piumatti sums up the situation thus:

> For the past two years, Suzana Werner has been perfectly content with her role as Ronaldo's trinket. She was famous because of who he was – she was the girlfriend of the world's most famous footballer, and not because of who she was. She was one undeniably attractive girl, but you see thousands of these on the

beach at Ipanema every day. It's true she appears in a soap opera on Brazilian TV but she was anything but a household name until her sudden notoriety. Overnight in France she started behaving how she thought a star should behave. Everywhere the paparazzi went, Suzana went too (rather than vice versa). Ronaldo might have imagined she was going to France to soothe his furrowed brow, but Suzana clearly believed she was there to further her television career.

In the acrid air of World Cup defeat, several players were keen to air their washing in public: none more so than roommate Roberto Carlos, one who, you might think, would be more sensitive to the plight of the young superstar. Roberto Carlos was happy to go on the record that he was in 'no doubt' that Ronaldo had 'chickened out' of the final and that 'he had become number one player too quickly. He cried because he was afraid. He couldn't stand the pressure.' Cutting words indeed from a teammate and quite why Roberto Carlos went on this rant no one is exactly sure. Was it jealousy? Perhaps. Roberto Carlos had been catapulted into the global footballing spotlight after his outrageous bending free kick against France in Le Tournoi the year before, one which he would dine out on thereafter. Perhaps his supersession by Ronaldo as the Brazilian media darling had gotten to him.

Watching the entire goings-on with a not-too-happy eye were Ronaldo's employers and lofty wage payers, Inter Milan. As naturally selfish as all big clubs, they had winced in anguish as their star asset laboured through the tournament, their medical staff being fully aware of the delicate nature of Ronaldo's knee, and looked on in exasperation as the events of the final unfolded. What condition would their man return to Milan in? President Massimo Moratti was characteristically forthright and gave the CBF both barrels. 'The CBF acted in an absurd manner. It was a serious mistake to play Ronaldo in those conditions. Even though he expressed a desire to play which is inevitable, I think someone should have looked at him more as a person than as a player. In general, he handles everything in an intelligent and balanced manner. This time, evidently, he wasn't able to do so.' Somewhat rich coming from Moratti, who had shown no compunction about using Ronaldo wherever possible for Inter, and had raised unsympathetic eyebrows whenever Ronaldo suggested he may need a rest. With Inter keen to go one better than their second place in *lo scudetto* the previous season, a fit and firing Ronaldo was the cornerstone of their plans. Without him their prospects were greatly diminished.

After Las Vegas, Ronaldo added more air miles with a trip to Cancun in Mexico, at the Quintana Roo resort. Although not scheduled to be back in Italy until 20 August for pre-season, he kept in contact with Moratti on a daily basis via his omnipresent mobile phones. For once, Ronaldo had the prospect of extended rest as he was suspended for the first two games of the new season due to sharp comments he had made about the refereeing in the infamous title-deciding Juventus game the previous season. This timely sojourn would give his troublesome knee as much time as possible to recover ahead of the onslaught of the *Serie A* season. But could his knee recover? Was it a case of merely letting it rest or was the damage caused by the innumerable painkilling injections now catching up with him? Again, the only person who really knew this was Ronaldo himself. Could the knee stand the rigour of another arduous season in *Serie A*, Ronaldo's second there and one where the uncompromising defences would be all the wiser to his game, and have even more preventative measures for him? Ronaldo returned to Italy at the end of August to join the Inter squad for pre-season. Although the fuss from 12 July hadn't and wouldn't die down for a while yet, Ronaldo's naturally boyish and straightforward demeanour helped him win back many observers who had abandoned him after the game; but on arrival in Milan the questions looming over him would not go away. Many wondered if he would ever get back to the player he was. Was there something under the surface that could rear its head at any time and induce another fit or convulsion? And then there was the knee.

CHAPTER 10

FRUSTRATION AND CONCERN –
INTER MILAN 1998–99

Amidst all the fallout still wafting around the football world from France '98, Ronaldo still had a job to do. He was being paid a king's ransom for his services and his paymasters at Inter wanted and expected him to deliver. Ronaldo had to get back to playing football, but the 1998–99 season would prove to be one of false dawns and frustration.

At Inter, the arrival of Italian folk-hero, the Divine Ponytail, Roberto Baggio created a welcome distraction for Ronaldo and meant that, at least for a moment, the spotlight was on the 1993 FIFA World Player of the Year, rather than the current one. Baggio, despite sporting some atrocious haircuts, was an Italian *fantasista* of sublime gifts who, along with Romário, had been the outstanding player at USA '94 and could perhaps sympathise with Ronaldo, as World Cup final disappointment was a subject about which he could speak with some authority. Having single-handedly steered Arrigo Sacchi's flaccid Italy to the final to meet Brazil, he took the field, like Ronaldo had in France, palpably unfit and with his right hamstring under inches of tape and bandaging. He laboured through the game and was unable to repeat the heroics and skill he had shown in the previous rounds, where some of his play had been quite brilliant. Alas, as the game went to a penalty shoot-out, Baggio needed to score to keep Italy in it. He didn't, and would be remembered as the fall guy for missing Italy's decisive penalty, thus handing Brazil the trophy. Although not quite as bad as Diana Ross's unforgettable miss from three yards in the desperately vulgar opening ceremony, it was a poor effort from a player of such quality. The image of lonely Baggio stood head bowed over the penalty spot having just blazed over, with Brazil's keeper Taffarel on his knees looking heavenwards, is one of acute polarities of sporting emotion. That moment of isolation and despair in front of the billions watching was something he candidly admits took him a very long time to recover from. He and Ronaldo had a lot in common.

Baggio's arrival also meant that Ronaldo could now acquire his coveted number 9 shirt, the pair of them taking the plum shirt numbers of 10 and 9 respectively. In this way, the increasing importance of shirt-numbering in the modern game was well illustrated at Inter, where Nike were now the kit suppliers after Umbro's deal had expired. Meanwhile, the Chilean Ivan Zamorano, not best chuffed at having to relinquish his cherished number 9 shirt to Ronaldo, came up with the novel idea of wearing the number 8 + 1, to make up 9. This would set an unfortunate trend of quite stupid numbering amongst some egotistical players.

The picture now looked to be complete. Ronaldo was adorned top-to-toe in Nike apparel, Inter had yet again had a merry summer in the transfer market and brought in the aforementioned Baggio, and all seemed set for another tilt at *lo scudetto* title. The fans were giddy with anticipation that Inter would finally deliver. But there was one minor fly in the ointment: Ronaldo wasn't fit.

The 1998–99 season at Inter proved anti-climactic in all sorts of respects. The rest of the squad were not slow in realising Ronaldo's importance to them as they struggled to make any impact on the league. Even Argentine Diego Simeone, for once exhibiting compassion, was compelled to admit that, 'Taking the field without Ronaldo is like leaving home in winter without an overcoat.'

On 6 February 1999, he had his first meeting, in Paris, with renowned knee specialist Prof. Gerard Saillant, but with Ronaldo claiming that the pain came and went without any sort of pattern, Saillant advised against surgery at this time as it could vitiate the whole situation. Inter's medical staff were also reluctant to put Ronaldo under the knife and a defensive strategy of extensive rest between games was adopted, more in hope of remedy than out of any concrete medical conviction. As such, Ronaldo's appearances were limited.

The situation with the CBF was also tenuous. As the CBF looked to sell their team around the world to fellow FAs in return for friendly fixtures, Ronaldo was again the jewel in the crown. There was also the contract with Nike which required Ronaldo to play. An injured Ronaldo hadn't ever been part of this thinking and the CBF, had they checked any available maps for a current grid reference, would have found themselves squarely located between a rock and a hard place. At the centre of this farrago was the unfit Ronaldo, being punted around like a prize exhibit, but unable to perform as billed, rather like ordering a bottle of Chateau Lafite from an impressive wine list and having the apologetic sommelier inform you they have none in the cellar.

But by now it was evident that his knee was a genuine problem. Its journey had been a tortuous one from the Osgood-Schlatter troubles at PSV, the long arduous season at Barcelona, the heavy, Nike-influenced schedule for Brazil and the pummelling of his debut season in *Serie A*. Not forgetting the intense, painkiller-assisted six weeks during France '98. This, combined with Ronaldo's trademark high-speed slaloming play, meant a breaking point had to come. No one knew this more than Ronaldo and he flew in old friend and physio Nilton Petrone from Brazil. Ronaldo was under pressure.

Apart from his obvious personal desire to play, his agents barely hid the fact that an injured, non-playing Ronaldo was of little use to them. Likewise Moratti, whose whole modus operandi at Inter hinged around Ronaldo. Being injured just wasn't on the menu. With Moratti's blessing, Petrone devised an extensive programme of physio-based rehab for the knee. Ronaldo remained patient throughout all this and calmly searched for answers.

To try to understand further the nature of Ronaldo's knee problems, I met with his press-officer, Rodrigo Paiva. Rodrigo, who bears an uncanny resemblance to Luis Figo, was invited to join Ronaldo after the trauma of France '98, when Ronaldo felt his life needed some professional organisation. Rodrigo, who had been chief media relations man at Rio club Flamengo, was seen as an ideal candidate and they struck up an immediate friendship. Rodrigo now also looks after press relations for the CBF. I caught up with Rodrigo in Rio's Leblon district and he explained the origins of the knee problem. 'Filé had made it clear that there was some serious problem with Ronaldo's knee whilst he was at Barcelona. Filé insisted that Ronaldo had to do a serious maintenance job on his knee back then to avoid serious problems further down the line. We asked the medical staff at Barcelona to ensure he had specific physio care but they never did it, and throughout the season Ronaldo complained about knee pain that came and went; it was very peculiar.

Then, when he moved to Inter Milan, we [Filé and Rodrigo] insisted to their medical staff that they took special care of him because of the knee issues. He was always having to take painkillers, both medicines and injections, to reduce the pain and allow him to play. It was a delicate situation. Because of the demand upon Ronaldo made by Inter, he was always having to play in pain, with sacrifice. It limited his movements; it limited his game. All the time he was trying to fix the pain with physio from Filé and from Inter's physio Dr Volpi, but it was not enough. Like Filé always maintained, he needed specific physio regimes, not just those that the rest of the squad received.'

By the end of April, Ronaldo felt sufficiently fit to be able to play again and, although doubts remained as to exactly how fit or not he was, he notched seven times in eight games at season end. Moratti, restless with impatience as his expensive misfits again failed to deliver success in the league, had gone through four coaches in the season. The previous year's incumbent, Luigi Simoni, was fired after a poor start. Mircea Lucescu resigned not long after, unable to stand the pressure, and Luciano Castellini had barely had time to put on his tracksuit before he was axed in favour of Englishman Roy Hodgson. Hodgson, although able to improve things, was unable to undo the mess that had preceded him and Inter finished a pitiful eighth – way, way off the pace of winners AC Milan. After a season not far off embarrassing, one wouldn't have wanted to be in the headmaster's study at term-end with Moratti that year. The season was a washout. Inter had been knocked out of the Champions League by eventual winners Manchester United in the quarter-finals, and dumped out of the Coppa Italia by Parma, and Ronaldo was again made a convenient scapegoat for the travails, his dodgy knee never fully allowing him to deliver the goods. This was a harsh assessment as, although his appearances were patchy, he had still managed to play in 19 games – effectively with one knee – and score 14 goals, but had not achieved the consistency needed to classify it as a good season. The strangely effective German Oliver Bierhoff, now at champions Milan, had again outgunned him with 19.

During this downtime, Martins and Pitta used every opportunity to punt Ronaldo around, sending him to festivals, launches, openings, promotional events, MTV appearances, anything where he could get profile while his principal vehicle of publicity, the football pitch, was not always available to him. Ronaldo was routinely wheeled out at big sporting events, such as Grand Prix where he was readily photographed

FRUSTRATION AND CONCERN . . .

with compatriot and Ferrari driver Rubens Barrichello alongside world no.1 Michael Schumacher. Italian motorbike sensation Valentino Rossi was also used for publicity, and that well known haunt of footballers, the Cannes Film Festival, was Ronaldo's next stop. At every turn, Ronaldo would be seen wearing Nike, Nike R9, or both.

Frustration began to set in as Ronaldo, in search of answers, only found furrowed brows and procrastination. His first season with Inter had been a success. Although not as barnstorming as his year at Barcelona, he had impressed all round. He had also played a burdensome 64 games and during the season had only realistically had four days off; a stiff workload for someone with a suspect knee. There was then the drama of the World Cup. For Ronaldo, a 'normal' day, as you or I would understand it, was a distant pipe dream.

He was then required to play in another of Nike's showcase games, this time for Brazil against Barcelona to celebrate Barcelona's centenary. The game, which ended 2–2, appeared tedious to all involved, and Ronaldo himself looked tired, jaded and disinterested in the whole event. But if you're going to throw a party, throw a good one, and for Nike, it was a roaring success with the Camp Nou packed to the rafters and sales of Brazil and (newly acquired) Barcelona shirts humming along nicely.

Ronaldo then rejoined the *seleçao* for the Copa America in Paraguay, sufficiently away from the media spotlight of Europe's hungry press packs and enabling him to reunite with his teammates with whom, in dire adversity, he had formed a solid bond after France '98. Also, by now his relationship with Suzana had run aground so the trip back to native Latin America was more than timely.

In the squad to contest the Copa America was another young face, also with a mouthful of teeth that would challenge the scope of dentistry, and with the same name: Ronaldo. As at the Atlanta Olympics in 1996, where the naive US organisers didn't know what to call Ronaldo and gave him the moniker Ronaldinho, the CBF were faced with a dilemma, as rather like with a private number plate or an internet domain name, the name Ronaldo was now taken. They came up with the new *nom de guerre* of Ronaldinho Gaucho, reflecting his southern Brazilian origins, with Ronaldinho to be used on his shirt. Hailing from Grêmio football club, Ronaldinho had caused a stir in domestic Brazilian football and was noted for his skill, trickery, pace and heady confidence. In other words, he was pure Brazil, and the fans took to him straight away. Rather like Roberto Baggio's arrival at Inter earlier that season, this was a welcome

111

distraction for Ronaldo, who would have welcomed anyone or anything that would divert the world's attention away from himself.

The Copa America is the South American equivalent of the UEFA European Championships and is a hotly fought prize. Despite his up-and-down fitness during the season for Inter, Ronaldo looked back to his devastating best during the tournament and was its undoubted star. But the fitness question as a whole remained a conundrum. Brazil opened their campaign in some style by thumping Venezuela 7–0. Ronaldo, prowling, menacing and hungry, scored twice, one a sublime piece of trickery to skin the full-back followed by a canny curling finish into the corner. But the game was remembered for the arrival of Ronaldinho, who scored a gem of a goal, weaving around several defenders and slotting the ball past the advancing keeper to rubber stamp the arrival of yet another classic Brazilian playmaker. Next up against Mexico, the *seleçao* won 2–1, but Ronaldo again looked troubled by injury and had a below-par game, and for the first time in the Brazil shirt got booed by certain sections of the samba contingent. Who said football fans weren't fickle? Undeterred, he scored the only goal in the next game against Chile, another trademark, skill-laden effort and, as group winners, Brazil would play the old enemy Argentina in the next phase.

These games are massive, of England–Germany proportions, but unlike the Anglo-Germanic struggles, they invariably have the cream of the world's footballers on view. On show for Argentina were most of the alumni from France '98, such as Juan Sebastian Veron, Javier Zanetti and the mercurial Gabriel 'Batigol' Batistuta. Added to this were up-and-coming stars such as Juan Riquelme, Hernán Crespo and Pablo Aimar: a glittering cast. For Brazil, Ronaldo and Rivaldo, who both had stand-out tournaments, were joined by the likes of Cafu, Roberto Carlos and Emerson. In goal, Taffarel, who was assisted out of the old folk's home for France '98, could finally hang up his gloves once and for all as a worthwhile replacement emerged in the shape of the imposing figure of Dida.

In a pulsating game, Argentina took the lead on 11 minutes through Juan Pablo Sorin of Paris St Germain, and Brazil were up against it. But since the nadir of France '98, the side now contained some seriously stiff resolve and a sense of unity that was missing on that night of 12 July. Brazil rallied and with Ronaldo releasing Rivaldo to equalise on 35 minutes, they went into the interval on level terms. Ronaldo again showed his priceless ability to score key goals when he notched the winner just after the restart to break Argentine hearts and send Brazil through. Argentina had again failed to deliver in a major tournament.

Ronaldo had had an outstanding game and, with a few days off ahead of the next game, he and his physio, Filé Petrone, decided to take a helicopter trip to the stunning Iguaçu Falls which form part of the border between Paraguay, Argentina and Brazil. They are quite simply breathtaking and an ideal and relaxing way to spend a day off. Ronaldo spent what appeared to be a contented day doing some sightseeing and shopping and then returned to the hotel. However, unable to avoid the headlines even at the remote Iguaçu Falls, a shopkeeper took it upon himself, no doubt in the pursuit of some cheap publicity, to claim that Ronaldo had bought over $50,000 worth of watches from his store with a view to taking them back over the border. Shades of Bobby Moore at the 1970 World Cup, and with various police called in it all threatened to get a bit nasty; however, as no watches were found either on Ronaldo's person or in his room, and as the shopkeeper couldn't produce any receipts to validate the alleged purchases, it soon blew over, but was a needless kerfuffle nevertheless.

Again, unperturbed, Ronaldo cracked on with the job in hand and helped steer Brazil to the final with a 2–0 win over Mexico. In the final, they would face old foes Uruguay. Uruguay, since their heady arrival on the world football scene in the 1930s, had fallen on lean times. But Brazilian football history contains one black cloud above all others – the cumulonimbus cloud of vast proportions better known as their defeat to Uruguay in the 1950 World Cup final at the Maracanã. A repeat of this would have been unlikely as Uruguay had been fortunate to reach the final and hadn't played with anything like the form of champions. Furthermore, their overly defensive approach in the final meant they never got out of first gear and were unable to thwart the combined menace of Rivaldo, who scored twice, and Ronaldo, who rounded the scoring off with a quite outrageous volley. Latching onto a bouncing ball about 30 yards out, he could have easily taken a touch and taken the ball on. But why do that when you can leather it into the top corner, first time, past a startled keeper? It was another final goal for Ronaldo (France '98 being the only omission from this set) and he was crowned *artilhero* for the tournament with five goals. It was the first thing he'd won in over a year. Throughout the tournament, Ronaldo had looked something near his best. The explosive pace and body swerves looked to be back in full working order and the sumptuous volley in the final suggested that confidence wasn't an issue either. But crucially, in the odd game, he had also looked distracted, as if his knee was giving him gyp that he couldn't quite fathom, reflecting his personal diagnosis earlier in the year to Prof. Gerard Saillant that it just came and went at random. A precarious situation.

Jubilant at their victory and bursting with pride and the South American bragging rights that their success now gave them, a few of the squad, Ronaldo included, went on for a celebratory night out in São Paulo. Full of beans and commanding attention, it wasn't long before a young girl slipped into the group and started enjoying the fun and games. The girl was Milene Domingues: petite, shapely, attractive, and in possession of the lethal ingredient that Ronaldo required as standard in all his women, *cabelos louros* – blonde hair. She was also the world keep-up champion with a vertiginous 55,178, and, having been brought up with seven brothers, had a natural affinity with football. When she was 14, she had been invited to do said keep-ups during the half-time break at São Paulo's Corinthians football club, and the money she earned from this helped keep the family afloat. Like Ronaldo, football had been a way to earn a living. They hit things off pretty much straight away and Ronaldo, showing a penchant for tasty blondes that Rod Stewart would have been proud of, now had yet another to adorn his right arm.

It was at this time that Ronaldo began his work with the United Nations. I asked his press-officer Rodrigo Paiva how this came about. 'After we won the Copa America in 1999, Ronaldo wanted to give his prize money away to a good cause, so he asked me to think about who should receive it. I thought long and hard and then arrived at the idea that kids with cancer would be a good idea: not only because it is a worthy cause in itself, but because the kids who suffer from it have their heads shaved for chemotherapy. As such, they can relate to Ronaldo, who also has his head shaved, so I thought this would be an ideal match to give them hope and self-confidence that having all your hair shaved off isn't so bad. They could identify with Ronaldo. We gave the money to various hospitals and it all went well. Having seen this and the positive publicity it created, the United Nations contacted us and said they wanted to do some work in Kosovo with Ronaldo and Zinedine Zidane, and use famous footballers as the focus. They wanted money to rebuild the heating systems that had all been destroyed during the fighting. Ronaldo said, 'No problem, you can have the money, but I want to go to see where it's going.'

FRUSTRATION AND CONCERN . . .

Cast your mind back to the Balkan crisis and Kosovo was certainly not the destination of choice for most multimillionaire superstars at the time. The UN were accordingly somewhat taken aback by this request.

Rodrigo went on, 'The UN were understandably concerned, but they wanted the money and after lengthy discussions to ensure this was do-able, we went. Inter and Moratti were going crazy, saying, "No, this is stupid, are you serious?" but eventually Moratti came round to the idea and lent us his private jet to fly to the area. It was amazing. Being Brazilians, we had never seen a war so close and all the devastation they cause. Everything was destroyed; everything. The most amazing thing happened when we arrived, in that everybody began to chant Ronaldo's name. Ron-al-do, Ron-al-do, Ron-al-do. Ronaldo couldn't understand it. They had no electricity, no TVs, no communications, but they somehow knew all about Ronaldo. How could this be? It was amazing. The news teams picked up on this and the next day the story was all over the world. Everyone was so excited by the whole thing. Then Ronaldo suggested, if everyone is so excited by all this, then why doesn't he become a UN Ambassador and help other children in need? Kofi Annan accepted straight away!

'Not long after, we were invited to a big UN reception in America. Lots of celebrities were there including Michael Douglas, Susan Sarandon, Muhammad Ali, Bono and that Spice Girl of yours. What's her name? Geri somebody. I don't know what she was doing there. What Ronaldo remembers is that he was in awe of all these great stars and Hollywood actors but they all wanted to be with him and talk to him. He didn't know what to do and didn't know why they all knew him. Even Muhammad Ali came over to have his picture taken with him. Bono came over and said Ronaldo was one of his idols. For us, it was incredible.

'Then, at dinner, Kofi Annan gave a speech about the danger of AIDS and the need for everybody to be more aware and to encourage the use of condoms. Out of all the star guests, he turned to Ronaldo and said, "If I ask Ronaldo to use a condom because AIDS is so dangerous, he will use one and send a great message to all people about the need to use protection." Ronaldo, somewhat bemused, laughed, and answered, "Yes, but I am not a good example, because if I did that my partner [Milene Domingues] would not be pregnant now!" Everybody fell about laughing. We have had some great times with the UN fundraising.'

CHAPTER 11

INTO THE ABYSS

Ronaldo's key role in the Copa America victory was a welcome return to the good times. The previous year had been an *annus horribilis* of trauma and uncertainty as he struggled to overcome the fallout from the World Cup final in Paris, and wrestled psychologically with the quirks of his knee. Now he was getting back to what he was more used to: scoring great goals and making the back pages, rather than the front pages, of the newspapers.

Whilst he'd been away in Paraguay, events had been hotting-up in Milan. Not one to lie idle for long, Massimo Moratti had brandished the Inter cheque book once again, this time capturing burly Italian striker Christian Vieri from Lazio for a whopping $52 million – a world-record fee. The Italian press began to salivate at the prospect of Vieri in tandem with Ronaldo, an extraterrestrial $84 million strikeforce – 'The Dream Couple', as they were tagged – linking up to score hatfuls of goals. Moratti had pulled off an even bigger coup by luring Marcello Lippi into the Inter coach's job, which, for years, had seemed like a poisoned chalice. Lippi, famously cool and a man of few words, had enjoyed years of success with Juventus and had led them along the golden path of *lo scudetto*, the Champions League and the Intercontinental Club Championship. He was justly regarded as one of the best coaches in the game and seemed the right man at the right time to galvanise Inter into championship material.

An assiduous character, Lippi demanded no more of his players than he was prepared to give them himself, and early in the job identified where he felt Inter had been going wrong, vowing 'to turn the Inter team into a Ronaldo-independent one'. Although this statement in itself was valid it was seized upon by the Italian media as being anti-Ronaldo. Their darling, nonpareil *Fenomeno* being forced to slum it with the hoi-polloi didn't stack up with them and Lippi was berated in the press for looking to pinion him. Here was the classic situation of a new, proven, high-profile coach at a big club versus a footballing superstar. From day one, there was friction between the two and they didn't get along. Lippi, a devout disciple of thorough fitness preparation, held no truck with Ronaldo's dodgy knee and put him through the same rigorous pre-season programmes he put the rest of the squad through.

Ronaldo didn't like this, again a reflection that only he knew how vulnerable his knee actually was. Lippi, perhaps sensing this, or even more so, wanting to stamp his authority on his new charges, caused a collective gasp of disbelief across Italy when he benched Ronaldo for the first game of the new *Serie A* season. Graham Taylor, the affable, highly entertaining but ultimately ineffectual England coach, had tried similar medicine with English national hero Paul Gascoigne after Italia '90. Espying an ego that may have been larger than his, Taylor had crassly dropped Gascoigne for his first game in charge versus the Republic of Ireland, citing tactical reasons and replacing him with nondescript journeyman Gordon Cowans. Lippi's decision caused similar disbelief in Italy as Taylor's had in England. What's more, Moratti, as startled as anybody by the decision, began to ask why expensive asset no. 1 was warming the bench and not warming the back of the opposition goal.

But the man doing the warming was Christian Vieri. For a striker of such obvious qualities, Vieri was surprisingly well travelled, having played for Juventus, Atlético Madrid and Lazio, all of whom he'd served well. He had worked under Lippi before, at Juventus, and despite one or two public spats with the obdurate Viareggian, they had since made up and he claimed one of the main reasons for him joining Inter was Lippi's presence there. Vieri got off to a flyer with a hat-trick against Verona. He left the field a hero and had completely overshadowed Ronaldo, who watched proceedings from the bench. For Lippi, it was a dream start, and initial vindication for his omission of the Brazilian.

Ronaldo, not best chuffed, sulked off to the Italian Grand Prix at Monza, where, with the sweetener of a $50,000 appearance bung from Brazilian oil giant Petrobras, he was happy to rub shoulders with all and sundry, much to the ire of Lippi. Even more annoyed was Moratti, who, fed-up with his lavishly paid stars swanning around, moved swiftly to quash all extra-curricular activity that took their minds off the job in hand. He was not happy and he wasn't messing around either. He forced Ronaldo to cancel two forthcoming commitments with outside sponsors. Ronaldo, Martins and Pitta were not amused. Nor were they used to being told what to do.

On the field, Lippi's charges further impressed by thumping Parma 5–1 and going top of *Serie A*. Lippi kept Ronaldo on the bench; Inter kept winning and Vieri kept scoring goals. None of this was in the script for Ronaldo, who had been so used to being the player claiming the headlines and scoring the goals. Perhaps looking for solace, and also off the back of the news that Milene was pregnant, Ronaldo proposed to her and they would be married in Brazil later in the year. It appeared to cheer him up as, in the next game versus Piacenza, he came off the bench to score in the 2–1 win. This goal was enough to persuade Lippi to start Ronaldo in the next game, the small matter of the Milan derby versus AC, and, at last, Italy had the chance to witness The Dream Couple starting for the first time together. Would they make it over the threshold OK? Ronaldo started well and was playing some of his best stuff since the Copa America. He duly converted a penalty to give Inter the lead but then disaster struck. Marking him that day was the feisty Argentine Roberto Ayala. No doubt not short of a few things to say about Ronaldo, Argentina–Brazil relations and, who knows, maybe some choice remarks about Ronaldo's expectant fiancée, the two of them were involved in a flare-up late in the first half, and both saw red. His frustration was tangible, and as the cameras spun round to the bench to focus on Lippi, the silver-haired disciplinarian remained as impassive as ever. He would have been livid though at Inter's ultimate surrender of the lead as Andriy Shevchenko (74') and then George Weah (87') nicked the game for the *rossonieri*.

His mood was not made any better when Ronaldo was next caught up in a wrangle between Inter, FIFA and the CBF. The whole thing proved to be a tawdry affair, with Brazil 'selecting' Ronaldo to play in a friendly against Australia in Sydney. Inter were understandably aghast at the prospect of the prized asset spending all that time airborne, for a meaningless friendly, at a crucial part of the season. They complained to FIFA but FIFA backed Brazil and Ronaldo made the trip. As it transpired, the CBF had sold the game to the Australian FA on the basis that Ronaldo would be there. Ronaldo's presence made the difference between bums being on seats or not and on confirmation of Ronaldo's presence, fifty thousand tickets were sold for the game in two days. His presence was key.

On arriving back in Milan, Ronaldo had the chance to cement his place in the side as Inter played lowly Lecce. Inter ran out convincing 6–0 winners, with Ronaldo scoring the fifth from the penalty spot, but then the first signs of trouble appeared. In chasing a through ball, Ronaldo felt something go in his knee, something his facial wince betrayed. Not wanting to provoke too much drama, Ronaldo hobbled off, complaining of a sore ankle, and was duly substituted. But the situation proved to be graver than first anticipated. Once Inter's medical staff had completed their full series of examinations the following day, it was evident that Ronaldo's patella tendon had gone. This tendon, between six or seven centimetres in length, governs the movement of the kneecap, and as such is a fundamental one. Again, the idea of an operation was resisted *pis aller* but it was soon evident that there was no alternative, so bad was the damage. Optimistic estimates suggested that, if all went well, Ronaldo would be back playing within four months. Language such as 'if all went well' was not what Ronaldo needed to hear.

In November 1998, Filé had presented a clear diagnosis of how he saw the problem with Ronaldo's knee and a long-term solution. The diagnosis was similar to the one he had made in 1996 in that the problem was Ronaldo's quadriceps – the assemblage of muscles in the front part of the thigh. Ronaldo's were larger than normal and his right quadricep in particular was larger, and in turn more powerful, than the surrounding muscles. This caused a series of disequilibrium and imbalances when Ronaldo was in motion. When contracted, the assemblage transmitted a large stress load to the patella tendon over the knee, which in turn transmitted through to the knee. As a result of these different forces, the patella, rather than just moving over its axis as it is intended to, also moved sideways whilst Ronaldo was running. Instead of working only in this axis/pivot mode, the patella had to make a bigger movement and suffered unequal stress as it had to absorb the lateral movement too. This created an overburden, which, combined with the other forces generated by Ronaldo's larger thigh and knee muscles, placed a massive load on the small patella tendon. In turn, the patella 'complained' with inflammation and pain, and it was this that had been causing Ronaldo such uncertainty and angst.

Filé's skill in identifying this imbalance was pioneering. Whereas an orthopaedist tends to look at the bones as a symptom of pain in the knees, Filé saw everything as a system that needed to be in equilibrium. He had alerted Ronaldo to this back in 1996 but was never really able to achieve the correct balance, primarily due to the massive demands of Ronaldo's schedule, which itself in turn had meant that the years of unequal forces upon the patella and knee were now beginning to cause acute problems. He had helped Ronaldo play as often as possible, with intensive physio programmes ahead of the big games to make sure he was fit, but the Lecce incident was a big warning sign that things were now becoming serious. The patella needed operating on.

Ronaldo travelled to Paris for the operation, which was undertaken by Prof. Gerard Saillant, who was by now becoming very familiar with Ronaldo's problem limb. For Ronaldo, whose year had been one of setback after setback, this took him to a new low, and the vexed frustration in his eyes was clear to see. Taking a leaf out of Roberto Carlos's book, Lippi cruelly stuck a boot in too, commenting that Ronaldo would not be missed, that he was a problem player and that he had little future now in football. Low blows indeed. As Ronaldo lay in his Parisian hospital bed, he had plenty to ponder. Unloved and unwanted by his manager, he could at least take comfort in his forthcoming nuptials with Milene. He was soon to be a father, and for the first time in his life, he had need to think beyond the white lines of a football field.

With the operation having gone well, Ronaldo took some time to recuperate back in Brazil at the CBF's plush Comary Farm training complex at Teresopolis, and rested back at his apartment in Rio. Whilst there, he married Milene, who by now was five months pregnant. The wedding, which was held in Rio's 'new money' area of Barra de Tijuca, was a relatively straightforward affair, without many of the garish trappings more commonly associated with a modern footballer. Despite the tension between the two families, the day went off well, and was brightened by the sight of Ricardo Teixera, head of CBF, being refused access by the security guards. Teixera hadn't been invited but had presumptuously made it his business to turn up. Security, under strict instructions to permit entry only to listed guests, duly did their job and stood firm. The hordes of paparazzi outside had a field day and Teixera's blushes were ultimately spared when, after 20 minutes of frantic 'Do you know who I am?' gesticulating with the heavies on the door, Ronaldo appeared and OK'd his entrance and the party carried on in earnest.

During the speeches, Ronaldo, as well as giving all the usual wedding-related banter, was keen to put a brave face on his current state of infirmity, stating that his unborn son will see him play football, and with the four-month recuperation period due to be finished by April, it was no idle boast.

It was during this recuperation that Ronaldo was summoned to take part in one of the more bizarre sequences in his already notable young life. Brazil were still smarting from their defeat by France in Paris. It was only the second time they had lost in a World Cup final, the previous time being the infamous reversal against Uruguay in 1950. For many years, the success of the *seleçao* has been shamelessly used by politics and politicians to hide the ills of the nation and give the 160 million or so Brazilian souls something to cheer about. This is known as '*Politica do pão e circo*' (the politics of bread and circus), a metaphorical phrase where the bread is the food and the circus is the distraction. For example, politicians will stage high-profile 'food for a dollar' days, where they will put on a good meal for Brazil's impoverished lower classes, often in front of the grand city hall, in exchange for BR$1 (about 20 pence). Camera crews and TV stations will be there in full force to broadcast to the nation the bottomless generosity that the politicians wish to convey, when all along the real problems of the *favelas*, drug and gun crime, and abject poverty go on unchallenged. The whole thing is a sham. Football hasn't been left untouched either by the politicians. For years, they have used the 'circus' of the supremely successful *seleçao* to distract the bulk of the nation from the fact they are living close to the poverty line and take their minds off the lack of bread.

The defeat in France was a poor showing by the 'circus' and had the double-negative effect of creating national disappointment and thus deepening the resentment regarding the lack of food (*pão*) and amenities. Although not quite on the scale of the 1950 trauma, certain sectors of Brazilian society were still not satisfied with the account of events given to them of what happened on 12 July in Paris: none more so than a little-known Communist congressman based in Brasilia called Aldo Rebelo. He had drawn up a petition in Brazil's House of Deputies to start an inquiry into the Nike–CBF contract, something he felt went against all that was good about Brazilian football, and an act he felt betrayed the sovereignty of the Brazilian game.

Rebelo possessed the distrust most Brazilians have of foreigners and foreign corporations – especially those who involve themselves in matters of such national interest as the CBF and *seleçao*. Rebelo was making it his business to find out what went on that day in Paris and how much influence and sway Nike had in it all. As a Communist, Rebelo would have had no qualms about waiting for the 18 months his petition sat in the bureaucratic queue in Brasilia. This wait actually worked in his favour, for it was during this time that details of the Nike–CBF contract, which had previously been guarded like the formula for Coca-Cola, were somehow leaked to the press.

Second, the former coach of the national team, Vanderlei Luxemburgo, was also under investigation for a range of offences broadly grouped under the corruption banner. With events akin to storylines of the many soap operas that clog the Brazilian TV channels, Luxemburgo had been sprung by his ex-mistress, the tiresome Renata Alves, who, seeing her shot at the big time, had blown the whistle on some of Luxemburgo's extra-curricular activities. Not only those in the bedroom (Luxemburgo was married) but also the way in which he used her as a proxy to buy umpteen items of status such as boats, houses, cars, jet-skis and the like. She also exposed how Luxemburgo had been selecting players for the *seleçao* with a view to raising their market value to Brazilian-mad European clubs. The fact that Luxemburgo was also agent for many of these players was again conveniently ignored by the powers that be.

But this exposé of Luxemburgo's activities, combined with the revelations of the Nike contract, which showed how the CBF had agreed to play a series of friendlies every year and play a minimum of eight Nike stars, only compounded people's view that the family silver had been hocked on the cheap. Rebelo was the crusader for justice.

Alex Bellos's brilliant book, *Futebol: The Brazilian Way of Life*, explains the events of 21 November 2000. First up in the witness box was Mario Zagallo, who gave a rather ruffled performance when pushed by his questioners. Their main line of attack was the role of Nike and what had happened to Ronaldo on that fateful day in Paris. Zagallo, although his performance was contradictory, didn't say anything to pin Nike. Nor did his fellow staff, Lídio Toledo and Joaquim da Matta. Zagallo, who always sees himself as the whiter-than-white patriarch of Brazilian football, was deeply affronted at his perceived grilling by the congress and became aggressive. He refused to accept any blame for the defeat, saying (as if to add indelible gloss to the whole affair) that the French medical people gave Ronaldo the all clear. What was he supposed to do? He would be pilloried either way.

INTO THE ABYSS

Next up, and relishing the moment, was Edmundo, who had been involved first-hand in the imbroglio that day. Edmundo, never one to shirk a good row, fingered Nike directly, his account of events receiving 'ooohs' and 'aaahs' from the packed gallery. Brazilian TV newswires buzzed with the revelations that Edmundo claimed it was Nike who tapped-up Ricardo Teixera on the night and said Ronaldo must play.

But then, two weeks later, the star witness himself arrived in the Brasilia court room: Ronaldo. During all this, one has to try to draw a parallel as to what was actually being presented here, in order to keep a grip on reality. Imagine David Beckham being called before the House of Commons to explain a missed penalty or why England performed so averagely at a World Cup. It is high farce indeed.

Ronaldo, dressed in a smart navy suit, entered the congress hall and his aura filled the room. It was evident many of the congregation were starstruck and most had pens and paper on hand just in case they got a chance to ask for an autograph. Rebelo, his big moment now arrived, then briefed Ronaldo as to what would ensue and told him he had 20 minutes to state his case before he would be cross examined. Ronaldo, ready to begin, paused for a moment and asked, 'Do I, as a witness, have the right to a glass of water?!' He is no mug, and knew he had the audience on-side. There was then a minor stampede from the sycophantic attendees to provide the superstar with the appropriate beverage.

Rebelo's main aim was to get to the bottom of the Nike situation and the whole question of the CBF 'selling out', but Ronaldo batted this back with confidence and backbone. Expecting Ronaldo to reveal all in such an official place as Congress, the congressmen were disappointed as Ronaldo gave a polished, reserved performance, saying, 'I would like to talk about it, and there's no great mystery in the contents, but this is an international contract which has a clause which prevents me from revealing the details, and I would like to respect that clause.'

When asked by Eduardo Campos if he had been tactically responsible for marking Zidane (who scored twice from corners), Ronaldo calmly responded, 'Do you really think answering that will help this investigation?'

'It will; I think it will,' responded an undeterred Campos.

'Well, whoever it was, they didn't do it very well, did they?!' answered Ronaldo, which was followed by a ripple of laughter around the auditorium that seemed to ease the rising tension caused by the banal questioning.

In a desperate attempt to get some answers about the Nike situation, Campos pushed Ronaldo once more. Ronaldo, by now running out of patience with the whole affair, answered, 'The relationship I have with Nike is very good, because it really never demanded anything of me, apart from using their boots during games, which is the least I could do, and, preferably, to score a few goals with their boots. That's the only thing that Nike has ever asked me for.'

Then Ronaldo provided his best sound bite of the whole pointless affair. Campos, coming to the end of his cross-examination, asked, 'Why, in the opinion of Ronaldo, the athlete, did Brazil not win the World Cup in France?'

Ronaldo, now fed up with the whole farce, almost lost his patience, answering, 'Why didn't we win? Because we let in three goals . . . because we lost. We lost because we didn't win . . . in football, in sport, you win and you lose. How many times has Brazil won the World Cup? Nobody asked why we won it. We lost, OK?' And with that, Ronaldo's role in the inquiry came to an end.

In Ronaldo's absence, Inter had continued to play well, with Vieri demonstrating superb consistency in front of goal. But alas, *lo scudetto* eluded them yet again. Who should lift the coveted crown but co-tenants AC Milan. Despite their ultimate disappointment once more in the league, Inter had performed well in the Coppa Italia and were set to face Lazio in the final at the Stadio Olympico in Rome. The final, on 12 April, came six days after the birth of Ronaldo's son. The proud father, rather like Franz Beckenbauer in calling his daughter Francesca, plumped for the inspired choice of . . . Ronald. But what this did mean was that, with Ronaldo having made exemplary progress from his operation, son Ronald would, as predicted, be able to see his father play. All concerned around Ronaldo, from Gerard Saillant to Nilton Petrone to the Inter medical staff, had been satisfied that Ronaldo was OK to play. He was training, was showing no signs of discomfort and was keen to feature. Saillant suggested 20–30 minutes would be OK and Lippi, showing more compassion towards Ronaldo than of late, welcomed him back to the fold with a place on the bench for the final. It would be Ronaldo's first outing since he limped off against Lecce. Ronaldo, buoyed by the prospect of returning to football, exclaimed, 'This will be a magical week. My first son has been born and I am returning to football. It's the only time in my life I've received two presents. Life is good.'

INTO THE ABYSS

The Coppa Italia, although not as popular or coveted as the English FA Cup, for example, has grown in stature over recent years in Italy and is now something the teams take far more seriously than they used to. The final, a two-legged format, saw Inter take on Lazio of Rome, who, under the calm and studious leadership of Swede Sven-Goran Eriksson, were having a season to remember.

The first leg was played at the Stadio Olympico in Rome, and all eyes were on Ronaldo. Lippi started him on the bench, and for once there were no complaints either from player or media. As discussed, the medical men had given Ronaldo the all clear to do between 20 and 30 minutes as part of his full rehabilitation and the final was seen as an ideal opportunity to get Ronaldo back into action. With the game deadlocked at 0–0 going into the second half, Lippi instructed Ronaldo to warm up. The stadium buzzed with anticipation. A huge throng of cameramen rustled into action in front of the Inter technical area as Ronaldo vainly tried to do his stretches and warm-up unimpeded. But it was a forlorn hope. Twelve minutes into the second half, Lippi signalled to Ronaldo to strip down and get ready, motioning to the assistant that Romanian Adrian Mutu's was the number to punch into the electronic gadgetry. Alongside it was duly punched in number 9 and the comeback moment had arrived.

A quick check of the studs and zoom, all eyes fixed upon the new boots Ronaldo was wearing. An updated variant of his own R9 Mercurial range from Nike, which he had so graciously exhibited around his neck after France '98, they were in eye-catching silver and were as minimal as a pair of running spikes. They were, to all intents and purposes, unique. Nike's marketing bods had delivered another *coup de grâce*. Knowing the whole world would be tuning in for Ronaldo's comeback, they had adorned him in yet another new model of boot. So he was ready; a quick thumb of the shorts, some brief tactical snippets from Lippi, the nod from the ref, the high-ten with the departing Mutu and on he went. The ground fell hushed as he skipped towards the Inter front line and waited for play to restart.

Before long, he had his first touch. He got the ball under control nicely, turned, and then BANG! Welcome back, Ronaldo. The uncompromising and often plain dirty Portuguese stopper Fernando Couto went clean through the back of him like a clumsy Sunday League veteran. Ronaldo fell to the ground, wincing in pain. There was silence. A collective, 'Oh my God, is he OK?' swept the Stadio Olympico. An angelic Couto stood over Ronaldo and mimed to the ref as if to say, 'Sorry, guys, don't know how that happened.' After what seemed like an age, Ronaldo, rather like a floored middleweight, stirred, got up off the canvas and rose to his feet. He was OK, gave a mystified look to Couto as if to say, 'Cheers, pal, don't you read the papers? I've been through the mill of late, you know, amigo,' and resumed.

With Couto in close attendance at all times, virtually doubling as Ronaldo's shadow, it wasn't the easiest of comebacks for him. Couto, never one to care for reputations and with a good dash of Portuguese–Brazilian rivalry thrown in for good measure, was tracking his quarry like a hawk. But then, 19 minutes into the second half, Ronaldo received the ball about 30 yards from goal. He turned and moved goalward, and his path was inevitably blocked by the imposing Couto once more. But then, in the blink of an eye, the trademark stepover returned, a feint one way and then the other and Couto, aiming a crude foul, was left behind as Ronaldo passed him like a zephyr. Twenty or so yards from goal, Ronaldo was back in the old routine: a blur of movement, defenders back-pedalling, goalkeeper nervously readying himself for an impending strike. Then disaster. Unimpeded, Ronaldo fell to the ground as if shot by a hidden sniper in the crowd. Wails of anguish and pain filled the Rome night air. Ronaldo was felled like a speeding gazelle, clutching his right knee in chronic pain. His right patella tendon, recently repaired in Paris, had snapped completely. His knee lay in ruin. This was serious.

Players from both sides, aware of the gravity of the situation, rushed to his side. Even ex-teammate Diego Simeone, now plying his sinister trade with Lazio, appeared compassionate. Fellow pros all, they shared Ronaldo's pain, many holding their hands to their faces in horror. As Ronaldo's shrieks of pain pierced the night air, the mood sank. What had been billed as his big comeback in the showcase final was now in pieces, a wreckage by the wayside. The image of Ronaldo sat on the turf, clutching his knee and with his face in a manic, incredulous contortion of pain, would be beamed around the world, a sight to churn the stomachs of footballers of all ages and abilities. As medical staff arrived on the scene – the severity of the situation reflected by the fact that Lazio's physio, Andrea Campi, speeding across the turf, was first there, closely followed by his opposite number from Inter, Piero Volpi – Ronaldo, still in hysterics, cried, 'Mother! Father!' and in complete despair he wailed, 'Why me?'

As the stretcher-bearers arrived, medical staff took a long time to evaluate the situation. Massimo Moratti, up in the stands, was ashen with shock. Players consoled each other as if at a wake. When Ronaldo was finally lifted onto the stretcher, he was cloaked in a blanket and he held his left hand to his face, sobbing uncontrollably. Then, amongst the despair and horror, something marvellous happened. The crowd, in a display of fantastic warmth, stirred from their shock and slowly began chanting, 'Ron-al-do, Ron-al-do.' As the chant took hold, its volume amplified and the crowd, both Lazio and Inter reflecting his universal popularity, raised the decibel level to the roof. 'Ron-al-do, Ron-al-do.' The whole Stadio reverberated. As the stricken Ronaldo passed in front of the Lazio 'Ultras', some of Italy's and football's most odious fans, the chant grew even stronger. 'Ron-al-do, Ron-al-do,' they boomed. A desperate event had demonstrated football's great power to unify.

One day later, Gabriel Oriali, an Inter director, further added to the magnitude of the situation. Visibly emotional, he told press, 'Ronaldo is not just about being an Inter player, he is the property of world football. With his wonderful goals and skill, he is something special and has conquered the hearts and minds of football people everywhere.'

As Ronaldo was ferried back to the dressing-room, his first action was to phone Milene, at home with young Ronald. Next to him, Inter's Dr Volpi was on the phone to Gerard Saillant in Paris, alerting him of the situation and the likelihood of Ronaldo needing his services. Inter had the team jet on standby, ready for the flight to Paris, but Saillant advised against this course of action, suggesting a night at home would be the best option. He could fly tomorrow. Ronaldo joined the rest of the squad on the plane home to Milan, his knee safely immobilised, and sat on the front row of seats. Fellow players on the plane describe a flight taken in total silence, the mood too sombre and pensive for light-hearted conversation. The game had finished 0–0, so there wasn't much to talk about there either. On board that night was Roberto Baggio, himself no stranger to knee trouble, and he was first to break the silence and offer Ronaldo some words of comfort. Baggio, a renowned Buddhist, told him, 'You are about to face a time that will seem lonelier than anything you've ever been through. But inside you, you will find the strength to recover. If you want to, you can do it.' Ronaldo acknowledged him with an affirmative nod.

Rodrigo Paiva, who'd been present that night at the Stadio Olympico for Ronaldo's big comeback, picks up the story: 'That day at the Stadio was supposed to be happy; Ronaldo's big comeback. I always say that when things happen to Ronaldo they happen in a grand fashion. For example, at the World Cup in France, he could have felt sick during the first round, the quarter-final or the semi-final, but no, it was the final itself. Same with his comeback; it was only six minutes into his return and the injury strikes. Why is this? I remember the night well, and will never forget what happened. When he was stretchered-off to the dressing-room, he was crying. Not mainly through pain but because he was nervous. He didn't know if the knee would repair. The dressing-room was like a funeral, everybody was apprehensive, even the other players were sick with concern.

'We then took a plane and got home at dawn and we decided we would go to Paris to see Prof. Saillant again to get his opinion on the new problem. The next day, we flew to Paris. Myself, Filé and Branchini, nobody else. We knew that something serious had happened but were not quite sure what, but Filé was convinced it was a full rupture of the patella tendon. It could be serious.'

The hospital which Ronaldo was taken to was the Pitie-Salpetriere hospital: a vast behemoth of a building first opened back in the reign of Louis XIV. There have been numerous extensions to the building over the years and it is a hospital in the grand scale, an imposing, somewhat intimidating building.

Rodrigo went on: 'I remember that Ronaldo was sad about the repercussions of his injury, which is of course absurd. Ronaldo's injuries could not be compared to, say, Ayrton Senna's death. For God's sake, let's not compare someone's death to a knee injury, but for the fans here in Brazil, the impact was the same; everybody was walking round as if somebody had died. But God gave Ronaldo the chance of a recovery, a resurrection, something that Senna did not have. I told Ronaldo this and he liked it; it seemed to give him some hope.

'We then sat down with Prof. Saillant and discussed the options. Saillant said, "You have a complete rupture of the patella tendon, and I will understand if you want to look for another doctor because you may have lost your faith in me." Remember it was Saillant who performed the previous repair operation. "But if you decide to do this, you must do it quickly as you have to be operated on within 72 hours, no later."

'Then Ronaldo looked Prof. Saillant in the eye and said, "Doctor, will I play again?"

'Saillant replied, "Yes, Ronaldo. I guarantee that you will. You are going to play again, Ronaldo. I am positive about this."

Flamengo FC's ground in the Gávea district of Rio de Janeiro, where Ronaldo was failed as a junior trialist.

São Cristóvão FC's ground in the Zona Norte area of Rio de Janeiro.

São Cristóvão FC club president Carlos Alberto Parreira Peixoto (back row centre) stands proudly with the latest batch of young hopefuls aspiring to emulate Ronaldo.

Ronaldo playing for Dutch side PSV Eindhoven, for whom he scored 54 goals in 57 games. (© Getty Images)

Ronaldo lifts the 1996–97 Cup-Winners' Cup after scoring the only goal of the game, from the penalty spot against Paris St Germain. According to Sir Bobby Robson, 'Ronaldo's arrival made a great team even better.' (© Getty Images)

Ronaldo in an unfamiliar strip, that of Rio Carnival garb alongside his girlfriend of the time, Suzana Werner. His regular trips to Rio would frustrate several managers. (© Getty Images)

Ronaldo caps a blistering display in the 1998 UEFA Cup final to score for Inter Milan against Lazio as he waltzes around Lazio goalkeeper Marchegiani with a sublime double stepover. (© Getty Images)

Catch me if you can: Brazil v. Morocco at France '98. This superb photo by Ross Kinnaird captures the glory of Ronaldo. (© Getty Images)

Shortly after the final whistle of the World Cup final at France '98, Ronaldo tries to piece together what on earth unfolded that day. In stark contrast, in the background Zinedine Zidane celebrates the French win.

(© Getty Images)

12 April 2000, Copa Italia final v. Lazio: Ronaldo's much-heralded return from injury is brought to a chilling halt as he collapses, writhing in agony clutching his right knee.
(© Getty Images)

9 December 2001: This wonderful photo captures the elation of Ronaldo's first goal since his horrific injury. In his first full start since returning, he scored a classy goal against Brescia, sparking waves of celebration across Italy. (© Getty Images)

Golazzo! Ronaldo whacks in the winner against Piacenza and it seems Inter are set to win their first *scudetto* since 1989. The joy is unconfined, with goalkeeper Francesco Toldo racing the length of the field to join the celebrations. (© Getty Images)

Poles apart: Ronaldo's feud with Inter's Argentine coach, Hector Cúper (background), festered through to the end of the season. This feud would be a key factor in Ronaldo leaving to join Real Madrid. (© Getty Images)

Obrigado, Oliver! Oliver Khan's uncharacteristic gaffe lets in Ronaldo, who gratefully taps home the German's blunder to give Brazil the lead in the World Cup final 2002. (© Getty Images)

Redemption: Four years on from the despair of France, Ronaldo completes his journey to the top of the world game and lifts the World Cup. Like Pelé and Maradona before him, he could now add a signature World Cup to his CV.
(© Getty Images)

Ronaldo completes a miraculous year by lifting the Toyota World Club Championship trophy in Tokyo. Ronaldo scored the first goal and was awarded the Man of the Match award.
(© Getty Images)

A familiar sight during the 2003–04 La Liga season: a floored goalkeeper, a bemused defender and Ronaldo wheeling away with another goal. However, the season would end in trophy-less despair for the 'galacticos'. (© Getty Images)

Ronaldo's ubiquitous face adorns a news kiosk in Rio de Janeiro outside the famous Jobi Botequim bar. The Nike campaign 'Vai Encarar?' translates roughly as 'Fancy your chances?'

Echoes of Steve Powell's famous Maradona photo from Spain '82 against Belgium. Here, Ronaldo is challenged by five Colombian defenders.
(© Getty Images)

Ramallah, West Bank, 16 May 2005: A bemused Israeli Army officer ushers Palestinians past his checkpoint who are awaiting the arrival of Ronaldo.
(© Getty Images)

In light of Ronaldo's recent short-lived 'marriage' to supermodel Daniella Cicarelli and the ensuing costly settlement, waggish Brazilian soccer fans display a banner which reads 'Ronaldo, please marry my sister!'
(© Getty Images)

INTO THE ABYSS

'Then Ronaldo said, "Doctor, I want you to perform the surgery. I want you to do it now."

'And with that the decision was made, and we OK'd for Saillant to perform the operation. It was a very stressful time.'

Rodrigo then explained the hysteria that was taking over the hospital with such a high-profile patient on site. 'Over 300 journalists were waiting outside the hospital; it was amazing. News teams and camera crew everywhere trying to get a picture or an update. Prof. Saillant performed the operation, which went well, and then the real suffering began. Filé has images from the surgery, which was unique; it had never been done before. Ronaldo himself was very low, the lowest I have known him, and the pictures were purposely kept from the press because Ronaldo was so low, he was defeated.'

Rodrigo explained to me the finer points of what Prof. Saillant had done. The operation was intricate, with Prof. Saillant having to rebuild part of the patella with reconstructed man-made fibres, mimicking the natural fibre of the remaining tendon. As we have seen from Filé's detailed long-term diagnosis, one of the main problems Ronaldo suffered from was the exaggerated nature of his quadriceps, especially his right one. These were, if you like, the pistons that had given him his jaw-dropping speed, but as He giveth, He also taketh away, and it was these V12 quadriceps allied to mere runabout patellas that had caused Ronaldo such grief. The two parts were not ideally compatible and the tendon had buckled under the stress-loads placed upon it by the quadriceps. Prof. Saillant had to ensure that the rebuilt patella was up to the job of dealing with this brute of a thigh muscle. The operation lasted over six hours, many brows were mopped, and eventually Ronaldo emerged, still heavily anaesthetised, and was ferried back to his room.

Rodrigo added: 'Don't forget too that his baby had just been born so Milene had to stay in Milan looking after him and wasn't able to come to the hospital very often. There were many nights when Filé and I took turns sitting outside Ronaldo's room. It was horrible because the hospital is so old and dark all through the night. Pitch black. Ronaldo was in the traumatology ward and alongside him were people with similarly serious injuries and problems, and in lots of pain. At night, we could hear people moaning and screaming in pain, and people crying. It was awful. And the dark corridors were very scary. It was like something out of a horror film.'

When Ronaldo came round, his mood was understandably glum. Despite the avalanche of cards and telegrams wishing him well and a speedy return, it was hard for him to see beyond the present, however much he tried. Words of encouragement flooded in from greats of the game such as Pelé, Zidane, Zico and Maradona. Zidane visited in person, something Ronaldo would never forget, and this would be the source of their friendship. Each day, there were groups of schoolkids at the hospital reception all keen to wish him well and leave cards, shirts, footballs, anything to convey their affection for him. Inspired by Baggio, he took some comfort and hope in more Buddhist writings and he vowed to not look back and concentrate on the future, never believing that he would not play again. Such talk wasn't allowed in his company. Also on hand was Inter president Massimo Moratti, who spent long hours with him, assuring him that it was a temporary setback, that Inter were with him and that he would again pull on the blue and black of the *Nerazzurri*. Back at Inter GHQ, their website was almost in meltdown as thousands of messages per hour were posted on there from all over the world, all wishing Ronaldo a speedy recovery. Ronaldo's army of sponsors, who had millions invested in him, also rallied round and expressed their support and ongoing patronage.

Inevitably, Prof. Saillant was quizzed by the media about Ronaldo's prospects. Well briefed, he remained positive and upbeat, saying there was no reason that, with the appropriate recuperation, rest and time, Ronaldo could not return to top-flight football. Few shared his optimism. Ronaldo's injury and the dramatic circumstance in which it occurred in Rome had shocked everybody. It was a ghastly injury and the thought of him even playing again, never mind returning to his former glories, was something few could imagine. Several obituarists were sharpening their pencils ready to draw a veil on his short but stunning career. Filé Petrone, the physio who had been by Ronaldo's side throughout his recent career, was distraught. All his work had been wiped out in six minutes at the Stadio Olympico. He complained of being unable to sleep, so acute was the pain he was sharing with his star patient. But he vowed to help Ronaldo return, and was already planning the comeback trail and schedules needed to get Ronaldo back to the big time. But as Filé and Saillant gave a united front and oozed positivity about Ronaldo's ultimate return, many of the world's press were sceptical. This latest knee blow, combined with the still-to-be-explained events of the World Cup final, left them unconvinced about Ronaldo's overall fitness and his mental capacity to cope with this latest setback.

At this watershed in his career, Ronaldo could look back with some pride at his achievements. Up until April 1998, he had played 386 games and scored 311 goals, at a strike rate of 0.81 per game; an awesome return. Even in *Serie A*, where his form had dipped and he had taken time to adapt, he had still banged in 63 in 89 at 0.7 per game. When this is lined up against the other great names of world football, it makes favourable reading. Maradona, considered by many to be the greatest footballer ever, scored 356 in 702 games during his career, a strike rate of 0.5. Alfredo di Stefano, whom many of a previous generation claim to be the best of all time, scored a whopping 893 in 1,126 games and can look back at a strike rate of 0.79. Di Stefano, who charmed audiences in the 1950s with his illustrious displays for Real Madrid, has not forgotten what football gave him, and in his garden has a statuette of a football with the words 'Thanks old friend' underneath – brilliant. Dutch legend Johan Cruyff scored 421 from 704 at 0.6. Above Ronaldo stood only one player: who else but Brazilian nonpareil Pelé, whose career figures are a monolithic 1,281 goals from 1,321 games at 0.97. Ronaldo was in good company.

But despite the comfort these statistics could give him as he now lay in a Paris hospital bed, he was a long, long way from a football field and the chance to add to these numbers. Playing football again was a distant dream. As the pony-tailed Buddhist Roberto Baggio had rightly observed, the journey now lay within Ronaldo himself.

Rodrigo described the mood soon after the operation thus: 'Ronaldo was depressed, very depressed. He did not know what was going to happen to him, if he would recover or not. The day he left hospital, you will see that there are no pictures of him leaving. We called for three ambulances, plus one round the back entrance of the hospital to fool the cameramen and journalists outside. We just wanted to get him away without any fuss, and we then flew back to Milan to try and start his life again, and set out on the recovery. It was a difficult time. We spent some time in Milan but then came back to Rio for the bulk of the recovery. Don't forget that Ronaldo was still very young, and hadn't really lived in Rio since he was 16. He had never been in Rio for an extended time with all the trappings of his new fame and fortune. To be back in Rio with all this was something new for him and there were too many distractions: late nights, beautiful women, parties. Everybody wanted a piece of him. These were things he hadn't experienced before in Rio. It was at this point that the first strains on their marriage appeared.'

CHAPTER 12

THE LONG ROAD BACK

Those who were confident that Ronaldo would play again gave initial estimates of January 2001 for a return to action. Considering his knee had been totally reconstructed, this seemed optimistic indeed. With Ronaldo now *hors de combat*, he had the one thing on his hands that he hadn't had before: time.

His career to date had been a whirlwind of progress and activity and he had mastered virtually everything put in front of him. His football spoke for itself, he had fabulous wealth, he was a global icon and he was now a family man. But the blight of injury had now put a line under all that for the time being, with only his family for immediate comfort. He had plenty to ponder and, inwardly, must have wondered if he would return. Outwardly, though, he remained positive and focused on the comeback route that had been devised for him by Filé, with Prof. Saillant's cooperation.

Although extreme caution was needed at this stage with the tendon so recently out of surgery, it was vital that Ronaldo started moving and got some mobility going in his limbs. But the distractions of Rio proved problematic, and as pressure mounted to stick rigorously to the recuperation schedule, Ronaldo's coterie of Filé and Rodrigo Paiva decided the best thing was to leave Rio altogether. But go where?

Rodrigo explained their next steps to me. 'It was decided we must leave Rio and for the recovery process to succeed, we went to the USA. We travelled to Vail in Colorado, a city famed as a ski resort but with one of the biggest and best orthopaedic clinics in the world. Nike helped arrange everything and with the clinic being well versed in various knee problems in skiers, it was seen as a logical step. Also, Ronaldo's anonymity in the US helped. Prof. Saillant was not too keen on the idea, though, but we figured as long as Ronaldo followed the programme that Filé and Prof. Saillant had laid down, it didn't matter if it was Vail, Jamaica or wherever.

'But, we began to have problems there too. Head of the clinic was an American doctor called Dr Richard Steadman. He realised early on that Ronaldo was in a lot of pain; pain so strong that it still made Ronaldo cry. We were a bit behind schedule in the treatment programme for Ronaldo and he was struggling to move his knee joint at all. Dr Steadman took objection to this and insisted the knee be operated on again. I said no, Filé said no and Prof. Saillant advised strongly against this. Ronaldo didn't want more surgery either; he was sick of it. But Steadman went ahead anyway and scheduled the operation. We were in a tricky situation. Dr Steadman insisted that the operation be undertaken but Ronaldo was dead set against this, so we phoned Prof. Saillant again and he said come to Paris. Without informing the American staff at Vail or Dr Steadman, we upped and left for Paris. We advised Nike that we were doing this but they did not understand why, as they agreed with Dr Steadman, but we left for Paris anyway. It was all a bit of a rush and we had to sneak out of the clinic.

'On arrival in Paris, Prof. Saillant brought in his colleague from the French Football Federation, a physio called Patrick Middleton. They concurred that Ronaldo's recovery was behind schedule but were still adamant he would make a full recovery. Ronaldo didn't want to go back to Vail, so I had to go back alone to get our stuff. It was a bit awkward because we'd left in such a rush that all our stuff was still there so I had to go back and get it all and let them know Ronaldo wouldn't be coming back. They were all a bit bemused, but that was that!'

I asked Rodrigo how Nike felt about all this as it was they who had set the whole Vail thing up. 'It wasn't a problem. Nike were fantastic throughout. The only thing they wanted was Ronaldo's recovery, so if he was happier in Paris, they were happy too. Some people didn't trust Prof. Saillant because he had operated before on Ronaldo and the op hadn't worked. But Ronaldo had 100 per cent faith in him and wanted to be closer to him. Once we got all our gear back to Paris, we then went down to Biarritz in the south-west of France to work with Patrick Middleton. Filé went too and the three of them worked together to get Ronaldo back on track and ahead of schedule. It was the best thing we could have done. Biarritz was superb and we were there for three months. Ronaldo fell in love with golf while he was there and Biarritz is always symbolic for us as it is the place where Ronaldo was first able to run after the operation. He recovered his self-esteem and confidence there.'

After the three months in Biarritz, the group returned to Rio. With Ronaldo now back home in his beloved *cidade maravilhosa*, Filé coaxed activity out of the painful knee with manipulative exercises, each time stopping when the pain or the effort was too much for the stricken star. With small steps is a lengthy journey undertaken and these were certainly small, but necessary nonetheless. It was a tough balancing act. Ronaldo had to get mobile again but further damage or even another rupture of the patella could have been irreparable. At this point, everything was a struggle for Ronaldo. Filé as well as Ronaldo had to tread carefully.

The next few months were long and tedious. Frustration was never far away and the long hours of mind-numbing, repetitive exercise meant that, at times, although they were good friends, things could become quite strained between Filé and Ronaldo. But they both knew the goal they were aiming for, were both professionals, and both knew turning back wasn't an option. With a view to creating the best environment possible for recuperation, Filé and Ronaldo sequestered themselves to Barra de Tijuca in Rio and Comary Farm. Home to both Filé and Ronaldo, and with a warm sunny climate, it made sound sense. A combination of work on the beach and lengthy, extended sessions at the CBF's training camp – a splendid, custom-built facility nestling in the foothills of Teresopolis two hours outside of Rio – meant Filé and Ronaldo could concentrate on one thing and one thing only: getting him playing again.

Even while crocked, Ronaldo was still an idolised figure to many: none more so than one of Inter's recent close-season signings, emerging Republic of Ireland star Robbie Keane. Keane joined Inter Milan from English club Coventry City, an unexpected transfer that had raised a few eyebrows at the time. He was interviewed by James Richardson for Channel 4's sorely missed magazine show *Gazzetta Football Italia* at his swish new Dia Dinarlo apartment not far from the San Siro. With Keane still visibly in awe of his new colleagues and surroundings, a well-informed Richardson prompted Robbie that he wasn't the only Inter resident of the exclusive apartment block. Robbie concurred, saying,

THE LONG ROAD BACK

'Yep, [Javier] Zanetti's got one [an apartment] downstairs, [Ivan] Zamorano's got one upstairs, and there's [Alvaro] Recoba's one a few floors above that.'

'Anyone else?' probed Richardson.

'Oh, yes,' remembered a smirking Keane. 'Ronaldo's got the top *two floors*.'

Nearly one year on from the operation and at the close of the 2000–01 football season, Ronaldo was in far brighter mood. The daily sessions with Filé were beginning to bear fruit and his mobility was coming back. He was still an appreciable distance from playing again, and who knew what the future might hold, but for now he was happier than he had been for some time. On a visit to Rome, he joined the Inter players for a training session for the first time since his operation, and although Ronaldo's involvement was extremely low key, it was another milestone on the return to fitness. Four hundred Inter fans thought it worthy of attendance and now the talk in football circles had begun to shift from asking *if* he would be back, to *when* he would be back.

Ronaldo was now mobile and able to play in training, and in March 2001 was invited to 'play' in a charity match for UNICEF at the hallowed Maracanã. It was a low-key, light-hearted affair and Ronaldo's medical team OK'd him to play. Ronaldo thoroughly enjoyed the big day out and showed he was somewhere near fitness with five goals which duly got the attention of the world's press. But Ronaldo was the first to pour water on the goal-fest, saying it was only a bit of fun.

On 8 July 2001, whilst back in Milan, he was given the go-ahead to play for an Inter XI in Bormio against a local side. This was a pre-season friendly in the truest sense of the word and was an ideal run-out for some of Inter's long-term injury list and new faces. Bormio proved more than amenable hosts as they shipped seventeen goals, of which Ronaldo scored two. It was all good fun in the Dolomitian town but hardly a litmus test of Ronaldo's state of health.

With the new *Serie A* season approaching, the pre-season games took on more importance, and quality. On 31 July, the San Siro played host to visiting Nigerian champions Enyimba FC of Aba. Ronaldo notched again in Inter's 7–0 cruise and was happy to tell reporters after the game, 'My knee is fine.' The 40,000 fans who had turned up to the San Siro that day saw no reason to disagree.

These pre-season kickabouts were one thing; playing top-level *Serie A* football was another. For him to have any realistic hope of playing in

Japan and Korea, he would need to put a good season under his belt at Inter, under the new Argentinian coach Hector Cúper. Marcello Lippi had walked out the previous year in tense circumstances. After failure to qualify for the Champions League and a dreadful league display away to Bari, he told an astonished post-match press conference, 'I don't put a team out on a pitch to play like that. They should be ashamed of themselves. If I were president, I'd take each one of them, hang them up on their changing-room peg and give them a good kick up the arse.' Words that didn't sit well with the Morattis, and Lippi was duly relieved of his role. The Italian legend from the victorious 1982 World Cup-winning side and he of the legendary goal celebration, Marco Tardelli, came in thereafter but couldn't achieve the results so craved by the *Nerazzurri* and they finished in a tame fifth place.

Cúper had risen to prominence at Mallorca, taking them to the 1999 UEFA Cup final against Lazio. He then surpassed this at Valencia, whom he took to two successive UEFA Champions League finals. But at Inter, Cúper, like Lippi, kept Ronaldo at arm's length, and before long it was clear that the relationship between the two was going to be strained. Cúper, like Lippi again, was keen to stamp his own hallmark on Inter Milan. They still hadn't won *lo scudetto* since 1989 and it was now becoming a Holy Grail, with even Lazio and Roma breaking their barren periods in the meantime. As usual, Inter's squad was brimming with the world's finest talent – Christian Vieri, Alvaro Recoba, Javier Zanetti and Francesco Toldo, for example – and they were ready for another tilt at the title.

Next up, ten days later, Ronaldo came on for the last 20 minutes versus Bastia in an Italian Cup game and scored twice to see Inter home 4–2. It seemed all was well. He certainly hadn't lost the goal-scoring touch.

Elsewhere in Brazil, further developments were taking place that would in turn play a part in Ronaldo's recovery. With the *seleçao* labouring under a lacklustre World Cup 2002 qualifying campaign, the CBF appointed their fourth coach in two years, Luiz Felipe Scolari. Scolari, faced with the prospective ignominy of being the first coach ever to have failed to take the *seleçao* to a World Cup finals – something deemed not far short of high treason in Brazil – was understandably exploring every avenue. Ahead of the important qualifier versus Uruguay, Big Phil convened a players' get-together with a view to getting to know everyone and doing some initial team-building. Ronaldo had been invited and duly turned up but his presence was not universally approved, with Romário churlishly telling local press that, 'His presence here serves only to confuse everyone.' With this nugget to chew on, the press looked for further displeasure among the camp, but Big Phil quickly put paid to their efforts by telling them, '*I* invited him, OK?' The pressure was not eased on the *seleçao*, though, as they lost to Uruguay, but Big Phil remained unfazed and told Ronaldo, 'You are a fundamental player in my plans for [World Cup] 2002.'

Scolari was facing a tough battle of wits with the Brazilian press and people. A number of them, still unconvinced by Ronaldo's fitness and still directly blaming him for the debacle in Paris, had put together a bandwagon of support for the hero of USA '94, the impish Romário. Romário's talents were undisputed and his career goal-scoring record ranks with the best. He is adored in Brazil and as a previous World Cup winner and FIFA World Player of the Year he had little left to prove in the game. At 36 years old, he desperately wanted to get one more World Cup under his belt. He was in prime form for Rio club Vasco da Gama and made no secret of his wish to be involved. But Scolari had his reservations and saw Romário as a divisive influence. Scolari had picked Romário for the qualifier against Uruguay, but was incensed at his comments relating to Ronaldo. What people didn't know at the time was that, if fit, Scolari wouldn't hesitate to take Ronaldo to Japan to form his preferred trident attacking option alongside Rivaldo and Ronaldinho. Scolari had selected Romário for the Uruguay game, keen to have a good look at him, but his comments and general attitude made Big Phil's mind up for him. He would go down the Ronaldo route.

Once Scolari had cleared this in his own mind, he then showed no hesitation in making Ronaldo aware he was key to his plans. This was something that Ronaldo would not forget down the line. We now had a situation where Scolari and Cúper each had different agendas for Ronaldo, and this would cause more dispute and headlines.

With the crucial, life-or-death qualifier versus Chile around the corner, Scolari wanted Ronaldo on board, and to cover every angle he flew to Milan to meet Cúper and get a full assessment of Ronaldo's fitness and readiness. Cúper, hedging his words carefully, was keen to seem in favour of a swift Ronaldo return, saying, 'Of course I would like him back in the team immediately, but over-eagerness can be a risk.' Cúper bristled at Scolari's enthusiasm for Ronaldo, and there was some national-coach versus club-coach friction. Scolari wanted Ronaldo playing for Inter and said as much to Cúper. Cúper, as much his own man as most big-name coaches, was not going to be told how to run his team, thank you very much, and Scolari returned to Brazil not much better informed than when he arrived.

But with the pressure mounting on Cúper from all corners to play Ronaldo, he couldn't hold him back much longer. Three weeks after Scolari's visit, Cúper listed Ronaldo in the squad to play against Romanian side Brasov in the first round of the UEFA Cup, Inter having again missed out on a Champions League berth. Ronaldo came on as substitute 18 minutes into the second half and expectation was inevitably at fever pitch. Could '*Il Fenomeno*' start weaving his magic? But, in a huge anti-climax, he limped off not long afterwards with a pulled thigh muscle. More frustration for Ronaldo but a timely slice of 'I told you so' for Cúper.

Again, this got the newswires humming and headlines of 'Ronaldo in more injury misery' were commonplace. His body, starved of first-team football for so long, was taking its time to readjust. Muscles which hadn't been tested in game conditions for over two years were taking time to stir back to life. The beast had been in dormant hibernation for too long and needed time to adjust its eyes to the dazzling spring light. Muscle strains became something that would dog Ronaldo's return: niggling, trifling injuries that, although minor and quick to heal, were irritants that impeded his progress.

However, unperturbed by this setback, Scolari duly picked Ronaldo in his squad for the game against Chile. This didn't go down too well with Cúper, who now saw Scolari as a meddler. Inter, with good reason still feeling a moral entitlement having paid Ronaldo's hefty wages and medical bills whilst he was *in absentia*, were very wary of anything that might affect their star's full recovery and felt the CBF were over-eager. Almost to prove this point, Cúper selected Ronaldo – now recovered from his thigh strain – for the following *Serie A* game versus Torino and left him on the bench throughout the entire game: an indignation Ronaldo hadn't suffered since his nascent times with the *seleçao* in USA '94, albeit a mere 17 years old. His mood wasn't good.

In the return UEFA tie against Brasov, Ronaldo also started on the bench and joined the proceedings at the start of the second half, but again pulled up with a thigh strain. The disappointment was tangible.

Although not quite back to the drawing board, it was clear that the engine needed tweaking, so Filé and Ronaldo got back down to some serious physio work to try to iron out the niggles and twinges. Ironically, the rebuilt knee seemed fine; it was the support cast that was fluffing its lines. Six weeks on from the last muscle pull against Brasov, Ronaldo joined the Inter squad for the *Serie A* tie at the San Siro against Lecce. This time, Cúper started him, but again, after only 13 minutes, Ronaldo limped off clutching his right thigh. Back to the physio room with Filé and a week's hard work.

November would prove to be a hugely frustrating month for Ronaldo as, seeming so close to being back, he was continually being thwarted by these thigh strains. He was passed fit again to play against Fiorentina and came on for the last 15 minutes, completing the game without any signs of further mishap. He spent the next two games on the bench and then got a 20-minute run against Udinese. Back to the bench for the duration of the Atalanta game and it was proving to be one step forward and two steps back. Nor was it doing much for Ronaldo's estimation of Cúper.

CHAPTER 13

CLUB V. COUNTRY – HECTOR CÚPER AND FELIPE SCOLARI

As December arrived, Ronaldo was still stuck in a see-saw situation with Cúper and his own fitness. It seemed when he was fit, he didn't play and spent 90 minutes on the bench, and when he wasn't fit he would be forced onto the pitch. But then his opportunity came. Cúper selected him for the away game against Brescia and informed Ronaldo that he would be in the starting XI. This was more like it.

It was Sunday, 9 December and a typically chilly and crisp Italian midwinter's afternoon. Brescia, for whom old pal and occasional psychologist Roberto Baggio was playing, were wearing their distinctive marine-blue strip with the white 'V'. As such, Inter had donned their attractive white away strip. With many of the players wearing gloves to keep the cold out, Inter took the field with the $84 million strikeforce at last in tandem and meaning business. They had waited a long time to see Christian Vieri and Ronaldo line up together. Inter had the better of the early exchanges and then, incredibly, in the 18th minute, Ronaldo scored. Linking beautifully with Vieri, he played a neat wall-pass off him and then stroked the ball effortlessly past Castellazzi in the Brescia goal as if he'd never been away. However, the stark truth is that it was Ronaldo's first goal in *Serie A* for a heartbreaking two years and one month. The expression on his face betrayed this and as he saw the ball strike the back of the net it took a few moments for this unfamiliar event to register; he'd almost forgotten what it felt like. But then, as it all began to compute, the right index finger emerged from its slumber, the gap-tooth grin reopened for business and Ronaldo wheeled away in sheer delight. He turned to share the magical moment with his illustrious teammates, gesturing to them as if to say, 'Did that really happen?' The image from that goal, of his teammates charging towards him in wild hysteria, desperate to share the moment, is one of the best Ronaldo pictures you will see. Vieri, Recoba, Cordoba *et al.* – superstars all – arrived on the scene with smiles and shrieks of genuine joy. It was a great moment.

At half-time, around the rest of *Serie A* when the scores were broadcast over the various tannoys, crowds erupted with cheers when they heard the news that Ronaldo had scored – a fantastic reflection of his popularity. When, on the 72nd minute, he was substituted, the whole Brescia ground rose to its feet to applaud him, chanting, 'Ron-al-do, Ron-al-do.' Visibly moved by all this, Ronaldo took his seat on the bench struggling to take it all in and keep the emotion in check. It was a big day for him.

He had played well, had looked sharp, and looked in synch with Vieri. Vieri had continued his great form with another two goals to give Inter a convincing 3–1 away win. Cúper too seemed to be coming round to the idea of Ronaldo playing a bigger role and in the next game against Chievo, Ronaldo played the whole 90 minutes, his first full 90 since late 1999. Chievo won 2–1 but Ronaldo had a good game, providing the pass which Vieri converted for yet another goal. Things got even better in the next game as Ronaldo banged in a cracking brace in the 3–0 victory over Verona in front of a delirious San Siro. Although it was visible that Ronaldo was still not fully back in the *ritmo do jogo*, he looked the best he had done since returning and, with three goals in four games, was starting to deliver the goods too. A two-year lay-off is a long time in any sportsman's calendar and inevitably it would take time for Ronaldo to reacquaint his body with the needs of top-flight football. Ferenc Puskas, the legendary Hungarian 'Galloping Major', provides an excellent example of such a situation. On signing for Real Madrid back in 1958 and being unveiled at the Bernabéu, he was sporting an unmistakable pot belly, the result of over 18 months' inaction due to a FIFA ban for his refusal to return to Communist Hungary to play for Honvéd. It took him several months to reattune to the rigours of pro-football (he was merely fat, not seriously injured like Ronaldo), but would appear to have rediscovered his bearings as his subsequent 240 goals in 260 games for Real bear testimony to.

Ronaldo would start in the next game, against Piacenza on 23

December, the last one before the Christmas break and the last one before his scheduled return to Rio to enjoy the festivities. He started well and won the penalty for the first goal, but then was forced to pull up with yet another thigh strain. His pulls and strains were proving much harder to shed than Puskas's belly.

The next few weeks proved equally as frustrating. Scolari had selected him for the *seleçao's* forthcoming friendly against Saudi Arabia, a pretty meaningless affair but one he wanted Ronaldo to be a part of as he assessed his chances for the World Cup. To acclimatise, the *seleçao* decamped on the sunny Spanish island of Majorca, but again, in one of the training games, Ronaldo pulled up once more with thigh trouble. As Japan and Korea approached, Scolari was starting to lose his patience. Between September 2001 and March 2002, Ronaldo had played in twelve games, but he had only started in one of them. For Scolari, so desperate to have Ronaldo on board for the finals, it was thin evidence that his key man was up to the job. He had to have more.

Ronaldo's stop–start comebacks had many wondering if this would now be the pattern of his career. Would his body ever fully recover and get back to full match fitness? Could he last a full season, or even a half-season? Could he last a tournament? To get the answer to this question, Scolari undertook a course of action that is pretty much unheralded, and would ultimately bear the biggest prize of all. He needed to know if his paladin Ronaldo would be sufficiently fit to take to the World Cup. It was time for answers.

Scolari had been roundly criticised for including Ronaldo in his original party for his first game in charge of the *seleçao* against Uruguay, being accused of romanticism for thinking Ronaldo would be up to it. Those same critics were warming up again for a similar dose of vitriol. During that game and in the build-up for it, Romário had been a general pain in the backside, was fractious and had generally made Scolari's life difficult over the Ronaldo issue. From that point on, Scolari didn't trust him and seemingly made up his mind that Romário would not be a part of his plans, much to the chagrin of many in Brazil, whose love affair with Romário is unconditional. But, from the moment Ronaldo had looked like he could recover and return from his horrendous injury, Scolari had backed him and shown every indication that he was his preferred option. Again, Scolari deserves credit here, for his central motive for doing this was psychological: to make Ronaldo feel wanted by the *seleçao*. Any player of any level needs to feel wanted by those he plays with, even if his name is Ronaldo. Cúper had spectacularly missed this trick at Inter. Scolari would not err likewise.

Scolari's focus was totally geared towards the World Cup. Back home in Brazil, the domestic game was all over the place. Ricardo Teixera, head of the CBF, had fallen out with footballing-superstar-turned-sports-minister Pelé, and the rumpus was causing a real stir, so much so that various CBF sponsors and investors were threatening to pull out. The Brazilian national league was as riven with hearsay and corruption as ever. It was a real mess. With all this kerfuffle to distract the CBF mandarins, Scolari, for once, found himself left in peace to plot Far Eastern success.

The cornerstone of his planning was Ronaldo. A large fly in the ointment was Hector Cúper. Ronaldo was fit again and at his disposal but, in the three months between January and March 2002, Cúper didn't play him. It seemed he wanted to win the title without him. Club versus country rows are a feature of the modern game and Scolari, exasperated with Cúper and Inter that they weren't playing Ronaldo and thus readying him for the World Cup, made a smart move. He persuaded them to release Ronaldo for a month, under the guise of receiving some minor treatment. Inter agreed and Ronaldo arrived in the *cidade maravilhosa* on 8 February. Scolari had stolen a march on Cúper.

Rodrigo Paiva was able to shed some intriguing light on this whole situation. Rodrigo, by now embedded as one of Ronaldo's inner circle, was virtually ever-present with him during these times. Both as a friend, press officer and general screen in front of Ronaldo, he was involved with all that went on around the player and was witness to what he perceived as the club versus country fight, plus Ronaldo's deteriorating stock in Milan. Rodrigo explained, 'The problems started when Cúper arrived at Inter. Ronaldo was fine, but Cúper wouldn't play him, and muscular problems began to creep in through inactivity. Also, Cúper's physical trainer, Galdino, was subjecting the squad to a new fitness programme. Many of the players at Inter had muscular problems, just look: Zanetti, Cordoba, Vieri, Emre – they all had problems caused by the fitness regime. Cúper started to make people believe that Ronaldo was never going to play football again. He didn't want him. He convinced Moratti about this, and he was doing a job on the Inter fans too, altering their mindset towards Ronaldo. Back in 2001, Ronaldo's then agent Alexandre Martins sought out Moratti to get an understanding of the situation. Moratti was very evasive but eventually agreed to meet

Martins. Why would he be so evasive with the agent of one of his star players? You tell me. Martins finally got some time with him and said that Ronaldo couldn't train with Cúper any more as it was ruining his fitness. Martins explained to Moratti that by the end of the World Cup [2002], if Cúper was still coach, he would ask Moratti to release Ronaldo to play for another team because he could not continue like this. Moratti said he understood the whole situation and he would present an arrangement that Ronaldo would be happy with. We took this to mean he would fire Cúper.'

The plot took a further twist when Rodrigo explained how they'd received a phone call. He continued, 'Round about Christmas 2001, we received a phone call. Inter officials will deny this but it is true. A friend of ours called Bruno Bartelloni, who was a senior figure at Inter at the time, telephoned. He said not to mention his name, but that we had to be aware that Inter didn't want Ronaldo any more because Cúper did not want him. He told us to start positioning a move for Ronaldo because Inter did not have him in their plans. It was a serious situation. For us too [at the CBF], the World Cup was approaching fast and we needed to get him playing some football to get him match fit. That's why we decided we had to bring him to Brazil and get him away from Inter and Cúper.'

Scolari had planned an intensive medical assessment of Ronaldo. If Scolari couldn't assess Ronaldo's fitness indirectly via Inter Milan, then he would do it himself. It was a bold and superb move. The moment Ronaldo landed in Rio, he was whisked off to a meeting with his physio Filé and José Luiz Runco, who had succeeded Lídio Toledo as head medic of the *seleçao*. The meeting lasted three hours. The following day, Scolari convened another meeting for Ronaldo, this time with nutritionist Silvia Ferreira, physical trainer Paulo Paixão and biochemist Alexandre Consendey. It was a cabal of the best medical expertise available in Brazil, and its sole purpose was to assess Ronaldo for Brazil's assault on the World Cup. Other footballing nations, take note.

Ronaldo was put through laboratory-level intensive testing. His whole biometric physical structure was assessed, analysed and processed to the nth degree. The goal was to assess Ronaldo's current physical state and, from that, to devise a programme to have him A1 by June and the World Cup. The programme was conducted in high secrecy. The whole thing took a month, during which time Ronaldo's body fat fell from 13.5 per cent to an impressive 8.5 per cent, something Puskas could only have dreamt of. A month later, on 9 March, all the tests and observations had been completed and the final analysis was ready for discussion. Scolari called a meeting of the five medical boffins and asked the simple question, 'Does he play?' Runco answered, 'He plays.' For Scolari, this was enough. He had his man and he could now plan the assault on the World Cup in earnest. As Rodrigo explained, 'Ronaldo was fully fit, no question. His sprint times and data were the same as when he was at Barcelona. Filé put him through the exact same tests and the results were the same. He was ready. But the problem remained Cúper.'

Ronaldo was now a lean machine, but still lacked that intangible ingredient so essential for a footballer: match fitness. Running miles on a treadmill is one thing, but the feel and pace of a game, the nuances of 90 minutes, is something only games under your belt can give you. Stood between Ronaldo and this was Cúper. Even worse, it seemed that Moratti, the renowned Ronaldophile, was also siding with Cúper, and rather than lending his presidential weight to a 'Reinstate Ronaldo' campaign, he was seemingly happy to let the Argentine run things his way.

Unfortunately, Ronaldo hadn't helped himself, as, after the conclusion of his bionic-man-style appraisal in Rio, he took time to enjoy the world-famous Carnaval, as a guest of his personal sponsors Brahma, one of Brazil's largest brewers. Brahma's VIP area at the parade is legendary in Brazil and guests in recent years have included the inevitable throng of Brazilian stars such as Giselle Bündchen and Rubens Barrichello, plus overseas luminaries such as Arnold Schwarzenegger, Dan Ackroyd and the mind-bogglingly wealthy ex-Microsoft mogul Paul Allen. At the Brahma gig, people party and they party hard, so when Moratti saw pictures of Ronaldo in the thick of it all, having a ball, he was not best chuffed. To add to the thick broth of mischief, on arrival back at Milan, Ronaldo was greeted with the headline in Italian paper *Tuttosport* that he was no longer required at Inter and would be sold in the summer. The club showing the most interest? Real Madrid.

When Ronaldo reported in for training, he requested a meeting with Moratti and Cúper. Rodrigo Paiva was again privy to this and told me, 'Ronaldo was in a tough situation. He wanted to play but Cúper was blocking him, so he called a meeting with Moratti and Cúper. He opened his heart, saying, "You don't like me; you don't want me. Why? I don't understand. You don't pick me to play when you know I'm fit. Why?" It was an impossible situation and Ronaldo still didn't get any proper answers. Soon after, Scolari picked him for the *seleçao*. Cúper reacted badly, saying it was a crazy decision, calling the CBF officials stupid, but he was only trying to defend himself from not picking him for Inter. We knew he was fit and ready. Dr Runco was happy with his fitness, countering Cúper's allegations, saying, "He can play; I know he can. He is ready."'

Things began to hot up. Scolari, satisfied with Ronaldo's fitness, now selected him for a pre-World Cup warm-up against Yugoslavia. The game was to be played in Fortaleza in the north-east of Brazil, which would mean another transatlantic flight for Ronaldo, something Inter would inevitably frown upon. Cúper reacted to Scolari's selection by saying, 'Ronaldo will only play for Brazil once he has played for Inter.'

According to Rodrigo Paiva, Cúper even phoned Scolari begging him not to play Ronaldo, saying, 'Please don't pick him, because if he plays for you and is OK, then he has to play for me here at Inter. You will turn the fans against me and create problems that I don't need. You can't do that.'

I asked Rodrigo if he felt it was a specific ploy to disrupt Ronaldo's and Brazil's plans for the World Cup. He took no time to answer: 'Of course he was doing it on purpose. He's Argentinean. He doesn't want Brazil to do well at the World Cup and he doesn't want Ronaldo to do well as it puts his position under threat. Argentineans hate Brazilians, don't forget. I never liked Cúper.'

Ronaldo played 45 minutes against Yugoslavia and looked impressive, doing a lot more than people expected. Cúper was now forced to pick him as Ronaldo had proved he was fit; but on returning to Milan, and as if to reaffirm his authority over Ronaldo and Scolari, Cúper duly benched him for the Fiorentina game and did not call on his services throughout it. Ronaldo was fuming. Scolari returned serve, saying, 'Ronaldo will continue to be selected for Brazil, no matter what Hector Cúper thinks.'

It was now mid-March and Cúper benched Ronaldo again for the full 90 minutes against Lecce and Roma. Tension filled the air. Moratti voiced his reluctance to release Ronaldo for international duty, saying, 'Ronaldo will play for Brazil after he has played for Inter. The interests of Brazil do not interest us. Scolari cannot go above the club.' Moratti had no intention of allowing, nor did he expect, Ronaldo to play any role in the World Cup. In his own mind's eye, he saw Ronaldo's full return coming at the start of the next season. Moratti and Scolari were poles apart in their outlook.

They say the Lord moves in mysterious ways and the very next day, who should pull up with a similar muscle complaint to those Ronaldo had been suffering from but Christian Vieri, further endorsing Rodrigo Paiva's view that the training at Inter was flawed. As the race for *lo scudetto* reached a thrilling climax, Cúper was obliged to look to Ronaldo as cover but still had this to say about the whole situation: 'At the moment, Ronaldo is preoccupied with his own future, not about the World Cup or playing for Inter. He has spent three years hardly playing and has barely contested a serious match, and he knows that he is still not 100 per cent right.'

Next up was Inter's crucial UEFA Cup semi-final against Feyenoord. Cúper named Ronaldo in the squad, but he would start from the bench. Two minutes into the second half and with the score at 0–0, Cúper instructed Ronaldo to warm up and get ready for action. As Ronaldo jogged up and down the touch-line, the San Siro crowd, who hadn't laid eyes on him in a football kit for 102 long days, roared in approval. They were desperate to see their *Fenomeno* return. But Feyenoord promptly scored and Cúper changed his mind, directing Ronaldo to sit back down. Not good. Twenty-five minutes later, Cúper finally signalled to Ronaldo and shortly he was on. Ronaldo only had 20 minutes to work with, but his performance oozed menace. Although he couldn't influence the result of the game – Feyenoord won 1–0 – he certainly made people sit up and take note, none more so than Gerry Armstrong, who was covering the game for UEFA's internet service. I spoke to Gerry about Ronaldo's impact and he explained, 'Having seen his performance, albeit only 20 minutes, I knew he was back.' Gerry adds, 'Coming on as a sub for the last 25 minutes or so, with Inter 1–0 down, he was just sensational, and I thought, bloody hell, he looks OK! He had the change of pace, the power, the acceleration, and the hunger looked to be there.' Despite Inter ultimately losing this tie over the two legs, Gerry earmarks this game as a watershed for Ronaldo as the one where he knew he could compete at the forthcoming World Cup.

A few weeks later, Gerry was co-commentator for Sky Sports, covering the Portugal–Brazil friendly, eager to see how the Ronaldo he'd seen impress against Feyenoord would fare in the national colours of Brazil. With Scolari deploying his preferred trident of Ronaldo, Rivaldo and Ronaldinho, this was potentially an excellent indicator of contention or otherwise for the World Cup, as Portugal were also fielding their strongest team. Gerry continues: 'Although Ronaldo didn't score, he looked a huge threat. So much so, on commentary that night I recommended that viewers get their money on Brazil to win the World

Cup and get it on Ronaldo to be top scorer.' Prophetic words indeed at the time, and ones that pocketed Gerry more than a few quid come July.

But Cúper remained impassive, saying, 'He is still not ready,' and benched him for the whole of the next game against Atalanta, which Inter lost 2–1: a very damaging result for their title aspirations. With four games left, Inter's first *scudetto* since 1989 lay tantalisingly within their grasp. It was theirs to win, but coming up on the rails were Juventus and Roma. Cúper needed nerve. Could he shake the nearly-man mantle and deliver the Holy Grail to the *Nerazzurri*?

These were tense, tense times for Inter Milan. They had set the pace all season but signs of nerves were beginning to creep in. On 14 April, Inter entertained Brescia at the San Siro as the race for *lo scudetto* was reaching its home straight. With Inter 1–0 down going into the last ten minutes, the success-hungry Inter fans were baying for a turnaround and the three points that Inter just had to gain that day. The tension was unbearable. Cue Ronaldo, who, in 3 magical minutes, sent the San Siro into orbit, scoring in the 79th and 82nd minutes, his second a rasping curling drive from the edge of the box that nearly burst the net. Pandemonium reigned. Shirt off (the first and last time he has ever done this, perhaps reflecting the wave of emotion within) and with the grin back on his face, Ronaldo was again mobbed by delighted teammates. The noise that erupted from the San Siro was deafening. It was incredible.

These crucial three points brought *lo scudetto* closer to Cúper's grasp. The next game was away at Verona to play Chievo. Chievo had proved nuggety opponents since their recent arrival in *Serie A* and had caused several big upsets already. Their sum was greater than their parts. Inter went 1–0 down in the 41st minute and the pessimistic *Nerazzurri* hearts sank in the crowd. It looked like Inter were choking. But then Stephane Dalmat equalised just after the break to give some hope. At 1–1, the tension was almost too much to bear, but then Ronaldo did it again, scoring in the 59th minute to send all and sundry crazy with joy. But then, from the ecstasy came the agony. Cúper, still proving peevishly stubborn, substituted Ronaldo in the 65th minute to reinforce his defensive options, and he must have thought the game was won as the referee's assistant posted 3 minutes' added time on the electronic board. Then, agonisingly, Cossato popped up with a minute to go to equalise, in true Chievo never-say-die fashion, and the points were shared. Inter were distraught and it would prove to be a costly two points they dropped that day.

Ronaldo scored again in the next game at home against Piacenza, the third in a tense 3–1 win, which meant Inter led *lo scudetto* going into the final game, away at Lazio. Inter's destiny was in their own hands. Up until this point, *lo scudetto* had been theirs to win. Now it was theirs to lose: a situation they had no experience in handling. And it showed.

Ronaldo had scored four goals in three games to keep Cúper's and Inter's dream alive, but the last-day visit to Lazio would mean a return trip to the Stadio Olympico, the ground where his world had gone dark in April 2000. It was not a lucky ground for him. Disaster was to strike again as, despite going ahead twice in the game, Inter imploded to lose 4–2 and ultimately finish third behind Juventus and Roma respectively. Cúper mysteriously substituted Ronaldo at half-time, a decision Ronaldo could not handle, and he broke down in tears once more, the world's cameras picking up on yet another nightmarish flirtation with this ground. Inevitably, the wreath of loser was hung around Cúper's neck to go with all his others. Again, Rodrigo Paiva has strong words for Cúper about his tactics that day: 'Why did Cúper substitute Ronaldo that day? The man is crazy. Ronaldo was the only one who looked like scoring in recent games and Inter had to win. Cúper was spiteful and took him off as if to blame him. He is stupid.'

It was a day where three teams – Inter, Juventus and Roma – could all have won the title. In a bizarre scenario, desperate to prevent city arch-rivals Roma from being crowned champions, the Lazio *Tifosi* were more than happy to cheer Inter along, many of them having bought Inter scarves and flags for the occasion. They had also gone out of their way to allocate as many tickets to Inter as they could. On the day, an incredible 40,000 Inter fans were welcomed to the Stadio Olympico with open arms and the famous stadium was decked out in blue and black; there was the surreal scene of a packed Stadio Olympico, with Lazio at home, all cheering on Inter. But even this wasn't enough to win it for them. A *Serie A* season that had promised so much for Inter, Cúper and Ronaldo had ultimately delivered nothing. It was a hammer blow to all involved with Internazionale.

Whilst in Milan, I spoke to John Moretti of the *Corriere della Sera*, who had been following Inter during their run-in for the title. When we spoke, it was a week or so after the Lazio game and the fog of disappointment still lay thick over the city. 'Jesus, don't mention the Lazio game around here,' advised John, with only the slightest hint of irony. He meant it. 'I know things are never over until they're over, but

CHAPTER 14

PENTACAMPEÃO –
FIFA WORLD CUP 2002

Ronaldo's redemption in Yokohama provided a wonderful, fairytale finale to the 2002 World Cup. Although not a great World Cup – too many of the star-laden nations failed to deliver – it was an exciting one, full of contrasts and played in superb, albeit somewhat charmless, hi-tech arenas. South Korea revelled in the opportunity to co-host the tournament and put on a real show, their delirious fans creating a dazzling atmosphere. The Japanese were more pedestrian and more mechanical in their methods.

The tournament's main letdown, that of tired players, was one not of its own making. The break between its commencement and the various climaxes of the European season was far too short, with, for example, the final of the UEFA Champions League being only 16 days prior. Several big names, notably in the French team, looked jaded and failed to deliver what was expected. Zinedine Zidane, reigning FIFA World Player of the Year, was unfit and unable to illuminate as he had in 1998. England travelled with a polarised squad of high quality padded out with Premiership wannabes.

Gerry Armstrong apart, Brazil for once were not everyone's pre-tournament favourites, primarily due to a lacklustre qualifying campaign. But when one sat down and examined their squad, it was difficult not to be envious of the quality at their disposal. There were the headliners such as the 'three Rs' of Ronaldo, Rivaldo and Ronaldinho, and although the jury was still out on exactly how good Ronaldinho was, in Ronaldo and Rivaldo, Brazil had two players oft referred to as geniuses, both of whom were previous FIFA World Player of the Year winners. Some of Rivaldo's feats at Barcelona, most notably his hat-trick against Valencia with a stunning overhead kick to win during the last game of the 2000–01 season, which guaranteed Barcelona Champions League football, were the stuff of legend in Catalonia. Most teams dream of one genius in their side, never mind two.

Pundits had pointed critical fingers at their defence, but again, on examination, they had three-players-in-one Roberto Carlos, a serial cup-winner with Real Madrid and noted dead-ball specialist. In addition, Cafu, the elegant Roma stalwart, who was appearing in his fourth World Cup, added finesse and attacking options down the right flank. Lucio had been one of the finds of the recent Champions League with his stirring displays for finalists Bayer Leverkusen, and their two ball-playing centre backs, Roque Junior and Edmilson, both played at leading European clubs. There was trickery on the bench in the form of Mr Stepover himself, Denilson, and the diminutive Juninho (Paulista), who had left such a warm impression in the English Premiership. For once, they also had a decent keeper in Marcos, with the massive Dida on the bench in support. In short, this Brazilian side had most, if not all, of the hallmarks that are admired and expected from Brazil: skill, flair and passion.

But 24 hours before their first game, Scolari and Brazil suffered what appeared to be a major setback. Captain and defensive midfielder Emerson Ferreira of Roma dislocated his shoulder in a freak incident. Scolari had wanted Emerson to perform the role Dunga had done so well in 1994, and he was a more than able player. During a light-hearted training game, he was playing in goal, of all positions, and dived to stop a ball – a good save, by all accounts – but landed awkwardly and dislocated his shoulder, thus bringing his World Cup to an end before it had even started. An incredible thing to have to live with and one wonders how he will broach that with his grandchildren in years to come. Painful indeed.

Scolari reverted to plan B and drafted in Gilberto Silva as cover. The quality of his play throughout the tournament would be reflected by his subsequent signing for English side Arsenal. For Scolari, it was pretty much a straight swap and the armband went over to Cafu. Scolari, although pilloried by the press back home and tagged a defensive coach, in reality proved far from it. Having backed Ronaldo, he was able to field him alongside Rivaldo and Ronaldinho, and with Cafu and Roberto

Carlos overlapping whenever possible, their attacking options were world-class. Scolari rounded on his critics, saying, 'I will never restrict an attacker's creativity. He is given tactics and a base from which he can improvise. A well-organised team finds it easier to play.'

Brazil, as they had in France '98, got lucky with the group draw, with Turkey, China and Costa Rica hardly being countries of enviable footballing pedigree. They were not to disappoint, as they got off to a winning start against the spirited Turks. The game was an interesting one in that nobody had expected that much of either Brazil or Ronaldo; people were perhaps just popping their head around the door to see how they both fared out of footballing curiosity. Surely he couldn't have fully recovered from that horrendous knee injury. For those who hadn't seen him in action since France '98, he looked bigger and broader, and with his boxer's neck resembled a no-nonsense middleweight.

Turkey had deservedly gone ahead and were causing Brazil a problem or two. But Brazil got going shortly after the start of the second half when Rivaldo, in space on the left wing, curled in one of his awkward whippy crosses into that area that goalkeepers hate: just in front of them and just behind the defence, and with plenty of pace on it, just asking for some contact. Although a tricky ball, it seemed it would be covered by the two Turkish defenders; but in similar fashion to his goal in the France '98 semi-final versus Holland, Ronaldo's anticipation was the difference and he burst between them and slid in to latch the ball into the goal. It was a goal for Ronaldo and Brazil – something not seen since Copa America in June 1999. The elegant brush strokes were beginning to return to a canvas that hadn't seen colour for over three years. Rivaldo secured the win from the spot in the 89th minute but the game, apart from Ronaldo's comeback goal, will be remembered for Rivaldo's dreadful play-acting over by the corner flag, clutching his face in agony when the ball had clearly struck him on the leg. This would later earn him widespread criticism and the laughable fine of just short of $5,000 from FIFA, money Rivaldo probably had on him.

The win sent a message around the World Cup that perhaps Brazil weren't quite in the disarray that many had suggested. Their play had shown swagger and flair and, should Ronaldo prove to be in the mood, they had that crucial component of any successful World Cup campaign (bar France in '98): someone who can get you five or six goals or more. One huge and not to be underestimated advantage that Brazil had over nearly all of the nations, especially the Europeans, was that they'd had the opportunity to spend a month together prior to the tournament training, bonding and acclimatising, and the benefits it had reaped in team spirit were clear to see. Before each game, they boarded the team bus a collection of smiles. Ronaldinho was rarely seen without his sambinha drum getting the mood rolling, and general bonhomie filled the air. Scolari had fashioned a fine squad into a team of stars, not just a string of individuals, and the mood was collectively stronger than it had been in the France '98 squad.

Ronaldo scored again in the next game as Brazil brushed aside the inept Chinese, and then twice more in the 5–2 win over Costa Rica – for many people, the most entertaining game of the tournament. Thus far, Brazil had played some cracking stuff and had scored a healthy 11 goals, but questions still remained over the quality of their defending. Played three: won three would do for starters, and now that Brazil had the world's attention, people began to take them seriously and talk about them in terms of favourites.

Brazil were again fortunate in their draw for the first knockout game, coming up against Belgium. Brazil prevailed 2–0, both second-half goals, and were reliant on two key contributions: one from their outstanding goalkeeper Marcos; and the other from the controversial Jamaican referee Peter Prendergast. One has to question the judgement of FIFA and their refereeing policy in appointing a Jamaican referee for a World Cup last-16 match, and his lack of experience and accompanying temperament was evident. FIFA would exasperate further when Spain's quarter-final versus South Korea would be officiated by the triumvirate of an Egyptian, a Ugandan and a Trinidadian. A highly contentious game would inevitably ensue, the vanquished Spaniards incensed at what they saw as primary-school refereeing. Italy would also join the chorus of referee bashers. I spoke to Brazilian ex-ref and current TV pundit José Roberto Wright about this state of affairs at world tournaments and he laments the dire situation. José Roberto, himself voted 'Best Referee in the World' by FIFA in 1990, is perhaps most commonly remembered as the ref who booked Paul Gascoigne during the semi-final of Italia '90. He cites the problem today as the fact that the age limit of international referees is 45, unlike the 50 of days gone by. As such, the stock of good referees is compromised by five years and FIFA have to spread the net wider to find officials. This, combined with their myopic desire to 'globalise' the attending officials (one way of satisfying lesser FAs), means that many big games are left in the hands of inept flag-wavers and whistle-happy incompetents.

Prendergast blundered badly on the 36th minute when veteran Belgian striker Marc Wilmots rose majestically above Roque Junior to head home and give Belgium the lead. It was a classic centre-forward's header. But somehow Prendergast adjudged Wilmots to have fouled Junior and the goal was chalked off. Prendergast at least had the good grace to concede he'd made a mistake to Wilmots during the interval, but for Belgium it was no consolation: goals against Brazil were precious gems.

Belgium continued to play well and forced a string of smart saves from Marcos – for some, a surprise selection ahead of AC Milan's Dida – and Brazil were for once looking bland. Belgium continued to press at the start of the second half and Marcos was again called upon to keep Brazil in it. His heroics were repaid in the 67th minute when Rivaldo took a Ronaldinho pass superbly on his chest, swivelled and crashed the ball into the roof of the net for 1–0. It had taken a slight deflection to confound de Vlieger in the Belgium goal, but it was a beautiful goal nonetheless. Ronaldo compounded Belgium's bad luck when he completed the scoring on 87 minutes, sidefooting a Kleberson pass under de Vlieger to maintain his impressive scoring record.

This win presented Brazil at last with a 'proper' tie against top opposition: a mouthwatering clash against Sven-Goran Eriksson's England. It is worth dwelling on the background to this game, as, for Brazil and Ronaldo, it was easily their toughest test yet.

England had attracted mixed reviews. Under the guidance of Sven-Goran Eriksson – a surprisingly refreshing appointment by the traditionally moribund English FA – the transformation of England's woeful qualifying campaign had been wonderful. England had gone on a winning spree, culminating in the never-to-be-forgotten 5–1 demolition of eternal foe Germany in Munich, in a game where England looked like a genuine team rather than just a collection of stars. England saved the best drama for last, as David Beckham's last-gasp free kick earned a draw with Greece and England were through to Japan. They had made their usual lacklustre start with a draw against Sweden, but then a stirring win over Argentina thanks to a Beckham penalty put them in charge of the group. A tame draw against Nigeria was not detrimental and then a comfortable 3–0 win against Denmark in the first knockout game brought them up against Brazil. England, then, were on good form, and they had world-class players in David Beckham, Paul Scholes and he of the wonder goal at France '98, reigning European Player of the Year Michael Owen. In the eyes of the team's detractors, however, the quality around these three, Rio Ferdinand apart, was thin and England's collective fitness looked poor. How would they fare against Brazil?

Inevitably, the game drew comparisons with the classic encounter in 1970, the game of Gordon Banks's save and the duel between Pelé and Bobby Moore. That game, revered as a classic, was probably the last time England had competed on anything like a par with Brazil. The optimistic suggested that this would be another. But again, when one looked at the teams on paper, there was no comparison. England had taken the gamble and ultimate mistake of arriving in Japan and Korea with several players not fully fit. Beckham had moved heaven and earth, and generated banal national hysteria, to recover from a broken metatarsal bone in his famous right foot, but was plainly not fully fit. Newcastle United's Kieron Dyer was unfit and he knew it. Manchester United's Gary Neville, a hugely underrated component in England's plans, had also broken a metatarsal and didn't travel, and was replaced *faute de mieux* by Danny Mills. Liverpool's Danny Murphy turned round halfway there as he broke down on the pre-tournament trip, joining the bizarre list of England's metatarsal victims, and was replaced with another workaday Premiership player, Trevor Sinclair. It was a good time to be looking for an England cap. England's one true gem, Michael Owen, was complaining of tight hamstrings. It was a sorry situation and, man for man, Brazil were by far the stronger side. For Ronaldo, he was up against the English defence which had proven to be one of the most parsimonious thus far, Sol Campbell and Rio Ferdinand proving perfect foils for each other, and, in goal, pony-tailed veteran David Seaman was thus far justifying his selection. Could Ronaldo continue his goal-scoring sequence?

For many Brazilian observers, this was a pivotal game in the tournament. Brazilians have a curious fear of England in footballing terms. Whether this is misplaced respect for the 'fathers' of the game I'm not sure, but many I spoke to were far from confident of the *seleçao's* safe passage. They felt if they won this, they would win the final. Scolari added, 'To be alive and not die. That was the only thought we had going into this game.' England were optimistic, thinking a victory was possible, and when they took a surprise lead through Michael Owen, it looked on. On the stroke of half-time, Rivaldo equalised with a goal so Brazilian the ball might as well have been wearing a thong as it zipped past David

Seaman. Ronaldinho's run to set up the goal was an iconic moment of the tournament, his mazy dribble totally bamboozling Ashley Cole. His inviting pass was then drilled home unerringly by Rivaldo and the teams went into the break on equal terms.

In the second half, England, bereft of know-how and ideas, succumbed meekly – the first time questions had been asked about Sven-Goran Eriksson's ability to motivate. Ronaldinho scored with a flukish free kick that England's ageing keeper David Seaman should have kept out, but he had no answer to it and probably never will – a shame, because he had kept superbly up until then. Ronaldinho was soon to see red as more questionable refereeing by Mexico's Ramos Rizo saw fit to remove him from the field of play, but England could find no way through and Brazil cantered home.

The only plus point England could take from the game is that they prevented Ronaldo from scoring – the only time in the tournament – and he was substituted on 70 minutes. Ronaldo hadn't had many chances and had been well marshalled by the aforementioned Campbell and Ferdinand. A game that promised so much, especially with England taking the lead, proved to be a huge disappointment, as England were quite frankly awful and the Brazilians were never required to get out of second gear to win the game.

Brazil proceeded to the semi-final against Turkey, whom they'd beaten in their first game. Ronaldo proved pivotal yet again as his sublimely inventive toe-poked goal on 49 minutes proved decisive. This goal combined several elements of Ronaldo's genius. Receiving the ball just inside the final third, he swivelled sharply to face goal, brushed Bulent aside and then burst away with a double stepover to leave his two markers trailing. As he bore down on the Turkish keeper, Rustu, he toe-poked it, surprising the goalkeeper by a fraction of a second. The ball went in off the far post. Although perhaps not the most aesthetically memorable goal that Ronaldo's ever scored, it was a brilliant piece of finishing, and assured Brazil's safe passage to the final to meet Germany. When I spoke to Gary Lineker about his favourite Ronaldo goal, he was adamant that it was this one, saying, 'Well, obviously there is the Compostela goal, but for me, as a fellow striker, it has to be the one against Turkey in the World Cup semi-final. Such a big game, and notice in how many big games Ronaldo scores. What I love is that he knew he only had a split second to catch Rustu unawares, and he took it with the toe-poke. Brilliant.'

As we have seen in Chapter 1, Ronaldo's cathartic brace put paid to the Germans and allowed Brazil to lift the cup yet again. 'Pentacampeão' ('Five-Times Champions') ran the headlines in the Brazil broadsheets and in an instant their shirts with four stars were obsolete. A record cumulative total of 45 billion people had watched the tournament according to official figures: a quite staggering number and I'd wager that most of them were happier with a Brazil win than a German one. The Germans were gracious in defeat and there is a wonderful image of German coach Rudi Völler, who had been so impressed by the unknown buck-toothed wonderkid all those years earlier, smiling with irony, shaking Ronaldo's hand and congratulating him warmly. That wonderkid had now equalled Pelé's haul of 12 World Cup goals and was closing in on Juste Fontaine and Gerd Muller. Time is on his side.

As the celebrations were in full swing on the Yokohama pitch, Ronaldo happily posed for photographers, clutching the World Cup aloft, beaming brightly and revelling in the ecstasy of winning the big one. His winner's medal was handed to him, appropriately, by Pelé and for a moment you had the two greatest products of Brazilian football, young and old, sharing mutual appreciation. Pelé was as happy as anybody.

Understandably, on departure from Japan, the mood was ebullient, the samba drums played hard and everyone was having a good time. Ronaldo, who had arrived for the tournament with the badly judged gesture of stretching his eyes 'orientally' with his fingers – something the co-hosts were not too pleased with – now took the fun one stage further and donned a mock-sumo skullcap. But who cared? He was Ronaldo and had just scored the goals in the World Cup final. He could do pretty much whatever he wanted at this point. Asked by reporters at the airport how he felt, he answered, 'It feels like I'm living a dream; it's incredible.' The mood aboard the Varig jet that took the *seleçao* back to Brasilia this time bore no resemblance to the sombre, gloomy atmosphere on the return from France '98. The plane was rocking to the samba beat and the champagne flowed for fun.

Ronaldo won the Golden Boot for his eight goals. As in France '98, he was now spectacularly back in the world spotlight, but this time for all the right reasons: football ones. On arrival back in Brazil, he was asked what he felt were the main reasons for Brazil's success. 'The Cup was won deservedly by a fantastic group of players. We were united all the way, and this was fundamental in helping us win the *penta*.'

Also, asked by a wiseguy Brazilian journalist, 'Which was more difficult, scoring the brace against Germany or going 40 days without sex during the finals?', Ronaldo, after some thought, answered, 'Not sure, but it was worth it to be World Champions!'

Ronaldo also had kind words for the Brazilian medical staff, and in particular Brazil's director, José Luiz Runco, saying, 'This win is a triumph for all the Brazilian medical staff who have helped me so much. But not just me, they got Rivaldo fit, they got Ronaldinho fit and they have assisted all the players throughout this tournament.'

Rivaldo, who had been injured towards the end of the season, had been given only a 50–50 chance of competing in the World Cup by Barcelona's physio, Ricardo Pruna, but Runco was having none of it and put him through a detailed programme of recuperation – as he had with Ronaldo – and got both the *craques* (star players) fit and ready for the finals. Runco confessed, 'Getting these two stars fit and ready for the *seleçao* and for Big Phil has been the biggest challenge of my professional career.'

Paulo Paixão also joined in the collective medical back-slapping by saying, 'We knew the moment we had Ronaldo and Rivaldo passed fit to play we had a good chance of winning the cup.'

Interviewed by Antonio Maria Filho in *O Globo*, one of Brazil's leading broadsheets, Ronaldo was asked, 'How does it feel to be called *Fenomeno* once again when many in the game had thought you were finished?' Ronaldo responded, 'It's been a long road and the two years since the Coppa Italia final have felt much longer. But I felt that good things were about to happen for me. Now, I want to remember this moment as the best of my life.'

Asked about Pelé's Brazilian record of 12 World Cup goals and his desire to overtake it, Ronaldo responded, 'Of course I would like to hold the record, but what is more important is that Brazil are World Champions and I want to be champion again. When we do this, the goals will come anyway.' He went on, 'It still hasn't sunk in about what we've achieved and that I scored the goals. I can only say that I am very happy, very very happy. I have no other explanation apart from that it is a gift from God. My family, as always, have helped me through difficult times, as have my friends and others who kept believing in me. They never lost faith in me. I have special thanks for my physio, Filé. He's been with me all along and never abandoned me or failed me. Although he's not here at the moment, I'm sure he is in Rio, celebrating. I'm here thinking of him for certain. I also have great thanks for Prof. Gerard Saillant [who was one of Ronaldo's special VIP guests at the final], whose skill saved my knee. Without him, my return would not be possible. I am very grateful.'

When Saillant was asked how he felt about his famous outpatient's return, he told Marcelo Senna of *O Globo*, 'Of course I'm happy. It was a success not just for me but for all involved, and nobody more so than Ronaldo himself. There were two years when we could only hope he would return. I am very happy for him. It's not easy to pick yourself up from the bottom, where he was, and arrive where he's arrived. Ronaldo is an example for all sportsmen, to young people, to everybody. He is an example to everybody who has a problem, of any kind.'

Filé was also touched by Ronaldo's gratitude. He had been through an extremely tough period himself of late due to tragically losing his 15-year-old son Ulisses to muscular dystrophy in 2001. Struggling to hold back the emotion, Filé thanked Ronaldo for his kind words and added, 'Today, I am certain, although I lost a son, I gained one in Ronaldo. My relationship with Ronaldo is not only professional; he is a friend, my confidante, and my son.' He went on, 'Ronaldo's return was not guaranteed. He worked hard; he did everything I asked of him, and more. He turned a page of medical history never turned before. Don't forget that.' Refusing to take full credit for Ronaldo's rehabilitation, Filé went on, 'Others take credit too. God, Gerard Saillant and the technical team put together by Felipe Scolari deserve much praise. They are all responsible.'

Not surprisingly, the Brazilian press in general had a field day and one name was on every paper's masthead: Ronaldo. Other journalists around the world were similarly gushing in their praise and respect for him – many of whom had previously doubted his fitness and durability. In every country, Ronaldo was the headline. In Italy, *Corriere della Sera*, *La Gazzetta dello Sport* and *La Republica* had no hesitation in comparing him to 'King Pelé'. *La Nacion* of Argentina, although not quite as word happy as other countries, and still smarting from their pathetic first-round exit, applauded Ronaldo as 'King of the World'. Spain's *Marca* hailed the Brazilians as 'Kings of Football' and the final as 'The Ronaldo Final'.

The Brazilian press were also warm in their praise for coach Felipe Scolari, for whom they'd had caustic words in the build-up to the finals. As discussed, the majority of them had campaigned for Romário's inclusion in the final squad and had not responded kindly when it was evident that the hero of USA '94 was not key to Scolari's plans. Romário was scoring goals with irrepressible ease in the Brazilian domestic game and was still a huge favourite with many. But Scolari's bold choice to build the team around Ronaldo paid the ultimate dividend possible. Scolari also became the first coach to win all seven games in the finals, something he wasn't slow to remind his former assassins in the press. He was also quick to praise his players, telling Marcos Penido, 'The secret of the victory was the attitude of the players – all of whom improved as the tournament went on. They formed a group of great unity, solidarity and commitment. The mixture of individual talent and hard work was the difference between us and other teams and I am convinced this team can help Brazil return to the vanguard of world football.'

He went on to explain some of his tactical thinking during the tournament: 'At the start of the tournament, and especially after our lacklustre qualifying campaign, I needed to re-establish the image of Brazil as winners and footballers. I studied hard our opponents in the opening stages – Turkey, China and Costa Rica – and decided that Juninho was essential to the team to create the right attacking image that Brazil's history is built upon. This player was fundamental at this moment. The team won its first three games and won back the respect and fear we needed. Juininho was crucial in this. Thereafter I needed to change things slightly and improve our defensive qualities as the games demanded. Kleberson was brought in to do this. Throughout, Ronaldo, Rivaldo and Ronaldinho were outstanding.'

Still acutely aware of the rough time he'd been given before the finals, and being no mug about the precarious life of a football coach, Scolari would ensure his fame and immortality among Brazilians by resigning whilst at the top and taking up the Portugal job.

Mario Zagallo, the granddaddy of Brazilian football and veteran of most of their previous campaigns, was for once not involved in 2002. But he was quick to add his praise to a job well done, saying, 'I wish to congratulate Big Phil for his humility in redirecting credit to Ronaldo. I was with him [Ronaldo] in '94 and then in '98 when he had his big problem. Afterwards, destiny had reserved for him two big knee operations and *O Fenômeno* arrived at the World Cup totally discredited by most in the game, and returned as Golden Boot winner. For me, and without wanting to put down the great contribution of Rivaldo, Ronaldo was the *craque* of the tournament.'

Romário was also not short of a few words, and in his customary controversial style was hardly overbearing in his praise for Ronaldo, but was willing to acknowledge his contribution, saying, somewhat grudgingly, 'I will not say that Ronaldo was spectacular because I know he wasn't 100 per cent fit. But he did score decisive goals in important games.' But then, in true impish Romário style, he had the last laugh, singling out German keeper Oliver Kahn: 'He was the best player, but he was also the ugliest.'

Brazil had proved to be rightful winners in 2002. With eighteen, they had easily scored the most goals, beating Germany's fourteen, of which eight had been scored in game one versus the clueless Saudi Arabians. Next up were Spain with ten. Brazil had conceded only four goals in seven games and made a mockery of those who said they were weak defensively. Admittedly, they were in a soft group and were only really tested later on in the tournament, but they had earned their respect with refreshing attacking football. Whereas most teams crave a player who can deliver five or six goals in the World Cup finals, Brazil possessed two, with Rivaldo scoring five and Ronaldo eight. All in all, it was an impressive campaign.

For Ronaldo, it could hardly have gone much better; perhaps only a hat-trick in the final could have provided a larger cherry to adorn the cake. Without the laser-like glare of the world's media that had focused on him in 1998, he had been given the chance to go about his business initially almost unnoticed. Nike were noticeably subdued in their Ronaldo hype this time round, perhaps wary of the adverse publicity they had unwittingly attracted four years earlier. For this World Cup, their TV campaign featured all their contracted world stars in a moody, futuristic game of five-a-side aboard a converted prison ship, under the instruction of Eric Cantona. As ever with Nike, the advert was a storming success, with JXL's remixed version of Elvis Presley's 'A Little Less Conversation' providing the theme tune and becoming the ubiquitous sound of the summer. Ronaldo played an almost apologetic role in this one and only featured towards the end. With chilling similarities to Nike's 1998 campaign, it was again the stars featured at the forefront of this advert, such as France's Thierry Henry and Italy's Francesco Totti, who had tournaments they would care to forget.

Unlike at France '98, Ronaldo had no unique boots of his own at the outset. I discussed this with Rodrigo Paiva. Rodrigo grinned widely and explained, 'About two years prior to the World Cup 2002, we had been at Nike in Oregon and they had these amazing new boots, super lightweight and silver coloured. Nike said these were the shoes they wanted him to wear at the next World Cup. But then, when the World Cup came around, the shoes they provided weren't the shining silver ones we had seen, but some darker ones, the Mercurial Vapour that the other big stars had. We didn't think much of it at the time, but when the semi-finals arrived, Nike contacted us and said, "We have the shoes, the silver ones, and we want Ronaldo to wear them." It transpired that Nike were waiting to see which one of their big-name stars shone at the World Cup so they could give them to him. Had it been Thierry Henry, for example, he would have got them first, or Francesco Totti, etc., etc. They did not have the confidence in Ronaldo to give them to him at the first game, after all his problems. It was ironic that he should get them anyway!'

The low expectation on Ronaldo's shoulders proved a huge bonus to him and allowed not only him to go about his business unhurried, but the Brazil camp too. Inadvertently, Nike ultimately got what they wanted – a Ronaldo and Brazilfest. As discussed, with 12 World Cup goals he now equalled Pelé and, at the close of the tournament, his 64 games for Brazil had yielded 45 goals at 0.7 per game. Healthy numbers all round.

As he took time off ahead of the forthcoming European domestic season, he could sleep soundly in the knowledge that he had scaled the summit of the world game once more and had written his name indelibly in the history books. But back in Milan, things weren't quite so rosy.

CHAPTER 15

THE REAL DEAL

Ronaldo was now back at the forefront of world football. It was a place he was more than familiar with and a place he enjoyed occupying. Not only did this massage his ego and reassure him that he was in fact one of, if not the best player in the world, but it also gave him the hand he needed to negotiate with Inter Milan.

Ronaldo's season with Inter Milan had been highly frustrating. Apart from the headline disappointment of losing *lo scudetto* to Juventus, Ronaldo's relationship with Hector Cúper was dysfunctional. Ronaldo, like many, expected Moratti to wield the axe against the manager after the last-gasp agony in the Stadio Olympico against Lazio, but instead he went for continuity and retained Cúper for another season. This was too much for Ronaldo to stomach. He couldn't face another season under the disciplinarian ukases of Cúper, the uncertainty of whether or not he would play and the humiliation of being benched for long periods. In fairness to Cúper, he had done much to improve Inter's fortunes and had taken them from being also-rans to genuine title contenders. He had galvanised a squad of high quality, but they had still come up short, and the piece he didn't want to accommodate was Ronaldo. Ronaldo had been vocal in his criticism, assuming that Moratti would replace him, and now his position within the Inter squad became almost untenable. He wanted out.

Not only would a move allow Ronaldo to be free of the Cúper impasse, it would also secure another lucrative payday for him and his agents, Alexandre Martins and Reinaldo Pitta. We haven't heard from this pair for some time as they had been forced to take a back seat during

THE REAL DEAL

Ronaldo's recuperation, but with asset no. 1 now back in action, they dusted down their calculators and started looking at the numbers again.

So where would Ronaldo go? Who could afford him? Who could give him the first-team football not guaranteed at Inter? It seems bizarre to think in terms of Ronaldo not being given a guaranteed start, especially as Golden Boot winner, but his time with Cúper had made him very wary of this prospect. The usual shortlist of clubs was drafted and Martins and Pitta got down to work. Nike, again, would play a role, but there was not the hysterical fervour of a complete Nike deal that surrounded his move from Barcelona to Inter Milan in 1997. Barcelona, Manchester United, Arsenal, Lazio and AC Milan were all touted as potential suitors and all had viable reasons to be interested. Apart from his football ability, Ronaldo's commercial value is staggering, and the recent World Cup had only served to rekindle this power. Shirt sales, merchandising and all the other general paraphernalia were crucial elements in the numbers involved with any purchase of Ronaldo. He was box office.

Barcelona were an obvious choice for him to talk to. He was still revered in Catalonia and he had spent a happy, although turbulent, year there. He enjoyed the city, the climate and the language. He also enjoyed the greater freedom *La Liga* offered his play. But it wasn't the Catalan giants who were catching Ronaldo's eye.

Over in Madrid, a revolution had been taking place. Real Madrid, whose team of the late 1950s and early 1960s contained such legends as Alfredo di Stéfano, Ferenc Puskas, Raymond Kopa and Francisco Gento, and had won six European Cups in ten seasons, were again the team of the moment. They had just won the European Cup in the May of 2002 – their third success in five years – with a goal of stunning technical showmanship by French star Zinedine Zidane, and under the self-styled presidency of Florentino Pérez, were embarking on a voyage to redesign the blueprint for how a major club should be operated. It is important to understand what was going on at the Bernabéu at that time and why Ronaldo was so keen to be part of it.

Here it gets interesting and the story is littered with footballing sub-plots. Let's wind the clock back four years to the 1998 Champions League final in the stunning new Amsterdam Arena: ironically, not long before Ronaldo's fateful World Cup final in Paris. Playing in the final that day were Real Madrid, then under the presidency of Lorenzo Sanz and in their first European Cup final since Liverpool beat them in 1981. Their opposition was Italy's 'Old Lady', Juventus. Ronaldo knew these two sides very well. The Real Madrid side was pretty much the one that Fabio Capello had assembled and had just pipped Sir Bobby Robson's exhausted Barcelona to *La Liga* title in 1996–97. The Juventus team, containing, amongst others, the irrepressible Zinedine Zidane, was the side who had beaten Inter Milan to *lo scudetto* that season – Ronaldo's first season with the *Nerazzurri*. Real Madrid had not won Europe's biggest club prize since 1966, an epochal wait of 32 years. For a club like Real Madrid, this was simply not acceptable and the long hiatus had become a weight around its neck. Even worse, arch-rivals Barcelona had had the cheek to win their first ever in 1992, and then Johan Cruyff's so-called 'Dream Team' had gone on an unprecedented run and had lorded it over Spanish football for most of the '90s, with Real only winning *La Liga* twice, in 1995 and 1997. Real Madrid simply had to win.

One goal was enough to do it, and this was provided by Predrag Mijatovic with a clever dink over Angelo Peruzzi in the 66th minute. For Real, this was such a seminal victory it is hard to define its magnitude, and this certainly won't be attempted here. But for a glimpse of its importance you need only to pay a visit to their fantastic museum at the Bernabéu, where Mijatovic's glass-boxed Puma Kings are virtually the first exhibit you see, pride of place amongst an Aladdin's cave of loot. This seminal game in Real Madrid's history, containing so many characters who would feature in Ronaldo's career, also meant the exit door for Juventus's coach . . . one Marcello Lippi . . . whose next job would be at . . . Inter Milan, where he would lock horns with . . . Ronaldo. Football is a funny old game, apparently.

Real Madrid, elated to win the European Cup after so long, had only finished a tame fourth in *La Liga*, and coach Jupp Heynckes had barely put his champagne glass down when he was fired. Irony abounds here, for the dismissal of Heynckes – an unfortunate victim of Real not winning the league – would be mirrored five years later by the dismissal of Vicente del Bosque. Del Bosque's crime? Not winning the Champions League. Del Bosque had won *La Liga* that season, but in those five years the climate of football had changed sufficiently that the Champions League was now deemed more prestigious (and more lucrative) than a domestic league.

Lorenzo Sanz had come to the presidential throne at the Bernabéu in 1995, succeeding Ramón Mendoza. Sanz was a property speculator who had acted as Mendoza's treasurer, and although Sanz's reign contained major silverware, he suffered, amongst other things, from a poor public image. He was never fully accepted by the *Madrileño* public. The emergence of Champions League football and its vast pots of gold towards the end of the 1990s was also key to the demise of Sanz and the emergence of Pérez. Sanz had been as lavish as any high-profile president, but in the process had racked up sizeable debts. These were often published in the Spanish tabloids as being in the region of $200m, but the real figure, according to Phil Ball in his book *White Storm – 100 Years of Real Madrid*, was more like $100m. When, in 1999, FIFA announced that clubs entering the Champions League would have to demonstrate their fiscal solvency and prudence, the bean counters at the Bernabéu swallowed hard.

Despite another fantastic European Cup win in 2000 – famously for the first time against a team from the same nation: Valencia – Sanz's time was running out. One of the new candidates for the job was also a property magnate: the head of ACS Construction, Florentino Pérez. Pérez was virtually unknown in footballing circles but he was very astute, very wealthy and, more importantly, very influential. His campaign for the presidency was built around two pillars. One, he would wipe out the club's debt, and two, he would bring the Portuguese player Luis Figo to the club. At the time, both of these pledges were seen as pure folly and nothing more than electioneering bluster, pie-in-the-sky claims from a chancer who fancied his 15 minutes of fame.

Luis Figo was regarded as one of the best players in the world at the time and had been the key component in Barcelona's *La Liga* titles in 1998 and 1999. He was very talented and seemed very happy at Barcelona. The *Cules* loved him. But incumbent coach van Gaal was reported to be getting on his nerves and he was not a big fan of Joan Gaspart, Barcelona's president. Seizing on this, and in another classic Real–Barcelona tête-à-tête, Pérez saw his chance. He helped structure a deal that reflected the free-spending times and lured Figo from Barcelona for a world-record fee of £37m, causing gasps of disbelief across Europe. It was a staggering move which surprised virtually all and whipped up further *morbo* (rivalry and passion) between Spain's two largest clubs. It was sensational. Imagine John Lennon leaving The Beatles to join The Rolling Stones or Mick Jagger going the other way and you have an idea of the shock; it was simply audacious. Pérez then duly swept to victory in the presidential elections. He had done it. He'd backed his word and done it, and now he was taken seriously.

For his next trick, he would, incredibly, clear Real's burdensome debt, but not without the raised eyebrows of many around the Spanish capital.

Using the influence and standing amongst Madrid's establishment that he had acquired through his property dealings, he negotiated the sale of Real's old Ciudad Deportiva training facilities to the local council. This prime piece of land close to Madrid's centre fetched a handsome price and at a stroke cleared all Real's debts. Not only that, there was also enough in the pot to build a brand new, state-of-the-art training complex on a piece of land that the council had earmarked. Many people scratched their heads in puzzlement. Some, such as Atlético Madrid and Rayo Vallecano in particular, were blue with anger at what they saw as favouritism. But Pérez had done it. His double boast was now reality. He further amazed the home fans the following season with the audacious swoop for Zinedine Zidane, again busting the world-record transfer fee at a stratospheric £44m, making Ronaldo's £18m to Inter Milan four years earlier look like loose change.

Using ex-stars Jorge Valdano and Emilio Butragueño as his mouthpieces, Pérez's philosophy became clear. Now he had the club on a sound financial footing, he would bring one global superstar, or *galactico*, as they would be tagged, to the club each year in a policy of quality, not quantity. The rest of the squad would be augmented by home-grown talent, a policy that was tagged *Zidanes y Pavons*, combining the surname of their most expensive *galactico*, Zidane, and their youth-team starlet Pavon. Come the summer of 2002, Real's playing staff included Zidane, Figo, Roberto Carlos and Raúl from the top ranks, ably supported by the enviable cast of, among others, Iker Casillas, Iván Helguera, José Maria Gutiérrez (Guti), Fernando Hierro and Michel Salgado. It was a classy place to play your football. He had created a private gentlemen's club for the cream of the world's talent, and they all wanted to play there. Their Champions League win at Hampden Park in 2002 affirmed their status as the best club side in the world and FIFA rubber-stamped this by then voting them Club of the Century. Like any exclusive club, membership had its privileges and was by invitation only. Next on the list was Ronaldo.

Time and circumstance can affect many a man's life, and these two intangible forces aligned to allow Ronaldo to complete his 'dream' move to *les Merengues*. For Ronaldo personally, he wanted out of Inter. For him, footballing matters came first – understandable for one who had spent the previous four years wondering if he'd ever play again. The fact that Inter had stood by him and paid his princely wages and medical bills was a mere side issue to Ronaldo. He had made his mind up; he wanted

THE REAL DEAL

to leave, and he wanted to sign his name in the members' book on reception and sink into the leather chairs at the Bernabéu. Massimo Moratti at Inter was not impressed, telling Italian daily *Corriere dello Sport* on 6 August 2002, 'There is only one truth: Ronaldo belongs to Inter and will play with us next year as well. That's that.'

Cúper also spoke in terms of wanting Ronaldo to stay and 'fight for his place' – hardly the burning incentive that would immediately change Ronaldo's mind. After much posturing, Moratti succumbed to the inevitable and agreed to talk with Real and Ronaldo's agents. Whilst still smarting from the outlay he'd bankrolled over the last five years for Ronaldo, he initially slapped a $100m price tag on his head. This came down to $60m before long and then the serious negotiations started. Valdano and the Real delegation flew to Milan to begin negotiations but soon they broke down, with Valdano and Co. returning to Madrid. Valdano told the Spanish sports daily *Marca*, 'Now that Ronaldo has returned to Milan [he had just got back from Brazil], we have withdrawn our interest in signing him and, as far as we are concerned, the matter is closed.'

This bluntness from Valdano and Madrid would be a feature in their negotiations and the on–off, 'shall we, shan't we' nature of the whole saga for a time became quite tedious and kept the world's media guessing. There was also now the advent of the transfer window – a finite thing – which meant any transfers had to be concluded by Sunday, 1 September, otherwise Ronaldo would be marooned at Inter until at least Christmas and be stuck under the argus of Cúper – exactly the thing he didn't want. As the clock ticked, Martins and Pitta cranked things up and got Real Madrid back to the table. But things broke down a second time, with Real Madrid claiming, 'Real Madrid states that insurmountable differences exist between the club and Inter Milan concerning the transfer of Ronaldo. It has been seemingly impossible to arrive at a satisfactory agreement during the friendly and frank negotiations this morning, which has forced both clubs to bring the talks to an end.'

As things stood, Real Madrid were offering €12m plus two players, each valued at around the €12m mark, from a list that included Spaniard Fernando Morientes, Brazilian Flavio Conceicão, England's Steve McManaman and Argentine Santiago Solari – a smorgasbord of world talent. Moratti, feeling this was derisory, said *non grazie*. Outside Inter Milan's headquarters, about 200 angry fans joined in a meaty protest and vented their anger towards their former idol. People shouted, 'Piece of shit, go home.' Banners were held aloft that read 'Traitor', 'Disgrace', 'Mercenary' and 'Ronaldo – Ungrateful'. I took time to visit Milan during this period to gauge the mood of the spurned Inter contingent and their mood was decidedly hostile. *La Gazzetta dello Sport* was stinging in its criticism of Ronaldo and one of its head writers and pal of Ronaldo, Candido Cannavo, was sick with disgust at the whole affair. He likened Ronaldo's actions to the 'last brick falling from football's disintegrating moral wall'. Cannavo, who had joined Ronaldo some time back on the United Nations-fronted tour of Kosovo, recalled the event and how Ronaldo had asked him what kind of world they were living in. 'Which world is he living in?' Cannavo fumed. 'He has betrayed us, and above all, he has betrayed himself.'

Inter's president, Massimo Moratti, felt the betrayal the hardest. Pretty much alone among Italian football owners, he is loyal to a fault to his players, aiming to uphold the liberal traditions of his Moratti family as set out by his father, Angelo. Ronaldo was a special favourite, and the player himself had at times referred to Moratti as a father figure, especially during the dark valley of his knee injuries. Ronaldo's transfer request galled him. It was hurtful enough that the Brazilian's many speeches in the aftermath of his match-winning exploits at the World Cup final contained not one word of thanks for the support of Moratti and his club. Ronaldo would also show distinct lack of tact as, throughout the whole transfer saga, he refused to enter into a direct dialogue with Moratti, shamefully using his agents instead, which perhaps reflected the personal embarrassment that Ronaldo felt about the whole situation. Candido Cannavo, now fully warmed up, described the situation as 'Nauseating' in *La Gazzetta dello Sport*.

At this point, things weren't looking good for Ronaldo. At Inter, he was training alone and was being advised of when the rest of the squad would be training. If Cúper had them in for a morning session, Ronaldo would be barred until the afternoon, and vice-versa: hardly the set-up the Golden Boot winner would warm to. Cúper then left him out of the squad to travel to Lisbon to play in the Champions League qualifier against Sporting Lisbon: again, hardly a reflection of Ronaldo's centrality to Cúper's planning. When Cúper was pushed that the whole situation might be an Argentina–Brazil feud, he laughed off the claim, saying, 'That's completely silly. I've no problems with Brazilian players, but I do have problems with players who don't feel happy to play for Inter.' It was not just in training that Ronaldo was isolated, and as much as Real Madrid wanted him, for Inter, they were happy to keep him, so neither side was really nailing down the negotiation. By now, it was the third week of August, with the deadline looming and the transfer window being pulled closed.

But then things kick-started again as Pérez and Valdano sat back down. Pérez wanted Ronaldo for his marketability as much as his footballing prowess. Valdano was aware of the added dimension Ronaldo could give their Raúl-dependent attack. Conveniently, there was a G14 meeting in Monaco and officials from both Inter and Real agreed to reconvene negotiations once the G14 business had concluded. Real began the negotiations by offering €36.5m plus their reserve striker Pedro Munitis. Inter were still not happy, and claimed, 'Neither the technical nor economic conditions emerged to allow the conclusion of the Ronaldo deal.'

With the clock ticking away, Barcelona and the Machiavellian figure of Joan Gaspart entered the frame. Gaspart, also at the G14 conference, had buttonholed Pérez and expressed his interest in buying Fernando Morientes. Pérez must have found it difficult to conceal his glee, as this would be the turnkey that enabled the Ronaldo deal. But, as ever in Madrid, beware of Catalans bearing gifts. Pérez smelt a rat and a familiar one at that. As much as he was interested in Gaspart's offer and had no reason to doubt him at face value, he kept another card up his sleeve just in case, and in his mind pieced together a plan B.

Pérez was fully aware of the potential meddling intent of Gaspart. Just as Lorenzo Sanz had been 'seduced' into a Real Madrid/Barça spat five years earlier, Gaspart could not resist getting involved. Not only was there the thick history between the two clubs but, on a personal level, Gaspart was green with envy over Pérez's demi-God-like status at the Bernabéu – something he could only dream of at the Camp Nou. Anything he could do to bring his opposite number down a peg or two would be seen as good political capital in his eyes.

Pérez suspected this. He surmised that Gaspart had laid a trap – a trap, he suspected, intended to scupper the deal and prevent Ronaldo, the former darling of Barcelona, plying his trade at the Bernabéu. Pérez conveyed his suspicions several times to Inter by phone during the course of the eventful day, but Inter naively refused at first to believe Pérez's hunch, citing it as Madrid–Barcelona paranoia.

Inter, keen to get the deal through, were happy to go with Gaspart's offer, and the deal, announced as a fait accompli on the Saturday in all the Spanish newspapers, was a cash-plus-player arrangement that read as follows: Real Madrid would 'give' Morientes to Inter, who would instantly sell him on to Barcelona. Real Madrid would also give Inter a large (undisclosed) sum of cash and then Ronaldo would move from Inter to Real Madrid.

During the Saturday morning, Barcelona started to haggle with Inter over Morientes' price, prompting Pérez to suspect that the Gaspart offer might be nugatory. Inter, still cocksure, ignored Pérez's warnings and were so convinced the deal would go through that they went ahead that very afternoon and signed Ronaldo's replacement, Hernán Crespo from Lazio, even before they had formally sold Ronaldo to Real: a hasty move from a club of such transfer experience.

At around nine o'clock that night, with three hours to the final deadline, Gaspart called Inter to say, surprise surprise, he and Barcelona had changed their minds: they no longer wished to sign Morientes. According to a Real Madrid insider who preferred to remain anonymous, 'the walls shook' at the Milan club, as the Inter dignitaries howled with rage at Gaspart's stunt. But, thankfully for Ronaldo, Pérez did not lose his cool. He had his plan B.

Pérez was straight on the phone to Moratti, whom he found in a mild state of apoplexy. He advised Moratti to stay calm, saying, 'Come on, let's get to work.' Impressively, these two titans of European business wrapped up in a matter of 15 minutes. Real agreed to pay €35m (£22m) to Inter, plus one of a choice of Real players – or a further €10m in cash – in December. One of the players available to Inter would be Steve McManaman, but their first choice – it was no secret – would be (another) Argentine, Santiago Solari. Argentines at Inter . . . do you detect a theme here?

So now, late Saturday evening, everybody seemed happy. But there was one further bizarre twist. As the Real officials waited at Pérez's mansion for Moratti and Co. to telephone back with confirmation of the above deal, they became agitated that the 'call you straight back' promise from Moratti was now nearly an hour ago. It was only when Pérez went upstairs to relieve himself and walked past his son's bedroom that he realised his son had hopped onto the Internet, thus downing the telephone line they were awaiting Moratti's call on. Can you imagine?! Pérez junior was swiftly disconnected and the phone soon rang, with Moratti having a go at Pérez for 'disappearing' for 40 minutes or so. Incredible!

Valdano told Spain's *AS* that, once the deal was done, he slumped into his sofa drained and exhausted. He would later confess that the Masters course on business negotiation he'd done at Harvard Business School was 'child's play' compared to the Ronaldo deal.

So the deal was concluded in the nick of time and, strangely enough, on the day Real Madrid thumped Feyenoord 3–1 to lift the European Super Cup. Ronaldo joined Real Madrid for €35m (plus the €12m player or cash situation) in a four-year deal and got his wish to join Zidane and Co. It was another juicy payday for Ronaldo and his agents, and at Adidas, the new shirts were prepared for printing. For the whole deal to complete, Nike and Ronaldo had agreed to revise their mutual contract, as Real Madrid's team kits were supplied by Adidas. As Ronaldo's personal contract stood with Nike, he could only play for a team wearing Nike kits and he had to be given the number 9 shirt to back up the R9 branding. One might think that Nike would resist such flexibility, but a lot had changed since the avaricious days of 1998. Nike had learnt a lot from the mixed publicity their Ronaldomania had spawned, and, in short, their hands were tied when their star man wanted to play for Real Madrid. Had they stood firm over their contract, it would have created a fairly stifled client relationship. As such, the contract was tweaked and Ronaldo was OK'd to wear Adidas. He would still wear Nike whenever possible, and continue to wear their footwear. As for the number 9 situation, this was the property of the bitter Fernando Morientes, who refused to give it up. Ronaldo, a bit older and wiser, was less perturbed by this these days and was happy to take the number 11 shirt.

Real Madrid made the following announcement:

> Real Madrid would like to announce that they have reached an agreement with Inter Milan for the transfer of Ronaldo and he will join the club on Monday [8 September 2002] to undergo a medical, and will then be presented to the media at the Santiago Bernabéu Stadium.

So there it was. Ronaldo now added Real Madrid to his CV of impressive clubs and had his vernissage at the Bernabéu in early September. The mandatory keep-ups out on the hallowed turf took place and all was festive. The image of Ronaldo juggling the ball with his head bears an uncanny resemblance to another south American legend, Alfredo di Stefano, voted by Real Madrid fans as their best ever player. The stance and posture are virtually identical.

Jorge Valdano, Real's accomplished sporting director and ex-World

Cup winner with Argentina, added to the mood, saying, 'It is a happy day for Real Madrid and we are very satisfied to have signed one of the most important players in the world to contribute to the prestige and spectacle in the Santiago Bernabéu.'

Club president Pérez hinted at the wider picture during Ronaldo's official presentation at the Bernabéu, saying, 'This is a great day for Real Madrid. The mixture of Real Madrid and Ronaldo is perfect because of the universal appeal that both possess.' Ronaldo had agreed to cede many image rights to the club and Pérez had also negotiated with Inter several clauses covering injury, should that happen. Pérez went on, 'One of the most important things for Real Madrid is its image. We all know Ronaldo is one of the best players in the world, but he is also one of the most universal images in the world. We will begin selling shirts bearing the player's name immediately and we are sure there will be a massive demand. In five years, we want to be in every country in the world.' Pérez was not wrong about the shirts, as in Spain alone, in the first three weeks of Ronaldo's arrival, a whopping 60,000 were sold. At €70 a time, this gave a healthy €4.2m early recoup.

Valdano was then swift to add, looking to praise Ronaldo, that the Brazilian had been willing to take a substantial pay cut (admittedly all relative in the stratospheric world of a top footballer) to join fellow *galacticos*. He went on, 'Of course, if Ronaldo had not made such a great effort, he would not be coming to the club. He was prepared to reduce his salary and showed great enthusiasm at wanting to play here.'

Valdano's kind words were well rehearsed and very intentional. The row over Morientes had upset a lot of the Madrid faithful, who held their established player in high esteem. Morientes was a proven goal-scorer, a Spaniard and an all-round nice guy. Many Madrid fans were still not convinced by Ronaldo's fitness and many saw him as mercenary and asked, 'If he can walk out on Inter Milan so easily, then what will stop him doing it to us?'

I was in Madrid at the time of the signature and the mood was decidedly cagey. I asked my good friend and lifelong Real fan Gustavo Gomez what he felt about the purchase, and he had mixed views, saying, 'For us, Morientes is a hero. We love him. Although not quite Raúl, he is hugely popular and is a good guy. His goals have been a big part of our success in the last few years, especially in the Champions League. To see the way he has been treated is not good and we want to show our support for him. OK, Ronaldo has had a great World Cup and everybody here remembers his season with Barcelona, but how fit is he? We don't know. If he breaks down again here, will he walk out on us like he's just done at Inter? They must be pretty mad about it over there. It seems a lot of money, too, for someone whose fitness is suspect. Of course we want to have players of that calibre, but he has a lot to prove. As we stand, the fans are not yet on his side.'

Rodrigo Paiva was closely involved in the whole move and he discussed with me the finer details of it and how Ronaldo felt about leaving Inter: 'All along, we had shown Inter that Ronaldo was fit and could play, but Cúper just didn't want him. Inter and their fans must know that Ronaldo was always straight and honest with them. He wanted to play for Inter. Ronaldo was frustrated but Inter made their choice; they trusted Cúper. Cúper and Moratti believed Ronaldo was finished, but he played eight games at the World Cup without a problem and they didn't trust him to play ninety minutes at the San Siro. Go figure! They had no faith in Ronaldo's recovery but had to stick to the same story to avoid the fans getting at them. How can they justify letting him leave when he was fit and the star of the World Cup? They never really wanted Ronaldo and had Crespo lined up. Remember how quickly the Crespo deal was agreed and confirmed? It was instant. It was all in hand. Another Argentinean.'

Once in Madrid, Ronaldo would have an uphill struggle for acceptance. Unable to claim to be from the *cantera* – the mystical Spanish football concept that confers special status on those who are part of local tradition, such as Raúl and coach del Bosque – he would have to do things the hard way, and for a striker, that means goals.

I spoke to respected Spanish journalist Guillem Ballague about the mood in Madrid at the time, and he echoed Gustavo's thoughts: 'He has a big job on his hands. Many here are questioning the need for such a player, and many are wondering if it is just a marketing move by Pérez. Fernando Hierro has said too that "footballers are not merchandise" and he has a point.' He went on, 'At Real, Raúl is king, and I do not see how Ronaldo can be accommodated unless del Bosque changes the style of play. Time will tell if he is a success and is accepted. Remember, it took Zidane, one of the best players around, over three months to settle, some would say longer.'

As the Spanish season got under way, Real Madrid made a steady if not spectacular start, and as September moved into October, Ronaldo still hadn't featured. The *Madrileños* were not amused.

CHAPTER 16

FIT FOR A KING – REAL MADRID 2002

The doubters were not assuaged either when, after his first training session, Ronaldo pulled up with a muscle strain. However, there was no Cúper to blame this time and it looked like the stop–start fitness shuffle would be his favourite dance in Madrid as well as Milan. As September passed by and he had still not pulled on a white shirt in anger, his debut began to seem like a mirage. Blessed with the finest assemblage of players of any present-day club side, Real had made only an average start to the season and come October were 'languishing' in fourth place. Del Bosque was under pressure to field the big new signing, but, admirably, he was not rushing things. He waited on the fitness thumbs-up from the Real medical staff and selected Ronaldo for the squad to play Deportivo Alavés at the Bernabéu on Sunday, 6 October 2002. I was in Madrid at the time and the expectation ahead of kick-off was immense. There had been several weeks of 'Is he? Isn't he?' in the press and amongst the fans but now it seemed certain that Ronaldo would feature, albeit from the bench, and tickets sold out accordingly.

Real Madrid had become '*Real*' (Royal) in 1920, when Alfonso XIII accepted their invitation to bestow his honour upon them. They were not the first team in Spain to acquire this prefix – Real Sociedad and Real Unión beat them by some years – but they are the team in Spain who have been traditionally linked ever since with the Spanish Royal Family, and Ronaldo, one of the princes of the modern game, was ready to make his royal entrance on the red carpet of the Bernabéu.

On a balmy Madrid Sunday evening, the stage couldn't have been better set. Alavés were not expected to offer much opposition and as Real Madrid took the field in their pristine white shirts it wasn't hard to see why. Zidane, Figo, Roberto Carlos, Makelele, Guti, Hierro – the list goes on. There wasn't a famous name on the Alavés team sheet and, within a minute, Zidane had given Real the lead with a masterly right-foot curling shot that nestled in the stanchion. It was poetic. Zidane was at his balletic best and, following the example of dads everywhere who have told us what an honour it was to see the likes of Puskas, Charles, Best, Charlton or Eusebio play, I took this moment to study the marvellous Frenchman, hoping one day to be able to repeat the paternal reminiscences to my children. Apart from his stunning goal in the first minute, what struck me about Zidane was his complete synchronisation with the game around him. He seemed to be able to absorb all the information the game was in the process of printing out. His slow-motion lope is hugely deceptive, for he consumes the manicured turf beneath his feet with ease. He will take a moment to run into spaces that others have vacated, then, with that automatic 180-degree left–right twitch of the head, he reconnoitres the area, assimilating all data and saving this information onto his hard drive for later. When the ball comes to him, his control is so instinctive that he rarely needs a second touch to position the ball for its next, his first touch has done that for him. With all the terrain and data stored and being processed, it is as if he is several passages of play ahead of everyone else, and with teammates alongside him of this calibre, danger is never far away. He is class.

On 30 minutes, fellow *galactico* Figo joined in with a penalty and it seemed as though a rout was on the cards. It was almost like, 'Right: Zidane, Figo – yep, you've got one. Who wants to score next?' But then Alavés got one back to quell Real's showboating and the sides went into the break at 2–1.

For the 75,000 of us inside the Bernabéu, this wasn't quite in the script, and when Alavés produced one of their better spells at the start of the second half, the mood amongst the *Madrileños* became a bit jittery. The opposition were then given the chance to draw level from the penalty spot but Iván Alonso's kick was superbly saved by Casillas. Then, on the 60-minute mark, del Bosque signalled his subs to go for a run and warm-up. Emerging from the smart Recaro-upholstered Madrid bench were Steve McManaman, Santiago Solari and, of course, Ronaldo. A huge cheer went up in the Bernabéu and a buzz of expectation zipped around the marvellous stadium like an invisible Mexican Wave. A few minutes later, expectation rose to fever pitch as the referee's assistant posted up the numbers on the electronic scoreboard. No R9 this time but his new number 11, and the moment was here. Sixty-three minutes into the Alavés game, Javier Portillo made way for Ronaldo, who crossed himself, touched the turf with his right fingers and jogged imposingly towards his striking berth.

Incredibly, 60 seconds later, he had scored and the place descended into pandemonium. From the left, compatriot Roberto Carlos swung in a cross towards Ronaldo, which, although inviting, was at an awkward shoulder height. Ronaldo, about 16 yards from goal, had to jump so he could stun the ball upwards off his upper-right chest – a difficult manoeuvre but one he managed well – and, as the ball then dropped to the turf, he shaped for the volley. There was one magical split-second moment where, having to wait for the ball to fall to volleyable height, he momentarily paused and, with perfect balance, right foot cocked and ready to deliver, he stood, motionless, like an assassin about to squeeze the trigger and take out the intended hit. Then, with the ball now ready, Ronaldo struck, the ball bouncing into the ground and then fizzing into the goal past the helpless keeper Dutruel. The Bernabéu went berserk, myself included. It was a fantastic moment and as Ronaldo's illustrious teammates rushed towards him to congratulate him, the buck-tooth grin was back again. Last seen in Yokohama, it seemed the boy from Bento Ribeiro could do no wrong once more. Not only was it a great goal for Ronaldo, it was a decisive one for Real Madrid as it put daylight between them and Alavés. Alavés were visibly done-in by the goal and their collective faces betrayed the view of, 'Christ, if they can bring Ronaldo off the bench to score, what hope have we got?'

Ronaldo's presence clearly lifted his teammates and now they were starting to play with the authority one would expect of such a bespoke team. Figo made it 4–1 on 72 minutes with a lovely finish, taken impudently with the outside of the right foot. Then, just when you thought it couldn't get any better, in the 79th minute, Steve McManaman, on for Claude Makelele, slipped a simple through ball behind the defence for Ronaldo to run onto. Rather like his Wembley goal against England back in 1996, the execution was over in a flash and with the minimum of fuss. He took McManaman's perfectly weighted ball with one touch, and, like a snooker player potting a long blue from its spot into a baulk pocket, he stroked it into the back of the net with a crisp right sidefoot of almost carefree virtuosity, the ball skimming across the green baize of the Bernabéu and into the corner. As he wheeled away, right index finger raised and the buck-tooth smile in full effect, mayhem erupted around the stadium. He turned to his onrushing teammates, grinning broadly as if to say, 'How about that, then?' It was wonderful, a great football moment. These expensively assembled *galacticos* had put on a show worthy of another planet. Alavés were simply blown away. This was football *in excelsis* and it was an honour to be there. Despite Alavés scoring a late consolation, the party couldn't be stopped and the buzz around Madrid that night was one of virile excitement and expectation. Real had put on a footballing jamboree of the highest order. Ronaldo was back in business and wearing white.

Once the hangovers had subsided the next day, Madrid's Monday morning press were gushing in their praise for the latest addition to the *galacticos*. They could have no qualms with Pérez's policy thus far as on the scoresheet were Zidane, Figo and Ronaldo, Pérez's three most expensive outlays. The Madrid sports dailies had a field day. *AS* claimed 'He's the King'. *Marca* hailed it as 'The Mother of all Debuts'. Ronaldo, showing marvellous wit when asked about which of the goals he'd enjoyed the most, paused for a moment then responded, 'Zidane's.' With the famous grin restored, he told *Marca*, 'I am happy, very happy. My goals are dedicated to the people of Madrid. I hope they made people happier. I hope to score plenty more.' As a PR exercise, goals were top of the bill for Ronaldo because in the Alavés game Raúl hadn't played due to a slight knock, but he would be back soon, and vying for Ronaldo's, or somebody else's, place.

Ronaldo vowed he would score 25 league goals that season. Bearing in mind his first game had only come in October, and with *La Liga* being one of the toughest leagues in the world, it was some claim. But in many ways it reflected the Brazilian's new-found confidence. Happy with his fitness, off the back of an outstanding World Cup and playing in a side as good as Real Madrid, he knew service and opportunity wouldn't be much of an issue. However, what he had done after such an imperious debut was to raise the level of expectation sky high in Madrid. The demanding Bernabéu crowd was now expecting this level of delirious entertainment every weekend.

Adding to this, they had not accounted for the impressive form of San Sebastian side Real Sociedad, who were surprising everybody by providing the main challenge to Real Madrid. With most onlookers eyeing Valencia or Deportivo La Coruña as the main competition, Real

Sociedad were able to put together an impressive opening to their campaign. Having nearly been relegated the season before, they made key reinforcements, with Dutchman Sander Westerveld in goal and the impish Turk, Nihat, up front. The signings bore fruit immediately. Real Madrid's arch-rivals Barcelona were in total disarray and 2002–03 would in turn prove to be one of their worst and most embarrassing seasons on record. Under Luis van Gaal, they slipped close to the relegation zone. He and Joan Gaspart would ultimately make way and, for the sake of Spanish football, Barcelona's season would thankfully be salvaged by able caretaker, the likeable Radomir Antic.

Once Madrid got into their stride, the season unfolded into a duel between them and Real Sociedad. But the autumn of the year, having started so fantastically for Ronaldo against Alavés, didn't run as smoothly as he'd hoped. Several things were still bubbling away under the surface that served to unsettle him. There was still no end of fallout from his move from Inter Milan. Ronaldo felt obliged to launch another broadside at the much put-upon Hector Cúper. He took a fierce swipe at the Argentine, claiming that he had put his career at risk. Having held his counsel for a time, he had become agitated by the continuing taunts of the Inter Milan fans who had been tearing into him, calling him a traitor and the like. Ronaldo aimed to justify his reasons for wanting away by having a go at Cúper, saying, 'He didn't play me when I was fit, and he made me train or kept me on the pitch when I wasn't. At times, he didn't even follow the advice of the doctors. I injured muscles four or five times [at Inter]. They were serious problems, not little ones. While at the World Cup, you saw that if I'm working well, I don't have problems.'

During two interviews Ronaldo did with Italy's RAI television and *Il Giorno*, he went on, saying, 'Cúper knew I was trying to recover from my knee problems and when I was close to full recovery, he didn't apply different work and fitness sessions and I had to suffer two injuries because of this. I risked my career with him.' He sharpened the knife by saying, 'I don't want to name names but 60 per cent of the team thinks like me – some of them probably detest him now, but they can't say that.' Ronaldo would later name players he felt shared his view of Cúper, highlighting teammates Emre Belozoglu and Okan Buruk as some of the others who sided with him in his rift with Cúper.

Ronaldo also admitted to being disappointed with Massimo Moratti, yet admitted he enjoys a close friendship with the Inter president. 'When I asked him to decide between me or Cúper, he told me that he couldn't sack him, but he told me to wait because things could change,' he said. 'But I have ended my patience and did not tolerate him. I hope he [Moratti] will stay a long time at Inter for the good of himself and the supporters. I have very good personal feelings about Moratti but he disappointed me.'

Then, with a Parthian shot at Cúper, and one he knew would hurt the Argentine below the belt, he went on, 'After five years, during which I never had any complaints towards the club, he [Moratti] preferred a coach who has never won.' Cúper would struggle to shake this nearly-man tag. 'I expected more faith – evidently it has not been so.'

Ronaldo then went on to add a personal message for Inter's fans: 'I love them and I'm not a betrayer,' he concluded. 'I'm worried because they think false things. My wish was to stay with Inter, but it was necessary to leave to eliminate a problem.'

Cúper, visibly fed up with all the handbags and keen to focus on Inter's *scudetto* campaign, would finally break his silence too, but with admirable grace refused to have a go directly at Ronaldo when he could easily have done so. He told the Italian press that Ronaldo's attacks on him were convenient as an excuse for him wanting to leave. 'I am the soft target,' he said. 'He won't attack Moratti or the rest of the squad, or simply admit that he wanted to join Real Madrid. So me, the coach, is weakest and is always the easiest target.'

CHAPTER 17

RECOGNITION AND RESENTMENT – REAL MADRID, AUTUMN 2002

Back in Madrid, the waters were getting choppier. The Bernabéu crowd had become expectant to the point of being assumptive about the success of their team. Their usual competitors were having very average seasons and, even better for Real, Barcelona were having a calamitous season of soap-opera proportions. But inevitably in football, nothing is ever a foregone conclusion, and Real Sociedad, as we have seen, emerged to challenge the men in white. When they came to the Bernabéu in November for the top-of-the-table clash, they played with admirable spirit and resolve and held the *galacticos* to a 0–0 draw, a result and performance that drew howls of derision for the home team. Real Madrid had won only once in nine previous *La Liga* and Champions League games and their autumnal form was shoddy for a team of such talent. Patience was wearing thin amongst the expectant *Madrileños* and the brunt of their ire was directed at Ronaldo.

During this match, Ronaldo had probably his worst game this far for Real Madrid and he was first to admit it. On Real Madrid's website, he stated frankly, 'I understand they [the fans] are angry and they protested, since that was one of the worst games I have played in my life.' Real Madrid's next game would be against the stricken Barcelona, and Ronaldo went on, 'My best form will return, certainly. Of that I have no doubts and my first opportunity will be in Barcelona. There, I think about delivering the goods and I want to score for many obvious reasons. But, by the end of the year, Madrid will be in the highest position because we have the best team in the world.' But Ronaldo wouldn't get the chance to put his rhetoric into action. That week, Brazil played a friendly against World Cup heroes South Korea in Seoul. They won an entertaining game 3–2, with Ronaldo scoring twice, but whilst away he picked up a nasty dose of flu, and was forced to pull out of the Barcelona game.

Ronaldo had travelled to Barcelona but then U-turned back to Madrid as his fever was too strong to play. Many Catalans cited this as him having bottled the game – his first against Barcelona for Madrid – and as evidence that he didn't fancy a repeat of the hateful abuse heaped upon Luis Figo, who had had a barrage of items thrown at him, including mobile phones and the odd pig's head, each time he went to take a corner.

I asked Sky Sport's Guillem Ballague, himself from Barcelona, albeit an Espanyol fan, about this and what his views were on the reception Ronaldo would have received. Guillem explains, 'For a start, I think he was genuinely ill and missed the game through a valid reason. As for the abuse he would have received, yes, it would have been bad, but I don't think he would've received the stick Figo got. You have to remember that Figo went directly from Barcelona to Real, whereas Ronaldo was at Inter for five years in between. Figo was adored by the Camp Nou, he won titles with them, they thought of him as one of their own. On the night of the game last year, there was a banner saying, "We hate you so much because we loved you so much". For me that sums the whole thing up.'

Ronaldo's fitness again became a huge talking point in Madrid. This time it was his physical bulk that was causing the headlines. Many thought him several kilos overweight and, to use boxing parlance, he did now look more light-heavy than middleweight. His neck was of Tysonesque girth and stories in Madrid abounded that his favourite eatery was the Hard Rock Café, where he allegedly consumed hamburgers and fizzy drinks with gusto. However, not only was he scooping up the quarter-pounders with cheese, he was also gorging himself on the cream of football's awards, collecting the European Player of the Year and World Player of the Year (for an unprecedented third time) within the same week. *World Soccer Magazine* readers also voted him their World Player of the Year. But, as he received this avalanche of recognition, many in Madrid still resented his presence there.

The award allocations were not universally well received and Ronaldo was deemed fortunate to have scooped the double after a patchy stop–start season. It was his performance at the World Cup which sealed the baubles but many, Johan Cruyff included, felt the awards were unjust. Speaking after Ronaldo's receipt of the Ballon D'Or European Player of the Year Award, Cruyff, a thrice winner himself, claimed Ronaldo shouldn't even have been in the top three and that, 'Thierry Henry, Roberto Carlos and Raúl all deserved it more. Ronaldo has had a great World Cup but he has played very few matches in the season, while Henry had a fabulous season.' He went on, 'Raúl [who amazingly is still to win and was overlooked in favour of Liverpool's Michael Owen the season before] has been playing very well for a number of years and Roberto Carlos has played very well again this year.' He had a good point.

Just before Christmas, Real Madrid jetted off to play in the Toyota-sponsored Intercontinental Club Championship in Tokyo. For Ronaldo, this would be an earlier-than-expected return to the Yokohama stadium that he had graced so thrillingly not six months earlier. His fame now assured in the Far East, Pérez was purring with approbation as Ronaldo stepped off the plane as a Madrid player and the sound of Japanese cash registers filled the air. Shirt sales were going through the roof. Ronaldo, his fitness now a weekly talking point, had declared himself fit and vowed to stay off the burgers. He gave an early warning to the opposition, Olimpia from Paraguay, that he was looking to add the world club crown to the World Cup-winners' medal. He told waiting reporters, 'It feels great to be back in Yokohama. To win the World Cup here was such a special achievement, but that's in the past and now I hope I can make some more history tomorrow. One of the reasons I joined Real was because of their long history. I always dreamed of playing in the Intercontinental Cup because it decides who the number one club in the world is.'

As ever from Ronaldo, nothing too earth-shattering in his comments, but good steady stuff. Real Madrid were keen to rectify the defeat in Japan two years earlier, losing 2–1 to a Martin Palermo-inspired Boca Juniors of Argentina. It was all set to be an auspicious occasion as Olimpia, like Real Madrid, were also knee-deep in centenary celebrations. Whoever won would have the perfect reason for further revelry. It was ultimately a dour game – when is the Intercontinental Cup anything but? – but again, Ronaldo showed his fondness for the big time by opening the scoring in the 13th minute, latching onto a Raúl through-ball to strike a right-foot shot past Ricardo Taverelli in the Olimpia goal. That's pretty much how it remained until the 86th minute when Guti, on as sub, headed in the second and that was that. Ronaldo was awarded the man-of-the-match award by the delirious Japanese and left the field weighed down by several huge trinkets.

For Ronaldo, it completed a quite extraordinary 12 months, bookended by goals of differing magnitude, but of equal importance to the Brazilian. Appropriately it had started with a goal, the much-heralded comeback one versus Brescia, and it had ended with one, the lucrative first against Olimpia. In between he had struggled with niggling injuries on the comeback trail with Inter Milan but had still scored invaluable goals to keep them in the hunt for *lo scudetto*. The World Cup needs no further coverage, and once the messy saga of his summer transfer to Real Madrid had been concluded, he got on with scoring goals for *les Merengues*. However – and this remains a fascinating insight into the machinations, traditions and expectancies of a major club and their supporters – he was still a long way from winning the *Madrileños* over.

CHAPTER 18

TIME TO DELIVER –
REAL MADRID, SPRING 2003

As 2003 arrived, Real Madrid were still struggling to find their best form either in *La Liga* or in the Champions League. Despite a virtuoso display in thumping Valencia 4–1 at a waterlogged Bernabéu, coach Vicente del Bosque was coming under pressure and the Madrid crowd were somewhat miffed that the unfancied Real Sociedad were giving them such a good run for their money. That humiliation of Valencia had seen Ronaldo and Zidane combine to lethal effect, both demonstrating the necessary technical brilliance to adapt their games to the treacherous surface. Each capped outstanding performances with goals.

Ronaldo went on to score a particularly crucial goal in the Champions League in early February to beat Borussia Dortmund 2–1, but he was still getting lambasted from all corners. His weight still looked on the bulky side and even German legend and know-all Franz Beckenbauer chipped in with his two-euros' worth when, observing the Borussia Dortmund game, he commented with typical Germanic precision, 'Ronaldo still looks about four kilos overweight. He did not look interested against Dortmund and even with his goal, his input was low. When he went off, Real Madrid looked a much better team.'

Ronaldo's lacklustre showing against Dortmund came a week after coach del Bosque had given Ronaldo an uncharacteristic dressing down at a coaches' conference he was attending. Pretty much unprovoked, he explained, 'At Real Madrid, we are a strong unit but there is one player who puts himself before the team.' As a ripple of surprise went round the room, del Bosque continued, 'All the players we have, with the exception of one, are very focused on working for the team. The only player who is different to the rest is Ronaldo.' It seemed a curious and unnecessary broadside at the time, and del Bosque was later quick to try to retract his comments, saying in true modern-day Blairite style that his words had been taken out of context and he had been misquoted. For Pérez, it was an unwanted lapse in camp unity and something he felt was very 'un-Real Madrid'.

The situation was becoming tense and a further incident towards the end of the Dortmund game in Madrid highlighted the ongoing tensions within the camp, much of them hovering around Ronaldo. Ronaldo, having scored what would prove to be the decisive goal, was substituted in the 73rd minute and left the pitch to a decidedly lukewarm reception. It was another of those games where his overall body language and demeanour had seemed disinterested, and his work rate patchy. This was a game Real Madrid simply had to win, and the rest of the team had run around like fireflies all night, none more so than Raúl, as Real Madrid struggled to overcome a typically dogged and resistant German outfit. For Ronaldo, it was a Románioesque kind of performance where, having done virtually nothing all game, he popped up to score the winner, giving him sufficient ammunition to quell his would-be critics. But the critics were still verbose and Spanish daily *AS* summed up the mood, saying, 'Every day, the Bernabéu is more Raúl's and less Ronaldo's. Possibly this game will mark a watershed in the relationship between the two players and the Madrid fans. Raúl left the pitch like a hero; Ronaldo, with more jeers than cheers.'

With only about four minutes left of the Dortmund game, Vicente del Bosque decided to make a substitution. He glanced up at Fernando Morientes, who had been limbering up in the rain for 20 minutes, and said, 'On you go.'

Morientes replied, 'On *you* go, you son of a bitch!'

Not a very nice way to speak to your manager, but one that reflected the divisions within what appeared externally to be a harmonious camp. Morientes had recently been brought back into the side and had been playing well, but he was clearly still smarting from his treatment over the previous summer and his puppet part in the Ronaldo transfer saga. He had played a major part in a run that had brought Real Madrid three European Cups in five years, and understandably would have felt he was an innocent pawn in a shameful injustice. Even worse, his beloved

Madrid had been willing to offload him to Barcelona; something he would never consider as a *Madridista*.

This perception of injustice was common among fans at the time of Ronaldo's signature and seemed to be taking hold again now, and despite Ronaldo's consistent goal-scoring record for his new club, they were siding with their own in Morientes. Rumours were circling that some club staff, as well as fans, felt Ronaldo was not pulling his weight, was not worth the king's ransom he was earning and was living on past glories. Stories also emerged in Madrid that Ronaldo preferred playing golf to training, that he was often seen out late at night trawling the town for action and that the burger habit was still in evidence. One report even claimed that a woman had filed a complaint to the police that her neighbour was keeping her up all night playing samba music until the early hours. She refused to name the carousing neighbour but said, 'He's a footballer who scores a lot of goals.' Even better for the tabloids was that she didn't live anywhere near Ronaldo's official home, sprouting a school of thought that he had a party pad in the centre of town.

The situation looked gloomy. The fans seemed against him and unappreciative of his goals, del Bosque, however badly or not he may have been misquoted, had berated him the week before and with the Morientes situation it was evident that there were factions within the Real dressing-room that would be happier without him. He did himself no favours either by picking up another thigh strain whilst playing golf when he should have been in Salamanca training with the squad. To add to the mix, rumours surfaced from Madrid that his marriage to Milene was also on the rocks. There was plenty to ponder for the Brazilian.

It wasn't just Ronaldo who was feeling the pressure in Madrid. Del Bosque was coming under fire too. Real's league form, although good, was still not stellar and they were in a right old dogfight with Real Sociedad. Likewise, their Champions League form had been unconvincing. One of the main reasons for this was that their defence had shown alarming vulnerability throughout the season. The veteran star Fernando Hierro was showing his age and one can sympathise with del Bosque, who had consistently pleaded with Pérez that, as nice as all these *galacticos* were to have in the side, it was a top-class centre-back that, as coach, he really wanted. His pleas would fall on deaf ears as, unfortunately for del Bosque, grizzly centre-backs don't sell many shirts and Pérez, soon after the Dortmund game, crystallised his modus operandi for the club in an indirect defence of Ronaldo, saying, 'Our strategy is very clear: at Real Madrid we have to have the best. Why? Because they represent the best return on your investment. And not only on the field of play. When you sign a star player, the club gains in its international projection and that translates into economic gains.'

Another reason for Real's misfiring was that, although their play was stunning in patches, it hadn't reached the consistency expected of such a great squad. Many saw this being due to their slowness to accommodate Ronaldo's style of play. Gerry Armstrong had been onto this all season and regularly explained what was needed during his Sky Sports co-commentary stints. I caught up with him again in February 2003 and we discussed the impact Ronaldo had thus far had.

Gerry explained, 'For me, Ronaldo's favourite position is lurking around the inside-left position, just inside the opposition half and on the centre-back's shoulder. What he loves is to be put through, use his explosive pace to outrun the defender and confront the keeper, and then have the option with his stepover of coming inside onto his right foot, or going the other way past the keeper and finishing with his left. What Real Madrid have been doing on the whole so far this season is playing the ball into Ronaldo's feet, whilst he is in that area just inside the opposition's half. He doesn't want it into his feet there as otherwise he has to lay it off and look for a one–two for him to run onto or he has to turn and take the defender on, for which, from a standing start, although he's still quick, he hasn't quite got the lightning pace he once had.'

It was fascinating stuff and Gerry cited several instances, notably in the horror show against Real Sociedad, where Ronaldo seemed to have feet of clay and couldn't get moving at all.

Gerry then went on to proffer accurate insights that would ultimately prove the catalyst to changing Ronaldo's whole career at Real Madrid: 'I sense that their style is changing, though, and one man has initiated this, and it's no surprise that it's Raúl – for me, one of the sharpest thinkers in the game and the first player to decipher Ronaldo's play. Notice how in recent games – and the Intercontinental [Cup] was one example and a goal came from it – Raúl has been putting in those balls behind the defence for Ronaldo to charge onto. I've noticed in recent weeks that their build-up play has been much more studied, more patient, with a view to waiting for the right moment to spring Ronaldo. I think, once the whole team gets used to this, Real Madrid and Ronaldo will become unstoppable, because, along with all the other attacking options they have, if they can utilise Ronaldo in the optimum way, they will be a frightening prospect.'

Gerry's prophetic words were soon statements of fact, as in Real's next game, away to our poor old friends Alavés, Real Madrid and Ronaldo struck top gear, thrashing them 5–1 with a blistering display of counter-attacking football. Ronaldo banged in a hat-trick, each goal from the classic Ronaldo archive, sprinting free from the inside-left channel, having been put in by who else but Raúl, charging down on goal and skinning the last defender with a trademark stepover then finishing with chilling ease. The third in particular was a Ronaldo scrapbook goal, culminating with a triple stepover to sit the centre-back on his backside. It was rousing stuff. Raúl netted the other two and it was a happy night for Real, this time wearing their black away kit as if to add to the solemnity of the defeat they had just administered. Alas, with Ronaldo's hat-trick coming against lowly Alavés, the Real Madrid faithful were still not fully taken in and suggested that anybody could score three against 'that' defence. They were proving to be hard taskmasters.

As March went on, Real Madrid's Champions League defence took them to freezing Moscow to play Lokomotiv. For Real, it was a must-win game, but the freezing conditions and corrugated pitch were not exactly to their liking. Real were lucky in this game: there is no other way to describe it. Lokomotiv missed chances galore and Iker Casillas had another of those games he always seems to have where he somehow gets in the way of everything. He also seems to have the uncanny knack of persuading attackers to hit gilt-edged chances straight at him. He was heroic in keeping his sheet clean, and with that, Real duly burgled a 1–0 win, with Ronaldo adding to his list of precious goals with a rare header and one which put Real Madrid through to the lucrative knockout phases. Wearing black tights underneath his white kit and with black gloves too, Ronaldo looked every inch the Brazilian in an unfamiliar climate. He didn't do much in the game at all but, inevitably, was there at the business end, getting on the end of Figo's cross in the 35th minute to break the hearts of the Lokomotiv faithful, who were desperate for a result against their illustrious visitors. Added to his winner against Borussia Dortmund, these two were worth over €15m to Real Madrid, as they propelled them into the next phase. Young Javier Portillo's 92nd-minute equaliser away against Borussia Dortmund was worth a few pesetas too.

Despite all the ruminations going on behind the scenes at the Bernabéu, the team had made it through to the quarter-finals of the

TIME TO DELIVER – REAL MADRID, SPRING 2003

Champions League yet again and had been drawn to play English giants Manchester United – a mouthwatering tie and, for many, one worthy of the final, to be staged that year at Manchester United's Old Trafford home in sunny Salford. Both clubs are giants of the world game and their history has illuminated European football for decades. Both have a justified reputation of playing attacking, flair-laden football and both are the envy of most other clubs for the way they have embraced the global marketing opportunities afforded by the modern game. In short, they are footballing powerhouses. But at the end of the day, it's not how many shirts you sell or how many hits your website receives; it's how good your team is and what silverware it brings home. This two-leg tie would prove to be a classic.

Sir Alex Ferguson would rant in typical style that the draw was a fix to eliminate Manchester United – myopic words he would subsequently be forced to retract – but it was United who had the favourable away leg first. The game, played in the Bernabéu on 8 April 2003, was a night to remember. A packed house witnessed Real Madrid treat United almost with contempt, United's 'Red Devils' seeming overawed by both the occasion and their opposition. Where United were insipid, Real were inspired, some of their football touching the highest peaks, with Zidane and Raúl in particular exhibiting a finesse and touch often missing in such do-or-die encounters. Real Madrid put on a spectacle and toyed with United as if it were an exhibition game. The first half in particular, for the neutral observer, was nothing short of fantastic. Even die-hard Man United fans must have secretly admired the mauling the men in red were subjected to. It reminded me of one of those warm-up drills so prevalent these days, where the team form a circle and one player goes in the middle. The aim of the drill is to prevent the lone player getting the ball. The only difference during this game was it seemed that it was the whole Manchester United XI in the middle, desperately trying to get the ball off the Real team effortlessly stroking it about around them.

Zidane was patrolling the left side with imperious, almost arrogant authority, ever aware of the shuttling runs of Roberto Carlos in assistance. Raúl and Ronaldo would provide the inside options and then, every now and again, Luis Figo would wander over as if to say 'Let me have a go' and then proceed to dazzle. Figo, keen to show his worth in the light of all the David Beckham transfer speculation, was outstanding and put his high-profile suitor in the shade, scoring the opener with a spectacular curling effort that arched into Barthez's top corner.

RONALDO

Real went into the break 2–0 to the good. It could have been many more. They went 3–0 up in the 49th minute when Raúl capped as good a performance as you'll see with a stunning shot from the edge of the box after he'd linked up so dynamically with the peerless Zidane. United, punch drunk, on the ropes and waiting for the referee to stop the fight, did the only thing they could do and came out fighting, staggering into the Madrid night looking to land a precious away goal. To their credit, they got it, thanks to the tireless Dutchman van Nistelrooy. United hadn't played well but they did create chances. They had the better of the second half and could have snatched a few more, but again Casillas showed his uncanny knack of standing in the middle of his goal and letting profligate strikers shoot straight at him. In truth, the game could have been 5–3, 6–5 or 5–4 – pick a number – it was such a festival of brilliance.

But one man hadn't shone like the rest of the stars in the firmament: Ronaldo. He looked distracted and was substituted, yet again, towards the end. The Madrid press snubbed him the day after by barely mentioning his name, their columns bulging under the praise for Zidane, Raúl and Figo. Ronaldo had left the field to a chorus of boos, the only negative feature amongst an otherwise fantastic night of grade A football. It was an incredible spectacle to see the *Madrileños* boo one of their own players, and Ronaldo at that, after such an overall display from their team. Personally, I find the Real fans tedious and to boo players of the calibre their team could boast is, among many things, plain rude. OK, these stars may have off-days now and again, but who doesn't? But booing them, or waving their craven white hankies at them? Come on. They should come to the English Premiership; then they'd really have something to boo about.

For Ronaldo, this was a pretty low point, but he tried to put a brave face on the situation, saying, 'I take the whistles and boos very calmly. You can't always be on top form. The Real Madrid crowd are very demanding, there's enormous pressure, but I can handle it. I'm sure that, with time, everything will work out.'

Although present at the party against Manchester United, he hadn't really enjoyed it, had not been able to join in properly and had left early. He was desperate to be fully accepted by the fans. He had come to Madrid to play with its illustrious cast and to play at a club where he wasn't the sole superstar, where he wasn't expected to score wonder goals every week and where the burden of expectation wasn't plonked squarely on his shoulders as it had been at Barcelona and Inter Milan. He had this at Real, the Manchester United game proving a perfect example as the other *galacticos* weaved their magic, Gary Neville referring to the game as like playing against the Harlem Globetrotters. But something was still missing from the jigsaw: he wanted to be accepted.

If I've discovered one thing about Ronaldo during my research for this book, it is that not only is he a very useful footballer, he also has immense self-belief. Because of this, he doesn't quit and he always looks forward. He needed these attributes during this period and, as the return leg against Manchester United beckoned, he was under increasing pressure from the Madrid fans who were initiating the process of giving up on him.

If the first game in the Bernabéu had been brilliant, then most of us had to reach for the thesaurus and seek new adjectives to describe the return leg at Old Trafford. It was as good a game of football as you could see. Almost like a *Rocky* film, these two heavyweights went toe to toe and slugged the life out of each other, like Creed and Balboa, blow after blow, rarely needing the solace of the canvas for a breather or to re-orientate. This was what footie is all about. What a game!

The match drew parallels with their meeting at Old Trafford in 2000, best remembered for Fernando Redondo's heavenly backheel-cum-Cruyff-turn that skinned Henning Berg and helped create Raúl's tap-in. Real Madrid went on to win the game 3–2 and progress to the final and the trophy. That night, they'd worn their black strips and, with some symbolism, they wore them again tonight. They had their healthy 3–1 lead from the first leg, but at Old Trafford anything can happen on a European night and, with the precious away goal, Ferguson's inspiration and Real's propensity to leak goals, United knew they had a chance.

However, Sir Alex Ferguson, again showing his recent tendency to leave his best players out, mysteriously benched David Beckham. Ironically, Steve McManaman, perennial bencher for Madrid, started, providing a complete reversal of their respective fortunes for England. For Ferguson, it was a decision that would prove folly and would again contribute to Manchester United's weak record in this tournament. For a club of their stature, wealth and Champions League experience, one win in nine attempts is not acceptable. This deficiency was regularly covered up by outstanding Premiership campaigns, something the Manchester United board and supporters seemed too happy to accept. As we have seen, Real Madrid tuned in several years ago to the real prize being the European Cup, with the domestic league being just a bonus.

Man United knew that they had to score at least twice to progress and came out of the blocks accordingly. They were hungry and looked in the mood. They'd taken some stick for the way they had been toyed with at the Bernabéu and were keen to show these *galacticos* that the Red Devils were a team of high talent too. United had the better of the early exchanges and almost took the lead when Ruud van Nistelrooy beat Michel Salgado only to see his fierce drive tipped over by that man Casillas. Old Trafford was buzzing and high on expectation. Its team had made a good start. But then it all changed and I do not recall in any game I've ever been to a goal of such party-pooping quality. It had been all United to this point. The crowd were right behind them, expectation was high and the Madrid defence had looked predictably vulnerable under the initial onslaught. But then Veron, looking every bit like a player who hadn't played for six weeks, was dispossessed on the edge of the Real Madrid area by Zidane. Zidane exchanged passes with Roberto Carlos and Steve McManaman and then found Guti. Then Guti, echoing the advice dished out by Gerry Armstrong earlier in the season, sprung Ronaldo with a perfect pass. Ronaldo, with Rio Ferdinand in vain pursuit, latched on to it, burst forward, then unleashed a bullet of a shot that zoomed past Barthez on his near post. Real Madrid were 1–0 up after 12 minutes, and 4–1 up on aggregate. Old Trafford went deathly quiet, a veiled hush suffocating all noise bar the joyous cheers of the Madrid players. Ronaldo had showed once more his ability to score goals of blistering quality. There were two split-seconds of flat-footedness, one from Ferdinand and the other from Barthez. Although Barthez was criticised for the goal because it beat him on his nearside, this was somewhat harsh, as, rather like his semi-final goal against Turkey, Ronaldo had surprised everybody by taking the ball early. This, and the pace and precision he imparted on the ball, made Barthez and Ferdinand look like dummies. It was brutally efficient and a withering blow to United's hopes.

United, as is their norm, refused to lie down and as the crowd got over the shock of the reversal, they began to play the attacking stuff they are famous for. A storming game unfolded, with the multitude of stars from either side each giving it their all. Solskjaer, the slayer of Bayern Munich back in 1999, was darting around and his combinations with van Nistelrooy were causing the relatively cumbersome Hierro many a problem. It was this combination that got United back in it just before half-time, with van Nistelrooy turning in a Solskjaer cross. It was 1–1 at the break and United still had the whiff of a chance.

Man United came out firing and again had some early chances, but once more their bubble of optimism was pricked by a piece of *galactico* magic, again against the run of play. This time it was Figo who embarked on a mesmerising run, with the ball never anything but fully under his command. He advanced on the United penalty area and caressed a lovely right-foot shot that thudded onto the bar, Barthez nowhere. The ball came out, United were unable to clear and Roberto Carlos squared to Ronaldo for a routine tap-in. It was 2–1 on the night; and 5–2 on aggregate. Out came the calculators and the UEFA away-goal guidebooks and it was clear that United now had the proverbial mountain to climb.

Undeterred, they came back at Real and forced Iván Helguera into an uncharacteristic error, turning a Juan Sebastian Veron shot into his own goal for 2–2. Many an observer had given up trying to work out how many United now needed and just got on with enjoying this feast before them. Boy, it was good stuff!

More chances came and went but then came the real moment of brilliance. In the 55th minute, Figo, again on one of his wriggly runs, fed Ronaldo just inside the Man United half. With the United defence now terrified of this awesome menace, they fatally back-pedalled. Ronaldo burst forward, a stepover here, a stepover there and then bang! A howitzer of a right-foot drive that screamed high and handsome past Barthez, scorching into the back of his goal like a fireball. Ronaldo's celebration was this time one of cool, measured satisfaction. There were no histrionics, no kissing or pile-ups, but the cold look of an assassin having terminated his prey. His trademark right finger was raised but the look in his eye said, 'That's the one. That's the one that will get them [the *Madridistas*]. That's the one they can't ignore.' And he was right. That hat-trick, so devastating and clinical in its execution, so debilitating to Manchester United, was the performance which not only took Real Madrid through, but finally seemed to have silenced the doubters among the *Madridistas* and convinced them that Ronaldo was the real deal. The Manchester United faithful were in no doubt either, and when Ronaldo was substituted late on, 67,000 rose to their feet to give him a rapturous standing ovation, something which momentarily startled him, and something he would remember with great fondness.

Vainly and hopelessly late, Ferguson brought on Beckham, who had been visibly squirming on the bench in his eagerness to get on. By now, speculation was high about his possible move to Real Madrid in the summer and many feel this was one of the reasons Ferguson chose to leave him out. Beckham had only just rid his ubiquitous face of the much publicised nick above his eye after Ferguson had landed a rogue football boot there after a dressing-room tantrum. But Beckham's impact was immediate as he curled in yet another masterly free kick and stabbed in a late goal to give United the game 4–3 on the night, but the tie was Real's, winners by a dizzy aggregate score of 6–5. It was one of those games that leave you breathless and many of the crowd needed a moment or two just to take it all in after the final whistle. Those present knew they had witnessed something pretty special: an effervescent chemical reaction of world talent, glowing like a freshly lit strip of magnesium ribbon. Had the game been classed as a substance, the box would have read 'Caution: Highly Flammable'. Safety goggles were needed to protect the eye from its incandescent glow. We had seen not just a cracking game, been privileged to sit ringside to watch a rare assemblage of talent, but also a hat-trick of stunning quality by one of the icons of the modern era. All this in one night was a treat indeed.

In the press conferences after the game, both parties were effusive in their praise for Ronaldo. Jorge Valdano purred with satisfaction, 'He had three shots at goal and scored three times. Other players may have more chances, but they can't turn everything they touch into gold.'

Sir Alex Ferguson put his disappointment to one side for a moment and admitted, 'You can't legislate for someone like Ronaldo. You just can't prepare for a player producing something as special as that third goal.'

I spoke to Sir Bobby Robson shortly after the Manchester United game and asked him what he thought of Ronaldo's performance. As proud of his old charge as ever, he said, 'Well, what can you say? Brilliant. What a hat-trick. But I tell you, he's still not fully fit, or at least he isn't quite the player he was pre-injury. He's 20 per cent less of the player I had at Barcelona, believe me, and he can still perform like that. Fantastic.' Fascinating words indeed from football's favourite septuagenarian but he does have a point, and it perhaps explains why, with the extra 20 per cent he had at Barcelona, Sir Bobby referred to him as being 'as good as Pelé'.

Ronaldo returned to Madrid a hero. The press soaked it all up and for the first time their praise wasn't caveated by snide remarks or jibes about his fitness. There was no suggestion that 'he could do better', for they had all just witnessed a hat-trick that couldn't be bettered. For the first time, he felt not just accepted at the Bernabéu but actually needed.

TIME TO DELIVER – REAL MADRID, SPRING 2003

This would be demonstrated in the semi-final against Juventus, now managed again by our old friend Marcello Lippi. The first leg took place on 6 May 2003 at the Bernabéu. The game came only a few days after Real had suffered a major reversal in their *La Liga* hopes, being stuffed 5–1 at home by Mallorca. It was a curious result, one of those rogue ones that can sometimes punctuate a season, but with visitors of the calibre of Juventus in town, it was a blip that couldn't be repeated.

Juventus were on their way to yet another *scudetto* and their side contained all the usual Juventus traits of organisation, discipline and toughness. Creativity and skill were provided by Alessandro Del Piero and the waspish Czech Pavel Nedved. Ronaldo and Real would have a game on their hands. The tie would encapsulate many of the differences and contrasts evident not only in Spanish and Italian football but also the different approaches of the two clubs themselves. The respective press had a field day, with Spain denouncing the Italian game as medieval, colourless and even barbaric, compared to the artistry and flair of *La Liga*. The Italians were happy to lap this up with a 'Let's wait and see, shall we?' attitude. The first game proved pretty dour, as Juventus inevitably came to stifle the match and then take the tie back to Turin. Del Bosque confounded and surprised many of his critics and went for a more aggressive formation and line-up, especially in light of the drubbing handed out by Mallorca at the weekend. Guti got the nod ahead of the more defensive Flavio Conceicão, something which drew surprise from, amongst others, Fernando Hierro, who was probably wondering where his extra defensive cover was going to come from on the night.

Ronaldo, now with the home crowd right behind him, opened the scoring in the 23rd minute after a smart one–two with Morientes (another positive addition to del Bosque's line-up) and a clinical side-foot finish into the corner of Buffon's goal. But then Juventus nicked one back just before the break, giving them that vital other Euro currency, the away goal. Del Piero had easily slipped a sluggish Hierro and pulled back for Trezeguet to score. Where a *galactico* had scored, a weak link in the armour at the back had undone the good work. Del Bosque would again rue his lack of defensive steel. Hierro had been a magnificent servant to Real Madrid and Spain, and was a player of the highest quality, but, at 35, Father Time was tapping him on the shoulder and the rigours presented by Champions League football this season looked a step beyond him.

But then that all-too-common side of the Italian game reared its ugly head. Ronaldo, buoyed by his new sense of belonging, was having a great game and running the Juventus back line ragged. 'Enough's enough,' the uncompromising Italian stopper Mark Iuliano seemed to think, and in the 40th minute went through the back of him with a scything challenge, causing Ronaldo to fall to the ground and writhe in agony. He was down for several minutes receiving attention and was clearly in trouble. Iuliano picked up a yellow card, thus missing the return game. Ronaldo spent the interval receiving treatment but, on the resumption, it was obvious all was not well and, in clear discomfort and disappointment, he was substituted in the 50th minute. Roberto Carlos slammed in a late winner to give the *Merengues* a slender advantage, but all attention was on the Ronaldo injury and whether he would be fit for the crucial next leg. Claude Makelele had also been felled and would definitely miss the return game in Turin.

The Madrid press were vitriolic in their overall condemnation of Juventus's methods. Smarting that, on balance, the scoreline definitely favoured Juventus, they climbed into the Italians in general and slammed them as a bunch of thugs with no understanding of how to play football the correct way.

With the return leg the following week, Ronaldo didn't have long to recover and ultimately failed in the race to be fit. He would start the game in Turin on the bench. As with all latter-stage Champions League games, this was a massive one. All sorts of things were at stake: club prestige and stature, footballing cultures, national pride and identity. It was huge. Juventus would start slight favourites, not just because of their away goal but also due to Real Madrid being slightly under-strength without Ronaldo and Makelele. Raúl would return to replace Ronaldo but was still not fully match fit after his bout of appendicitis. Juventus would also welcome back Dutch terrier Edgar Davids and Alessio Tacchinardi to firm up their midfield.

The Stadio Delle Alpi was packed and the snow-capped Alps peeked through in the background, providing a stunning backdrop. But Madrid looked sloppy and were soon behind, David Trezeguet poking in from close range. This stirred Real into life, and with Zidane starting to remind Turin of the magic he had graced them with for five seasons, they probed for the equaliser. Guti should have got it but shot straight at Buffon. Real slipped further behind when Del Piero again taunted Hierro and slipped a darting shot past Casillas to put Juventus 2–0 ahead at the break. Juventus had played easily their best football of their campaign.

TIME TO DELIVER – REAL MADRID, SPRING 2003

For many Mancunians, their presence in the semis left a bad taste as Manchester United had beaten them with ease on two occasions in the previous group stage. But they needed to be at their best to play Real Madrid. Real were 3–2 down on aggregate and del Bosque now needed some magic. In acute contrast to the season as a whole, where he had routinely substituted Ronaldo, he now called upon the Brazilian, who was still less than fully fit, to save Real's hold on the European Cup. Ironic indeed. Ronaldo came on in the 52nd minute but looked visibly restricted. Remember, Ronaldo had lambasted Cúper for playing him half-fit but he now had no similar words for del Bosque. The tie was moving into its final stages and Real Madrid needed something and needed it quick. Ronaldo managed to spring Juventus's rigid back line and burst into the box, whereupon Paolo Montero, the Uruguayan even more notorious than Iuliano, duly felled him. Referee Urs Meier had no hesitation in pointing to the spot: penalty Real Madrid. Ronaldo had done it again.

Talk about crucial pens! The kick was entrusted to Figo, Real's regular penalty taker. A goal would square the tie at 3–3, away goals even, and force extra time. With Real now in the ascendancy, they would be favourites to prevail. Up stepped Figo. Figo's penalty-taking technique is that of the stuttering run: waiting for the goalkeeper to commit and then planting the ball the other way. He had had great success with it, but tonight he was up against Gianluigi Buffon, the world's most expensive keeper, also currently regarded as the best, and surely the only keeper cool enough and good enough to get away with wearing a pink goalie jersey. The pair stood facing each other, motionless, eyeing one another up and down and posturing like a pair of Clint Eastwoods, 'Go ahead, punk' pulsing through their thought patterns. As Figo commenced his run, he did the famous stutter, but Buffon, fool in name only, was wise to it and stood firm, as if to say, 'Go on, Luis, you commit, 'cos I ain't.' Figo, flummoxed by this, arrived at the ball with Buffon still as yet uncommitted and it threw the Portuguese completely. Not knowing which side to put the ball and with his routine rumbled, he struck a tame shot that Buffon saved easily. Buffon had done him, and with it Real's and Ronaldo's dreams of reaching the final. It was brilliant goalkeeping.

Nedved scored a third for Juventus in the 73rd minute, giving them a 4–2 lead on aggregate. The importance of Buffon's save was highlighted fully when Zidane scored late on to make it 4–3, a goal which would have clinched the tie on away goals had Figo converted. For Ronaldo, it was more Juventus-induced heartache. They had robbed him of *lo scudetto* in 1998 at Inter, they had done it again in 2002 and now they had robbed him of his dream of the Champions League. For good measure, they had also injured him in the process.

Real returned to Madrid to lick their wounds and the Italian press wasted no time in thumbing their noses to their Spanish colleagues. The Spanish press tried to retaliate, highlighting the fact that, in the quarter-final, Real Madrid and Manchester United had shared 11 magical goals in a game few people would forget. In the other semi-final, the two Milan sides had to be prized apart by one measly, scratchy Shevchenko goal, in a game that few people would remember. But as the Madrid journalists knew full well, defeat is a tough position to argue from. It was a bitter blow to Real Madrid and to Ronaldo in particular, the Champions League being one of the few gongs that has eluded him. It was also a body blow to Florentino Pérez, who had expected victory and passage on to the final. Defeat was not a word in his vocabulary. Del Bosque and Hierro would lose their jobs over this at the end of the season, two guys of faultless *Madridista* pedigree being moved on in the quest for ultimate success.

The other gong to elude Ronaldo was a domestic title. He had been runner-up with Barcelona in 1997 and again with Inter in 1998. Once the disappointment of the Juventus defeat had waned, they had to get on with the business of winning *La Liga*. Real Sociedad had hung in there all season and the two teams were pretty much neck and neck going into the last few games. The situation was not dissimilar to the one Ronaldo had been through with Inter the previous season, but with Real, he was integral to the team plans.

Real's run-in was not the easiest, with away games against reigning champions Valencia and city rivals Atlético, then a home tie against Athletic Bilbao to close. A visit to Valencia's Mestalla ground is never an easy prospect, its steep vertiginous stands creating a cauldron-like atmosphere for travelling teams. Ronaldo, fit again after the Juventus upset, was cleared to start. Real were brilliant on the night and Ronaldo, yet again, was the difference, his brace sealing the 2–1 win. His first was a rare header; the second, for the winner in the 64th minute, was a trademark goal. Figo slipped him through and he motored towards goal, double stepovered to sit Canizares down, rounded him and finished in style. Pure Ronaldo, pure class.

Likewise, the visit to the Vicente Calderon stadium across town at

Atlético can prove to be a banana skin, as derbies always can be. Like all good footballing neighbours, Atlético enjoy nothing more than raining on any potential Real parade. But they proved flimsy opposition on the night, blown away by Real 4–0. Real, intent on avenging their Champions League exit by ensuring the title, were irresistible. Zidane, Raúl and Ronaldo were different class. Ronaldo scored twice, the first an irresistible left-foot smash that Atlético's goalie Esteban barely saw. The second was a routine tap-in from a Roberto Carlos cross and Figo and Zidane were the other well-known names on the scoresheet.

With a two-point cushion over Real Sociedad going into the final game, it was theirs to lose. Déjà vu for Ronaldo, who had been in a similar situation 12 months earlier, but he ensured there would be no repeat of Inter's capitulation. Real finished in style and secured the title with a 3–1 defeat of Athletic Bilbao. Ronaldo donned the woeful wedge hairdo he'd sported in the World Cup final, claiming it was lucky, and similarly scored twice to take his *La Liga* tally to 23. Including his 6 in the Champions League, he had scored 29 goals in all – a healthy return, in anybody's language. Gutted to fall just short of the 25 *La Liga* goals he had promised earlier in the season, he duly stood his bet and took the rest of the squad out for a slap-up meal. He looked happy and relaxed, although he would miss out on the 'Pichichi' Golden Boot award as Deportivo's Roy Makaay collected that for his impressive 29.

It may have taken Zidane and Co. a while to decode Ronaldo's play, but once they had, the results were impressive. This was especially evident away from home, where Ronaldo's game is perfectly suited to the counter-attacking nature of away ties. In 2002–03, Real Madrid scored a third more goals and won a third more points away than they had the previous season.

Del Bosque, in a volte-face from his broadside earlier in the year, was now full of praise for his leading goal-scorer. 'We are talking about the best player in the world,' he told Madrid's *AS*. 'What he has done is help make us better.'

Sporting director Jorge Valdano was also wholesome in his praise for Ronaldo, telling the English newspaper the *Daily Telegraph*:

> When Ronaldo attacks, it is as if a pride of lions is attacking you.
> He provides an overwhelming attacking force. Before, we had a
> team that chewed over its goal options. Now we have both
> choices. Over the season, his game and contribution have grown

consistently. His quality is guaranteed, so if he continues to enjoy good physical health, he will really help us stay at the top.

But all was not well at the Bernabéu. The disappointment of seeing AC Milan lift the European Cup (Real had beaten them 3–1 in their group game at the Bernabéu) was too much for many, their dull Italianate football grating amongst the Spanish press. It wasn't quite as dour as the *catenaccio* ('door bolt') of old but it was deemed little better in Spain. What really got the Spanish press was that the Milan side was littered with big names, all capable of playing attractive football, but they didn't play with anything like the flair of Real, or even try to. It was hard for them to swallow. *La Liga* did prove to be some consolation, but little more. Pérez and Co. upstairs expected the league; it was a given almost, a mere hors d'oeuvre before lifting the Champions League trophy. As a consequence, the likeable and honest del Bosque would be released, a reflection of the ruthless ambition of Pérez, who adventurously appointed Portuguese Carlos Queiroz in his place, who had been Sir Alex Ferguson's no. 2 at Manchester United.

Ronaldo could look back on a season that, as ever, had delivered a combination of highs and lows. Thankfully, there were far more highs this time, as once he'd got his weight under control and the dressing-room tensions had died down, he then only really had to get the crowd on-side. Not an easy task by any means at the notoriously demanding Bernabéu, even if you're the World and European Player of the Year and the World Cup Golden Boot holder. As we have seen, despite a steady stream of goals, it was only after the Manchester United game, where Ronaldo's sensational hat-trick had floored the Red Devils, that he was somewhere close to acceptance by the *Madrileños*. They'd proved demanding, almost impossible to please, but he'd got there in the end.

Ronaldo's play had been consistent rather than thrilling. There were moments of magic, of course, such as the Old Trafford hat-trick, the two Alavés games and his goal flurry at the end of the season to secure the title, but his game seemed to have moved into a different area from the one that everybody first remembers from his refulgent Barcelona days. The 'just give me the ball and I'll score' mindset had long been replaced, primarily out of necessity due to his horrific injuries. If Sir Bobby Robson is right, and he usually is, Ronaldo minus 20 per cent dictates that he has had to adapt his game to suit the body he now possesses. Since his full return, let's say from the World Cup 2002 onwards, his game has, at times, looked awkward – cumbersome almost – as if he didn't trust his limbs to execute the instructions his genius footballing mind was issuing them. Pre-injury, you would never see Ronaldo miscontrol the ball on the edge of the area or stumble into a wall of opponents, he would just burst through them with the ball stuck to his foot. There were also times, especially for Real Madrid, where his shooting was nowhere near as consistent as it had been, as on occasion he seemed to shovel shots, rather than delivering the unerring rifle blasts of before.

But, if these minor chips to the bodywork can be attributed to the 20 per cent lost during the years in the dark valley of injury, then the player that is with us today is still a mightily effective machine. His record bears testimony to that. He told the Spanish press, 'When I was at Barcelona, I was more spectacular, but now I am more effective. I'm getting better all the time.'

He is a different player now: Ronaldo II almost. He has learned to play economically, to be more apposite with his game, to save his energy, and with his added maturity is fully cognisant of when to use his gifts and hurt the opposition most. He scores with the minimum of movements, taking advantage of defensive mistakes or his superior awareness and reading of the game. His speed is still explosive, if perhaps not the slingshot blur of before, and he knows that given the opportunity he is too good for any defender. His belief in his ability has not wavered. Many felt that, given a full season to re-familiarise himself with the pace of the professional game, to settle into his new club and for his battered knee to re-groove, Ronaldo's second full season back would be the one to watch. As the summer arrived, Ronaldo was grateful of the chance to prepare for the 2003–04 season out of the spotlight. Why? A certain David Beckham fell to earth in Madrid as the latest addition to the illustrious *galacticos*.

CHAPTER 19

GOALS AND GOLDENBALLS –
REAL MADRID 2003–04

The hoo-ha that surrounded Beckham's arrival in Madrid was welcome respite for Ronaldo, as Beckham was, and is, probably the only current player who is a bigger media draw than himself. Goldenballs's arrival had actually proved a welcome distraction for all the players: so phenomenal was Beckham's profile and allure at the time that they all tuned in to witness the cavalcade of attention. Ronaldo and Co. looked on with raised eyebrows and minor bemusement as the circus rolled into town. Even for stars of their stature, Beckham is a notch above.

Pérez signed Beckham, like Ronaldo, for the dynamic combination of his football and marketability. For Pérez, it was yet another amazing footballing coup, and this one completed a stunning quartet. In four seasons, he had cherry-picked his fellow G14 members' best and most talismanic players: Figo from Barcelona, Zidane from Juventus, Ronaldo from Inter and now Beckham from Manchester United. Audacious signings all. If they were the G14, he was the G1. Who would be next? Like all great visionaries, he had made the impossible possible. Now the question was: could the club deliver the silverware to go with the hype?

Beckham had arrived just in time to join Real's tour of the Far East, and the hysteria that his presence created out there reminded many of Beatlemania back in the 1960s. It was quite extraordinary. But Beckham, far cannier than his wooden diction suggests, knew that despite all the fanfare, he was there to play football and that's how he would be judged by his new teammates, Ronaldo included.

On his arrival, many thought Beckham would take Figo's place on the right side of midfield, with Figo either being eased out or moved on, rather as Morientes had been to accommodate Ronaldo. Morientes, fed up with the whole situation, had accepted a loan move to Monaco and would not only enjoy an excellent season, but return to haunt Real in a way they would myopically not conceive possible at the time of the deal. Figo, though, was going nowhere. The early photos of Beckham, as pristine as ever, rarely saw him without Figo in attendance. At the time, one wondered, was this a classic case for Figo of keep your friends close and your enemies closer still? But as it transpired, it was nothing more sinister than the fact that Figo is a jolly good chap. He comfortably spoke the best English amongst the squad and had been tapped up by Queiroz to make Beckham feel welcome. Beckham's Spanish as yet ran to no more than a few pleasantries, but I'm pretty sure he would soon learn the Spanish for, 'I'm on free kicks, Roberto [Carlos], OK?'

Beckham's acquisition further embodied Pérez's philosophy of signing the best and bringing one superstar per year to the club. With the benefit of having Queiroz on board, who knew Beckham so well from his United days and spoke decent English, the England captain's integration would be swift and he would soon be wooing the Bernabéu crowd faster than any other import had in recent times.

Ronaldo looked fresh and ready for business as the new *La Liga* season arrived. The CBF had given him an exemption from the pointless Confederations Cup in France over the summer, and he had made the most of the free time this allowed him. Inevitably, he flew home to Rio to spend time with friends and family, and was also roped in to becoming a figurehead for Rio's optimistic 2012 Olympic bid. He spent time with his various sponsors, such as Telecom Italia and Brahma Beer, and also flew to Oregon to discuss equipment with Nike. He'd been as busy in the off-season as he had for a long time. Also, with his separation from wife Milene now confirmed, he joined Renault F1 boss and renowned libertine Flavio Briatore aboard his gin palace, the brilliantly named *FB1*, just off the coast of Sardinia. To help take Ronaldo's mind off his recent nuptial split, Briatore's girlfriend of the time, the curvaceous model Heidi Klum, had invited along a few of her model pals to join the fun.

As well as this fun in the sun, Ronaldo made a conscious effort to nail his weight down and, thanks to a tight diet of salads and high-protein foods plus regular exercise, he returned to the Bernabéu five kilos lighter than he had left it in June. Spanish daily *AS* greeted this with the imaginative headline, '*Cinco Kilos Menos*' (five kilos less). Ronaldo seemed full of beans and gave his annual prediction of how many goals he would score, saying, 'It's too soon to specify how many I will score, but it will be more than 30. I genuinely believe that. I'm in great shape to make this the best season of my entire career. I want to bring the Bernabéu to its feet.'

He had grown his hair a touch, making him look alarmingly like Scouser Craig Charles of *Red Dwarf* fame, and seemed at ease with all around him. He set out his hopes and ambitions for the season and told Spanish journalists, 'I am at the key moment in my career. The fact that I am a Real Madrid player is a luxury because it gives me the possibility to aspire to win every title each year. My will and power to win is strong and, in order to be part of a team so great, it is important that I demand the best of myself, to be prepared, to be 100 per cent, so as to not fail my teammates and the fans.' Looking to build on his excellent goal tally from last season, Ronaldo went on, 'Of course, if I can beat last season's total, that would be great, but the most important thing is to win titles. I hope this year we win the Champions League, as it is the only title that I am missing.'

The first game was against Real Betis at the expectant Bernabéu. Ronaldo had shaved his head again and took up his usual position in the formation just ahead of Raúl. The level of Beckham hysteria was quite staggering and I spent that week in Madrid marvelling at his pulling power. They simply loved him, and his couple of goals in the Far East, plus a rare header in the Spanish Super Cup, meant he was already way ahead of the acceptance curve.

For Pérez, Queiroz's quest was straightforward: the Champions League and *La Liga*. As simple as that. The arrival of Beckham had taken expectation to yet another plane, but Real still looked decidedly light at the back, having not reinforced their defence since Hierro's 'retirement', and were banking on Raúl Bravo, who'd been a loan-flop at Leeds United, to fill the breach. Again, it looked like the *galactico*s would be undermined by a porous defence.

The buzz around the Bernabéu on 30 August 2003 was sensational, not dissimilar to that almost a year earlier when we were all awaiting Ronaldo's first bow. Beckham started and promptly scored after three minutes – a simple tap-in from a Ronaldo cross – and the place went suitably gaga. Ronaldo added a second in the second half, showing excellent awareness to thump home a Zidane cross from close range: again, a good example of his new style of play where he simply gets himself in the right areas at the right times and uses his God-given advantage to deduce where the ball will be played. Like most good sporting things, the goal had looked simple, but the technical excellence with which Real Madrid had moved the ball around to ultimately locate Ronaldo was of the highest order. Ronaldo did the rest.

There was a further boon for Ronaldo later that week when it was confirmed he could regain his coveted number 9 shirt. Fernando Morientes, who had watched the Real Betis game moodily from the stands, was set to move to Monaco. It was a welcome conclusion to the whole sorry affair for Morientes, and he would go on to shine for Didier Deschamps' emerging side, setting the pace in the French league and also qualifying for the knockout stages of the Champions League. Not only was this a personal fillip for Ronaldo as he was reunited with his favourite number, it also meant another bumper payday for the Real merchandise shop as the new shirts rolled off the presses.

The next home game was against Valladolid, who, rather like Alavés the year earlier, were on the end of another footballing supershow. Real Madrid buried them 7–1 without compunction. It was brutal. '*El Inglés*' Beckham, playing as if he'd been a *Merengue* all his life, was outstanding. In fact, everybody was. Zidane scored a volley of the utmost technical impudence, up there with his one at Hampden Park, taking a 60-yard pass from Beckham over his shoulder and volleying it first time left-footed into the bottom corner. It was Rolls-Royce stuff. Ronaldo didn't miss out either and got on the scoresheet in the 67th minute. It looked as though the *galacticos* 2003–04 were now even better. The team that Pérez built, or '*El Florenteam*', as the Spanish press tagged it, was in huge demand. Tickets for the Bernabéu were like hens' teeth and sponsors were queuing up to align their name with the knights in white at the Bernabéu. Pérez's hope and vision, that his famous club would be the prism through which all other major clubs would be viewed, was taking shape.

For that vision to be fully realised, Real Madrid needed to win the Champions League again and then progress on to win the Intercontinental Cup. They were still sore from their semi-final exit the previous season when many, themselves in particular, felt they were the best team in Europe. They may well have been, but lifting the European Cup is a much tougher business than it was in the old knockout days when six wins got you the trophy. Their assault on the trophy in 2003–04 began at home against Marseille, who were back in the big time after their Bernard Tapie-inspired indiscretions of the '90s. After surprisingly going behind, Real and Ronaldo turned on the style to thump the French club 4–2, Ronaldo claiming a brace and the performance earning praise all round from the Spanish press. Despite the makeshift defence – Pavon and Bravo at its heart – Real had shown all their style and flair and the scoreline did not flatter them. It was a good start for Queiroz and his boys.

So, once again, Ronaldo was doing what he enjoyed most – scoring plenty of goals – but this didn't stop Queiroz substituting him with the regularity that del Bosque had shown. Ronaldo had had enough of this and said as much to Queiroz. Queiroz clearly took this on board because, as autumn unfolded, Ronaldo, enjoying 90 minutes per game, went on a scoring streak that was simply irresistible.

Despite the demolition of Valladolid, Real had made an average start to the season and had ceded the lead to Valencia. Valencia were looking more like the champions of 2001–02 again and would prove to be Real's biggest challengers. But with the arrival of October came Ronaldo's purple patch.

Vindicating his words, and those of others, that this season would be the one to really watch him, he set off on a run that saw ten goals in thirteen *La Liga* games, including a run of eight consecutive games on the scoresheet. He was on fire and started off with a brace against Espanyol to help Real win 2–1. Other highlights included a brace and an assist in the 3–0 canter against Athletic Bilbao, who must have been sick of the sight of Ronaldo by now. In that game, Ronaldo's second had brought the Bernabéu to its feet, another mazy run culminating in the effortless stepover to round the keeper and score. He looked happy and at ease.

I met with Carlos Queiroz to discuss Ronaldo and the situation at the Bernabéu that season. The charming Portuguese coach explained, 'Joining Real was a fantastic opportunity, a great moment. Working with such fantastic players like Ronaldo, Zidane, Figo, Raúl, Beckham and Roberto Carlos was a pleasure, as they were such a positive group. Our job as the coaching staff was to understand how to keep these players out in front, for they had won *La Liga* the season before, and our goal was to do it again and also add the Champions League trophy. Not easy! We devised strategies for each player as an individual, and also for each within the team and group set-up as a whole. There was a method for the individual and a method for the collective and Ronaldo was assigned his own plan accordingly. It was a very strong group, very professional, and with fantastic personalities. Ronie in particular, he loved to train. He trained very hard and in a very professional manner; but he always had time for a smile and joke where necessary. He is always enthusiastic, always happy. He lives to play football and he understands how significant football is in his life. For us, it was vital to get Ronie's preparation correct because of his unique physical characteristics and his value to the team. He is a unique specimen, yes, but he had had such problems with injury that we had to be very careful to develop the right plan for him. This took time, which is why we needed to substitute him to start with, but an athlete of Ronie's power soon got into shape, and we saw the results very quickly with his fantastic scoring spree. He became the team's talisman.'

Seville, Albacete and Osasuna would also pick Ronaldo goals out of their respective nets and then, in the next game – *el derbi* against Atlético Madrid – Ronaldo scored after 13 seconds. Not only was this a wonderful solo goal but it was also a curious one in that it was almost as if the referee had placed a stagger on the Atlético players, not allowing them to start the game when Madrid did. From the kick-off, they remained statuesque, allowing Raúl to find Ronaldo, who then went on a 30-yard run, virtually unimpeded, waltzed through the static back line and then passed the ball into the back of the net past a bemused Burgos. It killed the derby at a stroke and Real ran out easy 2–0 winners.

Ronaldo's streak continued in the return game against Olympique Marseille at their rowdy Stade Vélodrome. Beckham had given *les Merengues* the lead with another exquisite example of the art of free-kick taking but then Marseille levelled midway through the second half to set up a thrilling tie. Roared on by their manic following, Marseille exerted a lengthy spell of pressure, only to be foiled by the fantastic Casillas. Marseille sensed an upset, but the goal which floored them was yet another example of collective magic from Madrid. It was quite brilliant. Under the cosh, Real repelled yet another Marseille corner and the ball looped to what appeared to be the relative obscurity of the near touch-line. Beckham, continuing his gladiatorial early form for Real, galloped towards it and, with a sliding save, just prevented the ball from going out of play. He turned, carried the ball a short distance and then unfurled one of his pearling cross-field passes 60-odd yards to Zidane.

Zidane brought the ball under control as if plucking an apple from a tree and then slipped in Raúl, who had overlapped towards the byline. On reaching the byline, Raúl pulled the ball back to find Ronaldo, who diverted it into the goal with customary panache. The Marseille players sank to their knees. Sheer class had opened them up like a can of beans. On the bench, Queiroz punched the air with delight and satisfaction, as it was a coach's dream goal: from defence to goal in no more than six seconds. Watching the goal on the replay, not only could one marvel at the speed and execution of the move, but also the Jedi-like telepathy now evident between Raúl and Ronaldo. As Raúl headed towards the byline, Ronaldo charged forward too, defender in close attendance. But then, as Raúl reached the byline, Ronaldo applied the brakes and pulled off slightly to the left, thus slipping the attention of his marker, who carried on goalward. Raúl, in tune with this, instead of squaring the ball, pulled it back a yard or two into the space Ronaldo's nous had created. Ronaldo finished with the outside of his right foot and with the minimum of fuss. What a class goal and a textbook illustration of Ronaldo II. The *galactico*s had scored a *galactigol*.

I discussed this ability of Ronaldo's with Queiroz and he explained, 'Yes, he is fantastic at this. His orientation on the pitch is one of the key strengths that make him so dangerous. Just like the goal on matchday one versus Real Betis, his goal against Marseille was a perfect illustration of his timing. He knew exactly when he needed to be at that position to score the goal. He is able to arrive at very high speed to be in a tiny but critical area of the field at exactly the right time. With players of the calibre of Zidane and Figo around to deliver passes to take advantage of this gift, it is a very dangerous combination. It requires fractional timing that few possess. He knows his capabilities, he understands the game so well now, and he can change a game, on his own, in just a few seconds. He can go slow, slow, slow and then in just the right moment he pounces and hurts you – in some ways like Romário used to. There may appear to be no danger and then, bang! He bursts into life and it's a goal. He remains cool at the precise moment most other players get flustered in front of goal. In a one-on-one or a key scoring opportunity in a game, his mind arrives at a moment of calm and tranquillity as he executes the goal – he is totally at ease. His footballing brain is like a computer. Yes, he is special.'

Next up for Ronaldo and Madrid was the big one, perhaps the biggest league game in world football: the showdown against Barcelona at the

Camp Nou. Barcelona had made a tepid start to the season under their new coach, Dutchman Frank Rijkaard. At the time, Rijkaard was under a lot of pressure and can be thankful of the stoical support of his impressive chairman Juan Laporta. They had not won anything since 1999 and in that time, as we have seen, the club had descended in similar proportion to Real's ascent. Although this game will always be passionate, highly charged and alive with atmosphere, this meeting seemed virtually irrelevant from a football perspective, so far had Real left Barcelona behind in recent years. For Ronaldo, it was his first game back there since his playing days with them. Although the press tried to whip up Figo-like hysteria, Ronaldo's reception was nowhere near as hostile as the one the Portuguese always enjoys. The visit would also be a litmus test for the reception David Beckham would receive, having thumbed his nose at Barcelona during his transfer in the summer. Unwillingly caught up in the Barcelona presidential campaign as part of Juan Laporta's propaganda and bluster, Beckham had absolutely no intention of joining the Catalans. Real won 2–1, although not without some late scares and some more inspired/lucky (delete as you feel appropriate) goalkeeping from Casillas. Ronaldo scored the decisive second with a low, rasping drive that took a slight deflection, and Madrid returned home with the points and leadership of *La Liga*.

Ronaldo's streak went on until 3 January, when Real Murcia found a way to curb him. By then, he had scored fourteen goals in *La Liga* as well as three in the Champions league – an impressive first semester. Looking back at this great run, it is enlightening to see two things. First, the regularity with which Ronaldo scores a game's first goal, and often quite early, to put his team in the ascendancy. Second, and conversely, if he hasn't scored the first goal, he will invariably score the game's decisive goal, such as the Marseille classic.

This facet had been further illustrated in his displays for Brazil as their qualification campaign for Germany 2006 got under way. Brazil, who, due to another interesting FIFA directive, are the first World Cup holders required to qualify, began the process on 7 September 2003 with a tricky tie away to Colombia. Coach Carlos Alberto Parreira will be the first to tell you that qualification from the South American group is by no means a formality, and that the huge group is much tougher than many the European teams have to negotiate. He has a valid point, as there are few weak teams these days in South America, and even the ones that may be considered lesser nations present their own unique obstacles, such as

Bolivia, who play their home games in the thin air of La Paz. Likewise, any visit to the Naçional Stadium in Montevideo is not for the faint-hearted, as it is a decrepit relic, a health-and-safety assault course that has been barely touched since its completion for the 1930 World Cup finals.

Ronaldo continued where he had left off in Japan, with the first goal of the campaign in the 22nd minute. Aston Villa's Juan Pablo Angel levelled in the 38th and it was left to new sensation Kaká, who would enjoy a fine season at AC Milan, to provide the winner in the 61st. A tough first game had been safely negotiated. Three days later in Manaos, a Ronaldinho goal was enough to beat Ecuador and give Parreira the perfect start.

The next pair of games came in November with a tricky visit to Lima to face Peru first up. Brazil had much the better of the game and squandered a host of chances, Ronaldo included, and could only manage a 1–1 draw. Then, in the next game on 19 November in Curitiba, Brazil stormed into a commanding 2–0 lead against Uruguay. Ronaldo made the first for Kaká and then scored himself in the 28th minute. His goal contained a marvellous piece of awareness and improvisation. Latching on to a probing ball from Rivaldo, he bore down on the keeper, but with the ball taking an awkward bounce he was faced with a difficult and limited set of options. Ronaldo's talent found the answer as he steered the bouncing ball around the keeper with the front of his right shoulder blade, and then stroked the ball home with his left foot from a tight angle. This unorthodox manoeuvre was the only way he could have scored, and he had a split second to execute the touch as the keeper was almost upon him. For a moment, the keeper looked favourite to snatch the ball from Ronaldo's path, but Ronaldo outfoxed him, leaving him grasping at fresh air.

Ronaldo then hit the post four minutes later and Brazil were rampant. At half-time, it was 2–0 and it seemed Brazil would go on to complete a rout, but their complacency allowed Uruguay to get back into the game: Diego Forlan took advantage of some slack defensive play to level the scores and then a freak own goal by Gilberto Silva gifted Uruguay the lead in the 78th minute. I watched this game in a Rio *botaquim* – Brazil's distant cousin of the English public house. Howls of derision greeted Uruguay's third goal and vitriolic abuse poured forth in the direction of the TV screen. Uruguay are viewed as third-rate poor relations by Brazil and the scars from the 1950 World Cup-final defeat still refuse to heal.

To lose to them is considered a national humiliation, a footballing travesty, something that cannot even be considered, never mind tolerated. But with time running out, defeat looked more than likely. Ronaldo, however, again saved the *seleção's* blushes when, in the 87th minute, he was put through and had a one-on-one situation with Gustavo Munua in the Uruguay goal. The nation (and the *botaquim*) held its breath; this gilt-edged chance simply had to be taken. With trademark efficiency, Ronaldo buried the ball past Munua into the bottom corner with chilling accuracy. A wave of relief filled Curitiba's Pinheirao stadium and it was high-fives all round in the *botaquim*. Ronaldo had saved the day and spared Parreira some crimson blushes – and added two more to his burgeoning international tally.

Back in Spain, with Beckham settling in so quickly and Ronaldo proving irresistible, Real Madrid arrived at the New Year exactly where they wanted to be: leading *La Liga* and qualified for the knockout stages of the Champions League. Queiroz, in one of football's hottest jobs, was thus far delivering. He also had generous praise for his slimline number 9, saying, 'He could have kept his weight from last season and guaranteed us 23 goals and the title, which would not have been bad. But his work this summer and pre-season has been fantastic. Only a super-athlete like Ronaldo could have recovered from those injuries and be as good as he is today. I'm very happy with him.'

Queiroz had further reasons to be cheerful as Ronaldo continued his fantastic scoring form. A brilliant solo goal away against Real Betis salvaged a point and then he scored the winner in the 2–1 win at home against Villarreal. Then, in a pulsating tie away at Valladolid, he popped up in the last minute to score the winner in a 3–2 classic – Real having come back from 2–0 down. Two more at Espanyol and then another in the 4–2 thrashing of Celta Vigo meant Ronaldo was miles ahead in the Pichichi scorers' charts as, by game 28 on 13 March, he had scored a blistering 22 league goals and was well on course to bust the 30 he had promised.

Inevitably, such form attracted transfer speculation, and reports of a move back to Inter Milan became regular fare, although one struggled to understand why Ronaldo would contemplate such a move, unless for the unlikely, sentimental reason of wanting to return to the club who'd looked after him through his injury. The 2003–04 season had also seen the advent of London's Chelsea as a player at the big table, for one reason and one reason only: Russian oil kazillionaire Roman Abramovich had bought the near-bankrupt club off Ken Bates for a reported £55m – loose change when your personal wealth is estimated at over £8bn and *Forbes* magazine has given you the enviable title of 'The world's richest man under 40'. Abramovich had furnished coach Claudio Ranieri with unlimited funds and Ranieri embarked on a £110m trolley-dash across Europe that doubled Chelsea's squad almost overnight. With money no object, they were linked with everybody in the game and an ill-timed trip to London in February by Ronaldo led to an inevitable rumour that the Brazilian was next on Abramovich's list. The unauthorised trip would earn Ronaldo a fine from Real Madrid and much consternation. Real didn't like this parvenu from West London meddling around with their squad. Chelsea had already signed Geremi and Makelele, and Real were not going to let them get near Ronaldo.

Ronaldo would claim he was merely there on a photo shoot for one of his sponsors. Miffed about the fine, he would then defend his trip, saying, 'Before Abramovich, there would have been no fuss about my visit to London. I am very happy at Real Madrid and want to stay here. The club [Real] would not have asked for an explanation since I went to London to do some photos, but as there is this Russian who wants to sign everybody, everyone is afraid.' He perhaps could have left it at that, but he gave the press a few morsels to chew on by saying, 'Abramovich has never called me, but if he is interested in me, it is always good to feel valued.' Abramovich's power to strike fear into any club whose players drifted within snapping distance of Stamford Bridge was a reflection of what his wealth could achieve.

The Bernabéu's nerves were settled shortly afterwards when Ronaldo put the rumours to bed by signing a contract extension to keep him at the club until June 2008. He hinted that he would be happy to stay with Real for life, telling Real's website that, 'I'm delighted. There were grave doubts about my signing at first but, little by little, I've demonstrated that I'm worthy of a team like Madrid. We're going to look into something that ties me to Real Madrid for life. I love it here.'

He had now settled very well in Madrid. Inevitably for an individual with his wealth, he lived in a fine home in the exclusive La Moraleja area of the capital and could count, among others, outgoing prime minister José Maria Aznar as one of his neighbours. Looking through the keyhole for a moment, one can see that Ronaldo's drum was huge, tipping the scales at 12,000 square metres, with all the usual trimmings. His love of cars was reflected by the five parked-up in his garage, including two

BMWs (X5 and 745i), a couple of sponsored Audis and a hot Lancia, plus that new favourite of the loaded classes: the souped-up Hummer. His new-found passion for golf is well catered for with a floodlit putting green and the house boasts – count 'em – 12 TV sets. Loyd Grossman would have heartily approved. He has also recently acquired a grand residence in Jardim Pernambuco, one of Rio de Janeiro's most exclusive areas, which is currently undergoing a complete designer overhaul.

Life was pretty good for the Brazilian. He was now firmly established in the team and among the fans and was scoring with metronomic regularity. Real were playing some dazzling football and had opened up a healthy gap at the top of *La Liga* from Valencia. But injury would again return to haunt him. He was carried off during the semi-final of the Copa Del Rey against Valencia, having lain stricken on the turf for several worrying minutes. The look of dire concern on Queiroz's face as Ronaldo was receiving treatment told it all; he knew full well who his most valuable player was.

The injury proved to be a torn thigh muscle, and would rule him out for at least three weeks. It was a sickening body blow for Ronaldo. It meant he would miss several big games, including the return leg of the Champions League knockout game against arch-rivals Bayern Munich, and the final of the Spanish Cup against Valladolid. Real would ultimately negotiate Bayern but would lose a pulsating Cup final 4–2, after extra time. Losing their top striker was felt like a hammer blow, even for a club like Real. If Pérez's dream was to be realised, Real needed Ronaldo back quickly.

From being the subject of resentment not a year earlier, Real Madrid now realised what a vital piece of their plans Ronaldo was, with some Madrid news hacks suggesting Real Madrid had developed a 'Ronaldo dependency' – a turnaround indeed from a year or so ago. It also exposed the paucity of their squad, something that del Bosque had been at pains to point out to Pérez the previous season. Queiroz was now faced with the same problem. Without Ronaldo, Real's attack looked weak. Young hotshot Portillo was still raw and learning his trade, and Raúl was having one of his leaner patches. Some would argue that Raúl's barren spell was due to the fact that the team was now geared up to playing with Ronaldo and springing his play, and Raúl's game, in adapting to accommodate Ronaldo, had suffered in terms of scoring goals.

In Ronaldo's absence, a mini-crisis engulfed the Bernabéu. Now, of course, all things are relative when talking about Real Madrid, but when you lose two games on the trot (Copa Del Rey final 4–2 to Zaragoza and 4–2 away at Athletic Bilbao) for the first time that season, people start to panic and talk in terms of crisis. In this time, Real's lead at the top of *La Liga* from Valencia had been trimmed from six points to one. Next up was the crucial Champions League quarter-final against Monaco, with the first leg being held at the Bernabéu. The night before, AC Milan had thumped Deportivo La Coruña 4–1 in Milan and sent a message across Europe that they were not intent on relinquishing their grip on the trophy lightly. For Real, this was a large gauntlet thrown directly down on the welcome mat of the Bernabéu. They needed to show the Milanese that they were still the team to be feared. With the *Madrileños* desperate to hear good news about him, Ronaldo gave everybody a lift by his swift recovery and was selected to start against the *Monegasques*. As Milan had done the previous evening, Real Madrid went behind and it was only in the second half that they hit top form. In a performance that coach Queiroz would describe as 'Jekyll and Hyde', after the break Real Madrid played some of the grade A football for which they are famous. Iván Helguera bundled in a header and then Zidane squeezed the ball home from a tight angle to make it 2–1.

Ronaldo was looking especially sharp and, despite having missed a straightforward header in the first half, began to make amends in the second, where his constant running and availability proved too much for the Monaco back line to handle. A trademark mazy run and stepover was unceremoniously brought to a halt when Monaco's goal-scorer Sebastien Squillaci bundled him over in the area and the ref pointed to the spot.

Up stepped Luis Figo, who again, using his unconvincing stop–start technique, was almost foiled by Roma in the Monaco goal as Buffon had done a year earlier. Roma, desperately unlucky to see his fine block loop straight up, looked on in despair as Figo stooped to conquer and nodded the ball into the unguarded net, just in the nick of time as the defenders arrived.

Ronaldo then added one himself in the 79th when he took Zidane's through-ball and drilled a low left-foot drive under Roma. At 4–1, Real Madrid were cruising, and Queiroz promptly substituted Ronaldo, who left to a rapturous standing ovation. Oh, how they loved him now!

But then a late twist meant the tie would go back to the Principality as yet not fully settled, when returning favourite Fernando Morientes scored with a well-taken header to leave the aggregate score at a juicy 4–2 in Real's favour. Morientes, who'd received a rousing reception before the game, showed great dignity and restraint, for on scoring, he merely pointed heavenwards and said thank you, refusing to indulge in the crass celebrations so often seen by players these days returning to old clubs. He would receive another batch of applause from the home fans, who've never really forgotten him. It was good stuff, but one wonders why the *Madridistas* can't give their current squad the same backing.

Ronaldo's fantastic season continued the following Sunday in the home game versus Seville, who had unceremoniously thumped them 4–1 earlier in the season in Andalusia. Real Madrid put that behind them and at a sodden Bernabéu gave another exemplary display of high-quality football, whipping them 5–1. Ronaldo scored twice to take his league tally for the season to a superb 24. Beckham and Zidane were also outstanding. After all the talk of a 'crisis' at Real Madrid, the Brazilian press, who take any perceived attack on a Brazilian sportsman by foreign journalists as tantamount to treason, were as partisan as ever and hailed Ronaldo as the saviour of the expensive *Merengues*, with *O Globo* running the headline, '*Com Ronaldo é outra coisa*' ('With Ronaldo, it's another thing'). Ronaldo had looked very sharp the whole game and showed no signs of the muscle tear that had felled him just three weeks earlier. He could easily have had a hat-trick, and was unfortunate when his fantastic mazy run and shot was superbly saved by the Seville keeper, only to see Salgado drive home the rebound. Ronaldo received another huge ovation from the Bernabéu faithful and, with the gap now down to just one point at the top of *La Liga*, Real Madrid would need him to keep this form going through to the end of the season – as would coach Queiroz, whose position was coming under daily scrutiny. Top of *La Liga* and still alive in the Champions League . . . it's a tough game, top-flight football management. Things weren't about to get any easier for Queiroz and his men either. The next few weeks would prove to be a horrendous turnaround for all at the Bernabéu, with events off the field as well as on it causing much concern as the expensive wheels of the Real Madrid machine all came off at once.

Morientes' late goal at the Bernabéu had given the tie just enough oxygen to make the second leg worth watching, and to keep the game alive as a contest. It would surely have meant au revoir for Monaco at 4–1, but 4–2, although mightily difficult to overturn, at least gave them hope with that precious brace of away goals. What didn't assist Monaco's cause much was when Real went into a 1–0 lead on the half-hour mark in the Principality. Ronaldo was to the fore again in making the goal; his high-speed burst from just inside his own half put the Monaco defence on the back foot and, with them back-pedalling frantically towards the goal, he slipped the ball inside to the edge of the area, where Guti, having shaped to shoot, dummied the ball with supreme awareness, allowing it to roll effortlessly into the path of Raúl, who swept the ball home with his fabled left foot. At 5–2 ahead on aggregate and 60 minutes to play, there was surely no problem here.

That was about Real's last meaningful contribution of the game, and perhaps of their season as a whole. In a bizarre turnaround, Monaco, with nothing else to do but charge forward and fight for their Champions League lives, showed marvellous mettle – something that a horrified Pérez watching from the stands could've done well to take note of – and embarked on a staggering comeback. Spurred on by their talismanic captain, Ludovic Giuly, they equalised on the stroke of half-time, Giuly himself striking a neat volley which took a fortuitous deflection to squeeze in off Casillas's far post.

Deschamps must have put some Pernod or something in their half-time oranges, as his side came out for the second half like men possessed, foaming at the mouth and all set to be unleashed on Real Madrid. They ran Real ragged and the weary men from Spain were bullied into submission. Real's expensive, *galactico*-based season and the pitfalls of Pérez's vision of club-building could all be encapsulated in that second 45 minutes. Many factors played their part in bringing Pérez's edifice tumbling down. Beckham, whose prompting, running and energy had proved so impressive in the first half of the season, was absent due to suspension. At 4–1, with five minutes left in the first leg, he had tactically got himself booked on the assumption his pals would negotiate the second leg with ease and he'd be all set for the semi-final shorn of yellow cards to his name; something he would later do again for England against Wales in a World Cup qualifier, sparking predictable national furore. Morientes' late header made that unilateral decision look a bit hasty. Second, Real Madrid looked plain knackered.

In the second half, no one played with anything like the gumption needed. Ronaldo, after an impressive first half, faded into the background; Zidane is allegedly reported to have admitted to French colleague Giuly that they were all shattered; and the Real back line was simply all over the place chasing shadows. Morientes and Giuly completed the scoring to take Monaco through 5–5 on away goals – a cracking tie. Raúl had a marvellous header chalked off for a very dubious offside near the end but the writing was on the wall. Where Real had negotiated Manchester United the season before, just, 6–5 on aggregate, they had fallen short this time: 5–5 on away goals. Aggregate scores such as these aren't the stuff that European Champions are made of.

Furthermore, and the thing that seems so ironic about the whole Pérez dream, is that it was Morientes who really did the damage. His goal for Monaco's second was a towering, world-class header: one of the best you'll see. He rose above Real's static centre-backs like an eagle and planted a glorious header past Casillas. His two goals in the 5–5 aggregate proved critical in dumping out his beloved Real. One wonders why on earth the bean counters at the Bernabéu didn't exclude him from playing against Real as part of his loan terms. If it was an oversight, then it was a mightily expensive and embarrassing one and there must have been some red faces at the Bernabéu on Wednesday morning. It also showed the brittleness and fragility of Pérez's *galacticos* policy. How Queiroz could have done with Morientes to take some of the load off Ronaldo and Raúl and Co., who had laboured long and hard throughout the season. Morientes, unlike his admirably restrained celebration at the Bernabéu, showed no such sentiment this time and celebrated hard and ecstatically with the rest of his teammates. And so he should, too, after his shoddy treatment by the Spaniards. Also, where were the others, who'd been jettisoned to accommodate the *galacticos*? Claude Makelele was helping Chelsea negotiate Arsenal in a pulsating tie at Highbury. His holding-play skills would have been ideal to shore up Real in the second leg and help them defend the aggregate advantage. Queiroz, like del Bosque before him, was left to rue his president's seeming reluctance to free up funds for some world-class reinforcements, especially at the back.

It was a curious week of Champions League football. Real's exit was a huge shock, but some of the media focus would be taken off Queiroz and his team as, the following night, the highly fancied Arsenal crashed out; and then, even more amazingly, AC Milan sacrificed a 4–1 first-leg advantage as an inspired Deportivo La Coruña thumped them 4–0 to go through. These were the kind of results that just weren't supposed to happen, and they jammed the switchboard of European football, leaving people scratching their heads looking for answers.

In the managerial stakes, Arsène Wenger of Arsenal and Carlo Ancelotti of AC Milan were, prior to their exits, being publicly courted by free-spending Chelsea, who seemed ready to offload their affable

RONALDO

Roman 'tinkerman', Claudio Ranieri, as soon as possible. Ranieri, an Italian Graham Taylor almost, was, like Queiroz at Madrid, rapidly becoming a satrap under the gaze of an overbearing president. Defeat to Arsenal seemed the ready-made opportunity but now the Chelsea oligarchy of Abramovich and Peter Kenyon were left with egg on their face and Ranieri, enjoying an unanticipated reversal of fortune and struggling to wipe the well-earned grin off his face, was, for the time being at least, granted a stay of execution.

The defeat was a bitter blow for Ronaldo, who still is yet to win the Champions League. As he and his teammates returned to Spain, the pressure began to mount. It was no surprise that Real's stuck-up fans wasted no time in venting their disapproval. Right on cue, they were outside Real's training ground hurling abuse at all and sundry and chanting Morientes' name. Ronaldo in particular, who, having been their darling not ten days earlier and seeming fully on-side with them all, came in for the most stick and was victim of the 'fat' taunt again. It was a cruel turnaround for the Brazilian, whose blistering form all season had been the main reason for Real's success and their position in the league. He had had an off-night against Monaco but had still made the goal. The fans were proving impossible.

It's worth examining the question of Ronaldo's weight again here. To many, he does look on the heavy side, but most of these people have an image in their heads of Ronaldo when he burst onto the scene back at Barcelona, and then subsequently when his face was beamed around the world at France '98. He was only 21 then, with a lot of physical development ahead of him; it's inevitable that, with the passage of time, he has filled out a bit, and also his muscle sets have fully matured. He is now a big, fast, muscular striker, not the whippet-like specimen of six years ago.

Another fact of note is, next time you are either at the Bernabéu or watching a Real game on TV, count how many Brazil flags there are draped over the stands. It won't take you long, as you'll find that there are precisely none. In stark contrast to the delirious affection Ronaldo was held in at PSV, Barcelona and Inter, where sales of Brazil flags were rampant and the stadiums were always bedecked with loads of them, I have never seen one in all the games I've witnessed him play for Real.

Beckham, his honeymoon period with them now long gone, was also in the thick of some sordid personal allegations slung by his former PA, Rebecca Loos. His form on the pitch had also become mired and the

Spanish press, his amigos not so long ago, now christened him Forrest Gump. Harsh indeed.

Worse was to come that weekend, as, looking to find some solace in *La Liga*, Real were humiliatingly beaten 3–0 by Osasuna to provoke white-hanky time again at the Bernabéu, allowing Valencia to slip past them into a one-point lead. The fact that this was Real's first home defeat all season seemed lost on the 75,000 inside the Bernabéu. Even worse, it was an ex-Real Madrid youth XI coach, Rafael Benítez, who was shaping Valencia to win the league. Old friends were haunting Real at every turn. As bad for Queiroz was that Ronaldo, whose goals had been keeping the side afloat, hobbled off with another muscle strain. The look on Queiroz's face was again ashen with foreboding. Ronaldo's worth to the team, if not the fans, was immeasurable. It was a gloomy time to be around the Bernabéu, and Queiroz was up against it. He couldn't win either way. The squad at his disposal was wafer thin, as Pérez's lodestar of *Zidanes y Pavons* was clearly failing. On their day, and at full strength, yes, Real were irresistible, and some of the football they had played during the earlier part of the season was some of the best ever seen at club level. But over the course of a long season, with injuries and the vagaries of form, they were not quite the all-conquering Barnum's Circus they were expected to be. That season, they had signed only one player, the high-profile *galactico* acquisition of David Beckham, but had offloaded fourteen – a staggering number – which left Queiroz helplessly exposed should things go wrong. Emotionally and physically spent, the team had plunged into crisis.

Queiroz might well scratch his erudite Portuguese cranium and wonder what was conspiring against him. A month ago, they had been eight points clear in *La Liga*, they had seen off the tricky challenge of Bayern Munich in the Champions League and they were in the final of the Copa Del Rey against unfancied Real Zaragoza. The treble, and glory, was on. Pérez's vision was about to burst into bloom. And there lay the crux for Queiroz. Success was attributed to Pérez's vision and his *galactico* policy; failure was all Queiroz's. The team Pérez had built to conquer all with Corinthian style and ease was now bedraggled – and Queiroz knew it.

The crisis had been there for a while, lurking ominously like a grenade without its pin. Ronaldo had put the pin back in many times with his peerless finishing, but with his recent absence due to injury, the pin had worked loose again and the grenade was about to blow in Queiroz's face.

His team were knackered, but he was unable to rotate because, at Madrid, the stars must play because every night is gala night, and his inexperienced bench of young hopefuls were simply not up to it. There were no in-between layers, such as Makelele and Morientes, to bridge the void between *galactico* and young prospect. If Ronaldo didn't score, the deficiencies were exposed, and Raúl was having his quietest season for some years; not that you'll hear the fans hurl vitriol his way, though. Queiroz, feeling the strain, for once spoke up about his thoughts on the president's policy, telling the Spanish press:

> If we have to make up the rest of the side from the youth team, our youth system has to be the best of the best [something he'd seen exemplified at Manchester United]. We can't just go picking up kids who come and knock on our door at the Castellana.

Beckham, bought for his passing and flair, was having to help shore up the midfield, as the talented but lightweight dilettante Guti couldn't. With Helguera compromised at centre-back to fill the quality gap left by Pérez's apparent refusal to buy a class defender or two, the whole thing was coming crashing down.

I asked Queiroz about this heartbreaking reversal of fortune in the last month of the season. Visibly still miffed about what could have been, he explained his frustrations: 'Yes, the defeat at Monaco hurt very much, as did the disastrous end to the season. We were so close to a beautiful season. We had played so well but the squad was so stretched. In Portugal, we have a phrase "*Quando nao tive caoes, vai cacar com gatos*" ("when you can't hunt with dogs, you have to hunt with cats") and at Real, the president had got rid of all the dogs we needed as back up. Fourteen players were offloaded: Makalele, Macca (McManaman), Morientes, Flavio Conceicão, for example. The team was tired out and we had no way of resting key players for them to be ready for the big games. It is not fair to expect a young player like Javier Portillo, however promising he may be, to come in from 2B [the reserves] and fill the shoes of somebody like Ronaldo. It just can't be done. The same with Rubens and Pavon. The replacements need to have experience, to understand how to operate and perform in such big games and to assist in helping us rest the senior players when necessary. Look at things here at Manchester United [I interviewed him in May 2005, when he was back at Man United]. We have Christiano [Ronaldo], a great talent who we are trying to develop as best we can. This season, he has played in 82 per cent of the games and is doing very well. But last year, he only played in 50 per cent of the games. He is only 20 and it takes time to bring these players through to get them to the right level. For Portillo and the rest of the 2Bs to be expected to fill in was crazy. Everybody in the footballing world knew this; you didn't have to be a coach or an expert. Only the president [Pérez] seemed unable to see this and his ring of journalists who have to protect him for their own interests. It was crazy. We had no replacements anywhere.'

As the season closed, Real limped across the finishing line like a spent marathon runner, ridden with cramp and mineral deficiency, undignified and gasping for air, desperately seeking the solace of the foil blanket. They were hammered at home 4–1 by Real Sociedad and the sight of an empty Bernabéu was disgusting. There were so few fans in there that you could almost read in full the 'Real Madrid CF' written into the stands in white seating. The home fans had brought along extra supplies of white hankies to wave and as Pérez and Valdano squirmed in their plush seats as the humiliation unfolded, poor Queiroz was left isolated down on the bench to endure the last rites of his tenure. For Ronaldo, the game couldn't end too soon and there was the bizarre sight of the statistic being flashed up on the TV screen that throughout the game he had had zero attempts on goal and, as such, none on target.

Real ultimately finished fourth, just scraping a Champions League place, and had to face the embarrassment of a resurgent, Ronaldinho-inspired Barcelona finishing above them in second. Since the *el derbi* game earlier in the year that had seemed so irrelevant to Real, Barcelona had gone on a superb run, and with the canny addition of Dutch terrier Edgar Davids during the transfer window, they had burned up the league to overtake Real, beating them 2–1 in the Bernabéu along the way.

But who would come to fill Queiroz's tracksuit, should he be released? The susurrant noises within the Bernabéu were that he wouldn't survive into the next season: a shame, because he appears to be a coach of high ability.

Real's disappointing season had taken a lot of lustre off the Pérez dream and the attractiveness of Real Madrid as the world's most desirable club to manage. That they still may be, but boy, is that job pressured. If you were Wenger, Ancelotti, Eriksson, Mourinho or Capello, would you really fancy it? Surely you'd need some assurances, those same assurances that del Bosque and Queiroz had pleaded for in vain, that some world-class defensive reinforcements would be bestowed upon the squad?

A season that had started with the fanfare of Beckham's arrival and his 'Hala Madrid' clarion call, had ended in disaster. A season that as recently as March had seen the good ship Real Madrid cruising serenely over calm seas towards the double of *La Liga* and the Champions League, had been sunk by the combined fleet of Monaco and Valencia. As Pérez escaped in the only lifeboat available, Queiroz was left clinging to the flotsam and jetsam of a failed campaign. He would eventually drift up the Manchester Ship Canal and return to rejoin Sir Alex Ferguson at Manchester United – not a bad catch as your no. 2 – as Pérez moved swiftly to divert the blame and fired him without compunction.

Ex-player, ex-manager and ex-national coach José Antonio Camacho was brought in. Camacho, massively popular with the Real faithful from his playing days, has a less illustrious record as a manager. This self-styled Brian Clough of Spain (but crucially without the silverware) was welcomed by the fans as the man they thought would steel their overpaid stars who were showing (in their eyes) similarities with the 'Ferrari Boys' of the late '90s that included Clarence Seedorf, Predrag Mijatovic and Davor Suker. Pérez, understandably nervous about the impending presidential re-elections, also switched tack to assuage the fans. He effectively abandoned the *Zidanes y Pavons* policy with the panicked double-signing of Argentine hardman Walter Samuel from Roma and the injured Jonathan Woodgate from Newcastle United for the combined outlay of close to £30m. What would del Bosque or Queiroz have done for such transfer booty? Notice, too, and this is a crucial factor in the unfolding duel between Real Madrid and new kids on the European block Chelsea, that it is Pérez who is signing the players, not the coach. Say what you will about Abramovich and his 'Chelski' revolution, but he has been shrewd enough to get the best men in (Kenyon and Mourinho) and then leave them to it. He is merely happy to release funds when asked, and now that Chelsea have abandoned trying to copy Real and pursued their own path under Mourinho, they have prospered.

And what of Ronaldo? How long does he need or want to put up with derisory cries of *gordo* and be a prophet without honour? A country mile ahead in the Pichichi scorers' charts, looking lethal and playing with virtuosity, he must still wonder what he has to do to win the full acceptance of the Bernabéu. All Morientes had to do to get the unconditional adoration of the Madrid crowd was score twice against them, embarrass the whole club and put them out of the Champions League. Ronaldo's 60-odd goals for them in two seasons mustn't be quite sufficient. Fickle football fans? Let's not go there.

There were rumours of a swoop for a *galactico* such as Michael Owen, Francesco Totti or Patrick Vieira, but these merely appeared to be the bluster of a press keen to re-ignite the fun and frivolity of the previous *galactico* signings. There now seemed a more sombre, business-like mood around the Bernabéu. Jorge Valdano, who appeared untouchable as Pérez's mouthpiece, was also on his way out. Camacho had famously resigned from his previous tenure as coach at Real due to lack of funds and director-level support after 22 days, and one can only assume he received greater assurance from on high than he did back in 1998. The summer was a time for deep reflection.

CHAPTER 20

RONALDO PLC

It is perhaps an opportune time to divert our gaze from the football pitch for a moment to analyse and take stock of Ronaldo's awesome financial clout as a one-man industry. As he licked his wounds and reflected on a season that had promised much and delivered only heartache, he could perhaps take solace in the fact that, as a marketing commodity, he is, like his football, a phenomenon.

Ronaldo is marketing gold, a human brand that can virtually guarantee success and increased revenues for whoever has the wherewithal to attach his name to their product. As such, he is not short of offers and lucrative contracts and has some of the world's most respected companies queuing up to gain his endorsement. As well as the busy flurry of marketing activity that piggy-backed his rise to global stardom in 1997, there have since been several key deals struck that have cemented his wealth and presence on the billboards of the world. As of May 2005, these included Nike, Siemens, Audi, TIM (Telecom Italia Mobile), French supermarket group Carrefour and brewing giant AmBev.

This is easily explained by Ronaldo's broad appeal, not merely that gleaned from his football, but the general manner and demeanour with which he carries himself. He is very product-friendly, and in Brazil they warmly describe such people as having *alegria*: which can be translated as joy and passion combined.

Ronaldo's assets are rumoured to be in the region of £300m – making him one of the wealthiest sportsmen in the world – with a trusted team of advisers and executives looking after the day-to-day running of his financial affairs. Altogether, there are eight different companies employing 150 people both directly and indirectly, each of which is registered under the umbrella of 'Grupo R9'. Running this group are various executives in differing locations, such as Aloisio Freitas as finance director, who is responsible for Ronaldo's business investments in Brazil, and our old friend Nilton 'Filé' Petrone, director of Ronaldo's physiotherapy clinic in Rio.

Ronaldo has wisely chosen to use professionals rather than family to look after his affairs – avoiding this common pitfall of many South American footballers – and this is typified with his choice of Spanish law firm Garrigues (who also look after some of Beckham's Spanish interests), where Javier Ferrero and Julio Senn act as the key executives for him, and are reported to receive, on average, 20 proposals per month for Ronaldo's endorsement. Unlike many other footballers, Ronaldo likes to play an active part in all of this himself, and isn't merely the cheque-signer; he spends a lot of his time when not either playing or training in the offices, rolling his sleeves up and getting involved with the work at hand. He holds a weekly meeting with his advisers, is present for all things that require signature and has the ultimate veto over everything.

With regard to licensing, this is headed by Fabiano Farah, the commercial director of Grupo R9, who used to look after the licensing business of Brazilian Formula 1 legend and fellow national icon Ayrton Senna. His image rights are looked after by Luis Vicente, an old hand at this who also looks after Luis Figo. Elsewhere, Rodrigo Paiva has been responsible for Ronaldo's increasing involvement in charitable work with the United Nations, which, in a short space of time, has raised over £3m from benefit games that have seen some fine combinations of football and sports stars take to the field. Ronaldo's old friend, the French maestro Zinedine Zidane, has been involved in several of these too.

Ronaldo's roll call of endorsements is as solid as you would expect from such a star. He is an icon. Recently, respected Brazilian business magazine *Exame* ran a cover-story feature about Ronaldo's business empire, and published some figures as to exactly what Ronaldo yields from his various tie-ins each year. These were as follows: Nike – £3.5m; TIM – £3.5m; Carrefour – £1.5m; Audi – £3.5m; AmBev – £1.5m; Siemens mobile – £1.5m. Ronaldo sets stiff criteria for companies to which he lends his name and image. Each has to be the leader in its field, have a global reach and have sound ethics. In return, Ronaldo demonstrates sound loyalty (he's been with Nike and AmBev for over ten years) and has recently further demonstrated his value when a predatory bid from TIM's main network competitor in Brazil, Vivo (who list model Giselle Bündchen as their key figurehead), was rebuffed, with Ronaldo expressing a wish to honour his longstanding deal with TIM. TIM, despite being relatively unknown in Europe outside their native Italy, are huge in Brazil and have cleverly used their relationship with Ronaldo to gain a large foothold in the burgeoning Brazilian cellphone market. Ronaldo told *Exame*, 'When I give my image to a business or an activity, I have to be certain that it is something that is of high quality.'

With Siemens mobile, since their involvement with Ronaldo, sales of their handsets have increased by 27 per cent in Brazil, and sales are going so well that they are going to launch a Ronaldo-branded range of handsets later this year.

With AmBev, Brazil's largest, and now one of the world's largest brewers, Ronaldo is the figurehead for their Brahma beer, the most popular lager in Brazil. Ronaldo's face adorns billboards across Brazil promoting Brahma and he regularly features in TV adverts for them. When AmBev asked him to be guest of honour at the opening of their new plant in Guatemala last year, there was a mass invasion of the local streets by the Guatemalan public and the local TV network screened a two-hour prime-time special about his life. Three months after the opening of the plant and the frenzied reception for Ronaldo, AmBev had garnered a staggering 40 per cent of the local market.

Elsewhere, a recent survey by German consultancy 'Sport & Marketing' showed that Ronaldo is the most recognised sporting face in Asia, ahead of even Beckham and Tiger Woods. Spain's *El Pais* daily also had the surveys out recently and confirmed that, globally, Ronaldo's face is the third most recognisable in the world behind the late Pope John Paul II and American President George W. Bush: an amazing statistic for a kid from Bento Ribeiro.

The plaudits just keep on coming, with 'Starzone', one of Europe's leading image companies, extolling the marketing allure of Ronaldo, explaining that he has: 'The perfect combination of being an exceptional athlete, a humble personality, and is perceived as a dedicated father. Corporations love this mix. He is also remembered as the kid who left the *favela*, who had the beaming smile, who rose to the top, who conquered adversity – these are factors that people greatly admire in him.'

RONALDO PLC

As well as the above, there are two additional projects which Ronaldo has recently agreed to. One is a video game to be released next year, and the other is the exciting news that Fernando Meirelles, director of the brilliant film *City of God*, will be making a biopic about Ronaldo's life. Meirelles, who shot to global fame with his all-action portrayal of *favela* life in Rio, is due to start filming early next year.

Outside of football, Ronaldo has shown his appetite for wider business activity by involving himself in the recently formed A1 Grand Prix Racing series. This sub-Formula 1 series was recently founded and created by wealthy Saudi Arabian Sheikh Maktoum Hasher Maktoum Al-Maktoum. Al-Maktoum, a member of the ruling family of Dubai, has assumed the position of chief executive officer of the series. Ronaldo is the main investor in Brazil's team, and has appointed Brazilian F1 legend Emerson Fittipaldi to manage the pilot Brazilian team that is benefiting from Ronaldo's munificence.

The strength of the Ronaldo brand is quite staggering, and its global reach enables it to harvest the wealth that makes Ronaldo such a key player in world sport as a whole. He is in huge demand, and not just from the blue-chip companies listed above. Ronaldo's aura and popularity reach beyond the traditional footballing boundaries and into areas in which few, if any, other footballers can operate with any kind of credibility. For example, Russian president Vladimir Putin's recent visit to Rio ably demonstrates the clout of Ronaldo. Putin's visit was ostensibly to help engender improved trading relations with post-Soviet Russia and President Lula's new Workers' Party government. All the usual state shindigs were held and official duties performed, but the highlight of Putin's trip was his visit to the Maracanã stadium, where he was presented with a Brazilian national shirt – perhaps the country's most iconic symbol – with Ronaldo and the number 9 printed on the back.

More recently, Ronaldo visited the West Bank town of Ramallah in his capacity as a UN goodwill ambassador. The scenes that marked his visit were quite simply amazing and it was bedlam wherever he went. The crowds went berserk for him and it was interesting to note how many of them, men, women and children alike, were decked out in the various colours of Brazil, Real Madrid, Barcelona and Inter. These weren't the newly dished-out shirts of a hastily arranged PR exercise; no, these were the replicas of genuine fans, who had followed Ronaldo for years.

The affection and adulation that Ronaldo generates seems to be different in many ways to that of, say, Beckham, where it seems somewhat juvenile and superficial: rather like teenage fans at a pop concert. With Ronaldo, there seems to be a much deeper respect from those who come to get a glimpse or a handshake from their hero. The scenes were spectacular as his car struggled to get through the throng, with young and old yearning to get a sight of him or to touch him – almost like a messiah. Palestinian prime minister Ahmed Qurei was visibly starstruck and eager to make political capital out of his iconic guest; as was Israeli vice premier Shimon Peres, who chaperoned Ronaldo at the mixed soccer camp in Tel Aviv where Israeli and Palestinian children practise together.

When you actually dissect the magnitude of Ronaldo's visit, what he achieved and the imprint he left, politicians must marvel with envy at their own impotence, despite all their training, sound bites and posturing, to be able to match the superstar's rare gift: among the people, he is one of them; among the politicians, he is bigger than them; and among the kids, he is as innocent as them.

All this combines to make Ronaldo a commodity that is in huge demand, more so than any other footballer in the world today. The pressures on his time are immense, be it from his club, his sponsors or the UN and world governments, and the fact that he invariably manages to combine all the demands on him and still deliver on the pitch, all with that famous smile, are of great credit to him, and, in short, are pure Ronaldo.

CHAPTER 21

THREE MANAGERS AND A PRE-NUPTIAL – REAL MADRID 2004–05

For most of Ronaldo's colleagues at Real Madrid, there was little time to reflect on the season's disappointments as Euro 2004 in Portugal would see many of them turning out for their respective countries. For Ronaldo, he could take the summer off, even despite the Copa America being held in Peru. For an English observer, it seems bizarre that Brazil could rest Ronaldo for a tournament that is equivalent to UEFA's aforementioned Euro 2004, but rest him they did, plus several other key players. They duly won it, too, beating a full-strength Argentina in a classic final which saw them come from behind to vanquish their arch-rivals in a dramatic penalty shoot-out. Brazil's production line of fine talent was again in operation as Adriano took full advantage of Ronaldo's absence and spearheaded Brazil to victory with seven tournament goals.

On returning to Madrid for the new season, much had changed from a few months earlier. Camacho had been installed as discussed, with the luckless Queiroz making way. Morientes was back, perhaps sniffing a better deal under his old pal Camacho, and again, the competition seemed as tight as ever for forward places. This would be further compounded when Pérez, still craving his *galactico* fix, couldn't resist snapping up England's leading striker, Michael Owen from Liverpool, in what in fairness did seem like a good, if somewhat unnecessary, piece of business. So, at the start of the season, Camacho had at his disposal the outrageously talented quartet of Ronaldo, Raúl, Owen and Morientes. It was an embarrassment of striking riches and clearly not all four could be accommodated. It appeared that Morientes might be part of Camacho's plans as he starred in a 2–0 win during Real Madrid's Champions League qualifier by scoring both goals as they overcame Wisla Krakow 5–1 on aggregate. It wasn't the mere fact that he had scored, more the fact that, by playing him, he would then be cup-tied for all future Champions League games that season and his sale value would consequently diminish, an indication perhaps that he was back in favour at the Bernabéu.

Ronaldo got going in the home leg with a brace himself and Real were comfortably through to the initial group stages – an awkward mission accomplished that Pérez was visibly disgusted at having to negotiate. But this period was causing Ronaldo and several other observers at the Bernabéu concern. Pérez's strategy of *Zidanes y Pavons* had appeared to have been scrapped with the appointment of Camacho, the purchase of Samuel and Woodgate and the apparent forgiveness of Morientes. However, Owen had arrived to upset the balance and it was evident that the established stars such as Ronaldo, Raúl and Zidane were quietly wondering what on earth was going on. Beckham, after a disastrous Euro 2004, appeared to be surplus to Camacho's requirements and the mood around the Bernabéu and the training ground seemed to one of general disharmony. Camacho, who fancies himself as a bit of a martinet, seemed unable to get his ideas over to the players and bemusement and discord seemed to be on the menu. Not what was needed, with resurgent Barcelona making such a strong start to the league, again inspired by Ronaldo's countryman Ronaldinho, and ex-Real Madrid player, the Cameroonian greyhound Samuel Eto'o.

Worse was to come when, in Real's first Champions League group game, they were unceremoniously thumped 3–0 by Bayer Leverkusen with an insipid display that was pregnant with all the problems lurking beneath the surface. Camacho, best remembered for his sweaty rants during Japan 2002, was feeling the temperature rise once more, and after the 1–0 reverse at Espanyol later that week, yet again tendered his resignation at the Bernabéu. It had been another disastrous tenure for him, and it propelled the club into chaos.

Pérez, revealing his lack of deep-seated footballing knowledge, seemed at a loss over what to do. He'd tried *galactico*s and highly rated coaches; that hadn't worked. He'd gone back to brass tacks with

Camacho and that hadn't worked; so where did he go now? Again, the parallels as you looked across Europe at the big teams making the running were stark. Chelsea were starting to fire, as Mourinho and Kenyon gelled on and off the pitch. At Barcelona, another bright young chairman, Juan Laporta, wisely stayed out of things and let his emerging coach, the legendary Frank Rijkaard, do the work. Pérez was left wondering what to do and, in a laughable period for the great Spanish club, appointed the goalkeeping coach Mariano García Remón as Camacho's successor. How on earth he was meant to inspire the squad was anybody's guess, and for once, Pérez, who had sat comfortably in his plush Bernabéu seat for many months, was now looking just a little uneasy. Even worse, Barcelona were opening up a healthy gap in the league and were playing some breathtaking football. The balance of power in Spain which, only a year ago, had seemed so entrenched in Madrid, had swung, remarkably, back over to Barcelona.

Amongst all this, Ronaldo seemed somewhat bemused too. Looking across Europe once more, all the big teams had a coach or manager of enviable reputation and track record. Why were Real entrusting their season to an unknown goalkeeping coach? It didn't seem right, and quite frankly it wasn't.

The team soldiered on admirably, but there was clearly something quite badly missing in their displays. Ronaldo seemed distracted, as did the other *galacticos*. Real were fortunate not to slip fully out of contention in the league at such an early stage, even though they were now 13 points behind a rampant Barcelona. Their other challengers for the crown, champions Valencia, were having a lean time of things. New coach Claudio Ranieri had tinkered the heart out of last season's side, who now looked a totally different beast from the slick passing machine that Liverpool-bound Rafael Benítez had assembled. Ranieri brought in a string of expensive Italian imports who had little effect and he too, like Camacho, would be out of work before long.

All this confusion seemed to distract Ronaldo. His game lacked its usual potency and his figure again seemed somewhat Rubenesque, which inevitably was seized upon by the Spanish media. Yet again, he seemed to be the fall guy for the team's fortunes, despite the fact that they were collectively playing poorly and without much gumption. The Spanish press wasted no time in trotting out the *gordo* lines once more. There seemed to be a lot going on in his life at this stage. His new relationship with model Daniella Cicarelli had become common knowledge and this in turn led to some serious upheavals in Ronaldo's life.

Cicarelli, a fine specimen from the state of Minas Gerais to the north-east of Rio, was one of the most recognisable faces in Brazil at the time. A fully fledged Brazilian supermodel, her face adorned numerous billboards for face care products and the like, but also, she had been signed by TIM, with whom Ronaldo, as we know, has a huge contract. It is rumoured that they met on the set of one of these photo-shoots, became close friends and, in turn, lovers. Cicarelli, a statuesque, sparkly-eyed, toothy beauty, wasted no time in ingratiating herself with Ronaldo and very quickly they became a full-on item. However, not all was plain sailing, as it soon transpired that two of Ronaldo's most trusted aides and confidants, Rodrigo Paiva (his long-standing press officer/agent and friend) and César (who'd been with him since his Cruzeiro days), were now no longer on the payroll. Many at the time attributed this to Cicarelli's involvement. I tried to find some answers directly with Rodrigo Paiva but he wouldn't be drawn on the subject, preferring to keep his counsel, but it all did seem rather strange at the time and the Brazilian gossip magazines had a field day as the news broke. Later, Rodrigo would refer to the whole situation with resigned frustration as 'AC/DC', short for *antes Cicarelli/depois Cicarelli* – a very subtle play on words from Ronaldo's ex-press officer, but one which translates as 'before Cicarelli/after Cicarelli'. Rodrigo, clearly upset about the whole imbroglio, chose his words carefully for his interview with Rio sports daily *Lance!*, but he was understandably miffed, and demonstrated a friend's concern about the whole matter.

Ronaldo, not long separated from Milene, was now back in the limelight with some serious arm candy. Whilst I was in Rio, I tried to gauge the reaction of the general public as to their views on Cicarelli, and the overall impression was not favourable. She was a member of the São Paulo female high society and had had a string of tempestuous short-lived relationships with high-profile figures in Brazilian life. However, she had hit pay dirt with Ronaldo; and if she was covetous of his dough then she was fishing in the right pond as they don't come any bigger (or wealthier) than Ronaldo in Brazil.

Despite the public's misgivings, things seemed rosy. The couple were rarely seen apart and were happy to play up to the constant retinue of paparazzi that snapped away eagerly to feed awaiting gossip columns. The couple were big news and Posh and Becks-style hysteria developed in the gossip-hungry cities of São Paulo and Rio.

Ronaldo seemed clearly smitten and on the pitch he was happy to tell all the world how he was feeling with a newly developed goal celebration. Now, for someone like Ronaldo, who scores with such metronomic regularity, this was clearly going to get a lot of airtime, so it was no half-measure. It all started when he had the back of his left wrist tattooed with a 'D', a loveheart and an 'R'. After each goal, he would raise this wrist to his forehead and display the tattoo for everyone to see; his own variation almost on Raúl's famous wedding-ring kiss. It all seemed a bit unnatural and contrived, as it clearly was, and somewhat removed from the trademark right index finger that the world had grown so familiar with. But love can do strange things to men, as my father once told me.

Meanwhile, amongst all the furore of the Cicarelli hysteria and the upheavals at Real, Ronaldo was still in predatory mood for Brazil. His ability to do things 'in a grand way', as Rodrigo Paiva put it, remained undiminished with his hat-trick of penalties against Argentina in their recent World Cup qualifier. Only three people have ever done this in an international game, and Brazil won 3–0 to go top of the South American qualifying group and leapfrog the men from the Pampas. In an extraordinary game, with Ronaldo to the fore in virtually everything Brazil did, he actually netted four penalties, as his first one had to be retaken. The game was particularly symbolic for Ronaldo as it was played in Belo Horizonte, home of his first professional club, Cruzeiro. To score three was the perfect return to the place where he began to amaze the world and say thank you to the devoted fans. They showed their gratitude vocally as the whole ground reverberated with 'Ron-al-do, Ron-al-do, Ron-al-do'. It was a moving moment. I asked Leonardo Ferreira of Cruzeiro, who was at the game, about the atmosphere and he said, 'It was fantastic. To beat Argentina is always great, but for it to be our hero and idol Ronaldo who was doing all the damage and playing so well was just a dream for us.'

Ronaldo was suitably inspired and his rampant play was the difference between the two teams, as his blistering direct runs into the box led to fouls that resulted in each of the three penalties. He drew rave reviews all round. There was the inevitable wave of approbation from the Brazil camp, with teammate Ze Roberto saying, 'I wouldn't go so far as to say Ronaldo won the game single-handedly, but it wouldn't be far from the truth.'

RONALDO

Some, including coach Carlos Alberto Parreira, went even further: 'He is the best striker in the world today. Tonight, he made the difference.'

Ronaldo's consummate display was well timed, coming as it did in the wake of persistent rumours about his apparent weight gain. When asked about this, Mario Zagallo could not fail to see the irony: 'They say Ronaldo is fat. Well, I for one would love to have eleven "fat" players like Ronaldo in my side. To my mind, he's the best player in the world today.'

Even the vanquished Argentines were generous in their praise of the Brazilian number 9, with coach Marcelo Bielsa saying, 'He won the game for them; he caused all the problems.'

Javier Zanetti, Ronaldo's ex-teammate from Inter Milan, said that, 'The only way to stop Ronaldo is to catch him when he starts his runs, and then shout for help from some teammates.' The Argentinean also had this to say: 'During the game, he was giving instructions to his defence to try and sort things out. Some people say he's fat, but as far as I can remember he was even heavier when he was in Italy. As a human being, though, he is superb.'

Ronaldo scored again in the 3–1 win over Bolivia, his goal coming in the first minute with Brazil's first attack. He then bagged another brace in the 5–2 demolition of Venezuela. Brazil's progress to the finals in Germany was looking assured.

Back in Spain, Pérez needed to act and he needed to act fast to get Real's season back on track. Perhaps taking a leaf out of the books of the other clubs just mentioned, he appointed Arrigo Sacchi as general manager of football. As an ex-Italian national manager and the man credited with creating the great Milan side of the late '80s and early '90s that contained Gullit, van Basten *et al.*, Sacchi's CV is excellent and, importantly, he is hugely respected – something that poor Remón could only dream about. Sacchi was given the autonomy he needed to work in isolation away from Pérez and control over footballing decisions. He moved quickly to restructure the club on the playing side and wasted little time in securing a new manager. The appointment was bold and took a lot of people by surprise. Not many people outside of Brazil will have heard of the wonderfully named Vanderlei Luxemburgo, who was unveiled in late December 2004 as the new man at the helm. Luxemburgo, a tall, lapidary 52-year-old Brazilian, had been the leading domestic coach in Brazil for the last few seasons, winning five titles with four different clubs, and had also been in charge of the Brazilian national side that convincingly won the 1999 Copa America, in which Ronaldo was so devastating. Luxemburgo quit as boss of the Brazilian champions Santos to join Real and at the press conference demonstrated all his fêted PR slickness, saying, 'It is a very great personal satisfaction to coach the world's best team. What I will bring to Real Madrid is discipline, unity, hard work and professionalism. I cannot promise titles, but I have come here to win – I cannot say any different.'

Having one of the world's leading managers at the helm finally got Real back on track. Brazilian players are the best in the world, so why not Brazilian coaches? For some time, Brazil's coaches have been sneered at for being part of the oft-derided Brazilian domestic league that is riddled with corruption and suffers from a non-stop merry-go-round of sackings and re-appointments; but Luxemburgo's record of success back home was better, result for result, than any current European coach. Sacchi deserves credit for being alive to this and for having the courage to execute the appointment. Luxemburgo is credited with shaping well-disciplined, very fit teams that play organised attacking football; just the type needed at the Bernabéu. His first task was the rather bizarre assignment of negotiating a six-minute game against Real Sociedad, as the original match had to be abandoned due to a bomb scare. It seemed tedious for all involved, but it proved a vital fillip for Luxemburgo in getting off to a winning start, as Ronaldo, with only seconds remaining, burst into the box only to be clumsily upended. Zidane converted the resulting penalty. 'It was the best start I could have had,' Luxemburgo told local press. 'At that moment, the players started to believe again.'

Believe they certainly did, and Real set off on a seven-game winning streak that not only racked up points, but restored much-needed respect to the club, which was on the verge of descending into a state of derision, much like Barcelona had done in the final throes of the van Gaal/Gaspart era. It got their league campaign back on track and showed that Luxemburgo was a coach to be reckoned with. Suddenly, it became the norm to see morning and afternoon training sessions, which were rare in Europe but common currency in Brazil. Some players complained, but not for long, and within a short space of time Real were celebrating their lack of injuries and much-improved physical form. However, Luxemburgo's appointment didn't initially go well for Ronaldo. One might expect that having a fellow Brazilian in charge would have sat well, but things seemed frosty to start with and, with Ronaldo's form dipping alarmingly, Luxemburgo showed he had no difficulty in dropping the striker, whose weight seemed heavy again. Luxemburgo held no truck with lazy superstars; he wanted the best out of them, as he expected to offer them nothing less from himself, and his hardline stance had shades of legendary American Football coach Vinny Lombardi's brilliant quip: 'If you're not fired with enthusiasm, then you'll be *fired* with enthusiasm.' The *Madrileños* implored him to '*darles cana*', literally meaning 'give them the cane', or, more accurately, 'kick them up the arse'. Slowly but surely, he was getting his message across to the *galactico*s. Again, Ronaldo seemed miles away, as off-the-field events seemed to be clouding his focus and judgement. To compound matters, the place where he could always escape whatever life's slings and arrows were throwing at him was also letting him down, as he went on the only prolonged lean spell of his career, and didn't score for 12 games. Again, we need to stand back and look at this poor run in its true context. Ronaldo's barren patches are rare; very rare; in fact, rarer than an Alan Hansen article without reference to his Liverpool days. Ronaldo's 12-game dry spell included *La Liga*, Champions League, Copa Del Rey and *seleçao* games, so it wasn't perhaps quite as bad as many observers were making out. But the frustration was visibly getting to him and Ronaldo blew his top after Luxemburgo subbed him again towards the end of Real's game against Mallorca after a lacklustre showing. Ronaldo was struggling to regain his old tempo and, as George Michael will tell you, guilty feet have got no rhythm. On being hauled off, Ronaldo bypassed the dugout and went straight for the tunnel, where he was caught on film whipping his shirt off and flinging it away in disgust. The game was particularly poignant for Ronaldo as, yet again, he had looked sluggish. Furthermore, not only had he failed to score, he had failed to score against his old adversary: the Argentinian Hector Cúper, who was now in charge of Mallorca.

Slap bang in the middle of this dry spell was all the brouhaha that surrounded Ronaldo's 'wedding' to Cicarelli. This was one of those sagas that must have had the coaching staff at the Bernabéu rolling their eyes with bemusement and frustration. The event had been temporised on three separate occasions and the staff were understandably perplexed at the big distraction it was creating. To have a full-blown showbiz wedding in the middle of the club's toughest and most important part of the season was not high on Pérez's, Sacchi's or Luxemburgo's wish list. They knew the bulk of their squad would be on the guest list and they were not happy. The 'wedding' was finally scheduled for 14 February: a romantic gesture, you may think, but more a puerile one when you understand that

THREE MANAGERS AND A PRE-NUPTIAL . . .

Valentine's Day isn't a big deal in Brazil, so the Brazilian lovebirds were merely paying homage to a European tradition with which they were not that familiar.

But, familiar or not, the 'do' was an incredibly lavish affair that, by all accounts in Brazil, was all of Cicarelli's bidding. Ronaldo's usual agents of action, Paiva and César, were shabbily overlooked (this was a factor in their subsequent fall-outs) and the planning went ahead for a spectacular bash at the sumptuous Château de Chantilly, about an hour outside Paris. I can only assume my invite was lost in the post, but I'm reliably informed. It was a *Hello!* magazine-style wedding to end them all. Irish rockers U2 were scheduled to provide the music, with Ronaldo calling in a favour from his old pal Bono. The catering alone was thought to be coming in at €2,135 per head, and a fleet of sponsored Audis was on-hand to ferry guests around. Even *Footballers' Wives* couldn't have scripted it.

But in the end, the event turned into a fiasco. As it was, Ronaldo's divorce from Milene wasn't official and hadn't come through yet, and, more alarmingly, it transpired that Cicarelli was a feme covert, as a whirlwind marriage to a mysteriously anonymous Brazilian some time back was also, as yet, not annulled. As such, there could be no official service – a bizarre, but somehow rather Brazilian oversight. With everything booked and in place, being Brazilian, they decided to go ahead and throw a massive party instead. Events got even more bizarre when, at the evening do, Cicarelli unceremoniously kicked gatecrasher Carolina Bittencourt out of the place, creating a right old rumpus in the process. The source of her pique was that the fellow model (an old sparring partner from the Brazil *Maria-chuteira* circuit) was on the arm of Daniella's ex-boyfriend João Paulo Diniz. By all accounts, it was a hugely embarrassing situation and one that Ronaldo didn't seem best chuffed with. It seemed to be a case of 'she doth protest too much' and rumours immediately re-ignited that Cicarelli was still hung-up on Diniz, a wealthy supermarket heir. It was a very inauspicious start for the couple, and Ronaldo further rocked the boat back in Spain by returning a day late and then arriving late for training, which promptly got him dropped for the game against Athletic Bilbao and landed him a club fine. Things would get worse several weeks later when Cicarelli miscarried the baby the duo were expecting.

Luxemburgo set about getting his prize striker back to scoring goals. Real were now looking solid and organised again, not the ragtag bunch that were shaming the shirt under Camacho and Remón. Owen was putting his early-season frustrations behind him and scoring with regularity when the chances arose; Raúl was playing some of his best stuff in a long time and Beckham looked back to his Man United swagger once restored to his familiar berth at right midfield. However, problems still surfaced at the back. Woodgate was extending his highly paid sojourn in the capital and looked nowhere near doing a full training session, never mind making the starting line-up. His joint buy, 'The Wall' Walter Samuel, seemed Jerry-built and was having a miserable season, looking slow, cumbersome and inept – a trinity of attributes you wouldn't perhaps expect in a £16.5m defender – and, as an impulsive shirt-puller, was finding the referees less lenient in Spain than he had at Roma and had chalked up a whopping 17 yellow cards.

To get Ronaldo in shape and focused again, Luxemburgo, not unlike Scolari before Japan 2002, got his hand-picked backroom staff of fitness experts and dieticians to get cracking. These included his right-hand man and physical trainer Antonio Mello, and the nutritionist Patricia Fernandes Teixera. It was Teixera who really got hold of Ronaldo and is credited with getting him back to the lean machine he can be, helping him to lose six kilos. She explained her concept to the Spanish press as, 'There are no forbidden foods. The diet is individual, respecting each player's preferences and balancing elements such as proteins, fibres, carbohydrates and so on. Sports nutrition is something we have been doing for a while in Brazil but it seems to be a new concept here.'

In a short time, Ronaldo got back to his optimum weight, which he feels is 82 kg. The evidence was clear to see when he and his 'wife' posed for a surprisingly tasteful black-and-white shoot that featured in Brazilian *Vogue*, with Ronaldo stripped down to his waist displaying a taut six-pack.

But things got worse before they got better for Ronaldo and Real Madrid, with the thing they really loathe at the Bernabéu: exit from the Champions League. In a titanic struggle that went to extra time, their irascible rivals from Turin edged them out with only four minutes left, Marcelo Zalayeta scoring the clinical winner for Juventus. Real had admittedly put in a lacklustre performance in Turin and should have taken more out of the first leg than just the 1–0 lead. In that first leg, Real had played with real verve and passion, with only some typically inspired keeping by Buffon and the woodwork restricting the score to its surmountable level. For the deciding return leg in Turin, Real huffed and puffed but couldn't blow down a thick black-and-white wall. Ronaldo played as well as anybody, hitting the post and having one chalked off for offside, and as his frustration grew, he fell for a sucker punch from Alessio Tacchinardi, who lured him into a row off the ball. For Ronaldo, it was going wrong all at once – the pressure of his off-the-field problems, plus his ongoing goal drought, which seemed to be being extended by uncooperative woodwork in game after game – and he swung a rash kick at the Italian and got his marching orders (along with Tacchinardi) for only the second time in his professional career. Juventus had done them again. Lifting the European Cup for the tenth time continues to be a Gordian task for Real. The Italian press loved it.

Having scored just four goals in three months since the arrival of Luxemburgo and been roundly booed by the *Madrileños*, Ronaldo finally ended the drought that had been so alien and distracting to him. And what a way to end it. With the disappointment of the Champions League exit to Juventus still bugging them like a wasp on a summer's day, Real had only one thing left to play for and set their sights on reeling-in Barcelona's lead at the top of *La Liga*. Barcelona had similarly been dumped out of the Champions League in a feisty tie against Chelsea. It had knocked the stuffing out of them for a time, allowing Real to get back into contention. Admittedly, it needed a major stumble for the Catalans to cede the crown that had seemed to be theirs for the taking all year long, but Luxemburgo had instilled that winners' mentality in his men and, despite the long odds, the mood was positive. And what better dent to put in Barcelona's lead than by beating them at the Bernabéu?

The game proved to be one of those *La Liga* classics that everybody loves. A packed Bernabéu gave Barcelona an especially hostile reception and Real got off to a dream start when Ronaldo jinked his way down the right flank, picked his spot and floated over an inviting cross for Zidane. The Frenchman showed admirable bravery by launching his bald pate full length at the ball and planting it in the back of the net, fractionally before he collided with the far post. There was a moment of concern as the maestro lay stricken in the goal mouth, but he rose to his talented feet and the panic was defused. Then Beckham, having perhaps his best game of the season, delivered one of his trademark crosses (something he was doing more and more now that he'd been restored to the right flank under Luxemburgo) and Ronaldo nodded in a header to thankfully close his irritating drought. His delight was tangible and it visibly lifted him as he went on to have his best game for about three months, tormenting the Barcelona back line with his buccaneering runs and bullish strength. It was a humdinger and the quality on show was breathtaking. Samuel Eto'o gave Barcelona a lifeline four minutes later when he scored a brilliant solo goal, but then Raúl, likewise having an authoritative game, latched on to Ronaldo's pass and restored the two-goal cushion on the stroke of half-time. What a game!

Then Beckham produced a moment of sublime brilliance to put the match beyond doubt. On the same night that Tiger Woods unfurled perhaps the best golf shot ever seen, caressing an outrageous chip into the 16th cup at Augusta to reaffirm his place at the top of golf's world order, Beckham similarly adjusted the loft on his equally fêted tool of choice, namely his right Adidas Predator, and dinked a dreamy through-ball into the path of his galloping England colleague Michael Owen. Demonstrating his alarming one-footedness for a striker of his status and record, Owen, in charging onto the pass, was forced to adjust and twist his body shape to get the ball onto his right foot; but he did so with great skill and instinct, and then flicked it past Valdes into the Barcelona goal. Bedlam ensued and Owen, in a massive release of pent-up frustration, wellied the ball into the far end as it came back out, before scampering off towards the crowd in a display of well-earned delirium. Real were alive and kicking. Undiminished, Ronaldinho stroked home a lovely free kick to make the final score 4–2, but Real had sent a message: 'Rumours of their demise were premature.' As Luxemburgo double-punched the air in celebration of a brilliant win, Barcelona knew they were in a race to the tape. The game was marvellous, and I challenge anybody, apart from Liverpool fans, not to consider it a shame that these two brilliant footballing clubs had been eliminated from the Champions League at this stage.

In a thrilling finale to an excellent *La Liga* season, Barcelona held off Real to take the crown for the first time in six seasons. Real had run them close but their crass errors, both on and off the pitch, in the early part of the season cost them dear. Barcelona were rightly crowned champions and took possession of the Spanish bragging rights. Revitalised, sharp and lean, Ronaldo had gone on another of his scoring streaks and he had that *pistolero* glint back in his eye, rattling in seven goals in as many games to take his league total to twenty-four – not sufficient to bag him another Pichichi award (Uruguayan Diego Forlan won that on the last day, just pipping Samuel Eto'o), but another fine return nonetheless.

THREE MANAGERS AND A PRE-NUPTIAL . . .

So the *galacticos* concluded another season *sans* silverware. Sacchi and Luxemburgo had restored a lot of sanity, order and pride to the dressing-room and the club as a whole. Ronaldo handed in yet another outstanding card for goals scored and, without the fun and games around Valentine's Day, he could well have been lifting yet another Pichichi award. He could look back on a season of ups and downs; one where he had performed to his usual outstanding standards but let himself get far too distracted at times. As the season came to a close, it had one more bizarre twist. It was announced that Ronaldo had severed ties with his 'wife' Cicarelli. In what had proven to be a union worthy of any of Brazil's ubiquitous *novelas* (daily soap operas), it was announced in late May that Ronaldo had called it a day with his tempestuous girlfriend. Amid reports of some quite spectacular mood swings and tantrums, it was revealed that Cicarelli had been spending a lot of time back in São Paulo hosting her MTV show *Beija Sapo* (Kiss the Frog), which was allegedly getting Ronaldo's back up and making him think more and more about the sage advice handed out to him by his close allies at the outset of their relationship (who, in time, Cicarelli had managed to alienate). The dragon's teeth had been sown with Cicarelli's attendance at João Paulo Diniz's party in São Paulo – a fact that was only made known to Ronaldo by acquaintances who had spotted her cavorting around in the early hours. Ronaldo had begun to doubt Cicarelli's temperament after a story broke that she'd thrown a mobile phone at Ronaldo's driver, Pappi, when she found some condoms in the glove compartment. Despite the explanation that the French letters were for Guti's use, the mobile clattered poor Pappi flush on the forehead as Cicarelli went bananas. Now, Ronaldo had had enough and called it a day.

The split may put a dint in Ronaldo's coffers, as it is said that they have a pre-nuptial agreement that gives Cicarelli $5 million in the case of 'divorce'. Not a bad haul for a three-month roller-coaster ride. How the respective lawyers will interpret the 'marriage that wasn't a marriage' back in Paris, I'm not sure, but it could make interesting viewing.

CHAPTER 22

LOOKING AHEAD

So what does the future hold for Ronaldo? In early 2005, Rodrigo Paiva confirmed to me that Ronaldo was very happy at Madrid and wants to see his contract out there through to its conclusion in 2008. However, a lot has changed since then, and if you take your eye off Real Madrid for a moment, then you do so at your own risk. As the 2005–06 season unfolded, trying to make predictions and pass accurate comment about the famous club became a mug's game.

After ending the previous season on such a fine run of free-scoring form, Luxemburgo, perhaps feeling more secure in his job, decided to flex his ego and his tactical muscles and switched the system to his preferred, but somewhat bizarre, 4–2–2–2 'boxes' system. In doing so, he wrought confusion, head-scratching and, in turn, a loss of form.

Michael Owen was offloaded to struggling Newcastle United, albeit for a lively £16 million, which yielded a nice £8-million profit in 12 months. Owen could look back with pride on his stay in Spain, which, although not establishing him as central to team planning, brought him his usual batch of important goals.

The club would rue selling him, as, within a short space of time, both Raúl and Ronaldo were injured. Ronaldo had started the season in blistering form. He looked lean and fit and scored some typically outrageous goals. His season got off to the perfect start, with a goal after three minutes in game-one, versus Cadiz. By game-seven, against neighbours Atlético Madrid, he had seven against his name and was about to make it eight and seal his hat-trick when Atlético's Perea went through the back of him with a crude challenge as he shaped to shoot. Perea's challenge would ultimately concede an own goal and deprive Ronaldo of his hat-trick, but far worse was that Ronaldo was stretchered off with a badly damaged ankle. It took the gloss off an impressive derby victory which had bought Luxemburgo some breathing space, but the truth is that Real's start to the season had been poor. Their football lacked any real conviction – the tactical straightjacket of Luxemburgo's 4–2–2–2 system suffocating all the flair out of the team – and it was only Ronaldo's goals once more that were saving the club from complete anonymity.

But with Ronaldo now ruled out for a month, Owen counting his money on Tyneside and new signings Robinho and Julio Baptista struggling to settle, Luxemburgo, like Queiroz and del Bosque before him, saw how valuable Ronaldo was to him. Real's form was all over the place, with them winning and losing games with equal measure, and they were thumped unceremoniously by Valencia and Deportivo la Coruña. Their Champions League form was also patchy, and the club was again hovering close to ridicule.

Things came to an embarrassing head on 20 November, when Barcelona visited the Bernabéu. After a slow start to the season, Barcelona had recently struck top gear and made their way to the top of *La Liga* with the sizzling football that had won them the league the previous season. Some of their play was quite brilliant, with Samuel Eto'o and Ronaldinho again providing most of the dazzling colour, and the latest 'next Maradona', the floppy haired Lionel Messi, suggesting he could join the greats too. Luxemburgo knew that defeat would put his job under almost critical strain. Gambling, he brought Ronaldo back from injury before he was match fit and also ushered the ailing Zidane back too soon.

Defeat against Barcelona is never easy to take for Real Madrid, but the stuffing that Barcelona inflicted on them was not far off a public flogging. Ronaldinho was at his insulting best and scored two goals of high-speed brilliance, his second leaving the isolated Casillas completely emasculated. His super-show heralded a rare standing ovation from the hard-to-please Madrid crowd, but many feel it was not only a show of fulsome appreciation but a pointed gesture towards their hapless board of directors to fully compound their unease and embarrassment. Barcelona were now the undoubted darlings of European football. They had a young team, a young board, a young coach and, in Ronaldinho, they had a talisman who could do no wrong. Everything about them felt fresh and vibrant. In stark contrast, Luxemburgo's Madrid seemed sclerotic and, not surprisingly, he paid for it with his job, as Pérez, like a desperate scientist wrestling vainly with his malfunctioning *galactico* invention, sacked him soon after.

Ronaldo was clearly not fit for the Barcelona game and was a mere onlooker throughout, observing his friend and compatriot Ronaldinho perform with the verve and elan he had himself once shown for Barcelona. He would miss the next few games as his ankle took time to fully recover, and his much-heralded World Cup year was now looking somewhat in jeopardy. He desperately wanted to put in a good season and tee himself up for Germany, but, again, his niggling fitness worries and the pantomime-horse antics behind the scenes at the Bernabéu were casting a shadow over the whole situation.

The Barcelona game was a watershed for many things at the Bernabéu. As discussed, it lead to Luxemburgo's removal and highlighted many of the shortcomings at the club. Respected *AS* columnist Alfredo Relaño had some intriguing observations around this time about Real's dependency on a fit Ronaldo. If Ronaldo isn't quite the swashbuckling player of old, his goals and sheer presence are of vital importance to the team. Relaño refers back to the Atlético Madrid game when Ronaldo was initially injured, saying:

> After Atlético, the injured Ronaldo left Madrid as leaders, five points ahead of Barca, who were then sixth. Eleven rounds have passed in which Ronaldo has not played or has played whilst injured. Now Barca are top of the table, with a thirteen-point lead over Madrid, now in sixth. . . .
>
> Ronaldo is all Madrid has, whether they like to admit it or not. If he's in the team, there are goals, expectations, intimidation, optimism. If he's not, they're left with a bundle of makeshift forwards; discussions re Guti 'yes or no?'; re Sergio Ramos here or there; four crosses from Beckham and three shots on goal from Roberto Carlos. Coaches come and go, and Madrid cannot rid itself of this extraordinary dependence on an even more extraordinary player. He produces a lot from very little. He doesn't run, doesn't track back, doesn't pressurise the ball, doesn't head the ball, doesn't participate, or even train! But with three runs, he scores two goals and wins a match.

LOOKING AHEAD

What to do with such a player? Madrid need to let him recover, and recover fully, and in the meantime cross their fingers. Or buy a genuinely good centre-forward, who won't be like him because there aren't any (except Samuel Eto'o, who was allowed to go [from Real] to Barca), and try and survive his absences in the interim. Such is the reverence for Ronaldo, conscious or subconscious, that in the last eighteen months Madrid have bought eleven players (and got through four coaches) but they haven't devised a solution, not even a provisional one, for Ronaldo's absences.

As Luxemburgo returned to Brazil in a huff to rejoin Santos, Pérez appointed Juan Ramon Lopez Caro from the reserve team. Arrigo Sacchi also left, citing personal reasons, but one felt that he found the current reality uncomfortable and restrictive. Barcelona sailed on merrily ahead at the top of the league, and Lopez Caro's first job was to get some discipline and belief back into the team. He reverted back to 4–4–2, which everybody seemed far more at home with. He also wisely reinstalled Beckham to right-midfield and instructed him to cross the ball at will, something Beckham's right peg needs no second invitation to do.

The situation was virtually identical to the farce that unfolded 12 months earlier with Camacho's exit. Real were similarly 13 points adrift of Barcelona and had similarly appointed a caretaker from within. But, in fairness, Lopez Caro seems to have far more about him than García Rémon and has got the team playing some eye-catching stuff once more. In a policy turnaround from days gone by, they made signings in the January transfer window and brought in the highly rated São Paulo full-back Cicinho and Italian hothead Antonio Cassano. This apostasy from Pérez went against one of his most touted maxims: you don't sign players in the January window, as it is a reflection that your pre-season strategy has failed. Not for the first time, Pérez was being forced to make humbling U-turns.

Meanwhile, and to the surprise of many, Lopez Caro had got Madrid playing football again. Beckham was playing some of his best stuff since arriving in Spain, Robinho was getting his tricks out, and with the return of Woodgate came a flurry of clean sheets. All looked good for the visit of Arsenal in the last 16 of the Champions League. Could Madrid 'do a Liverpool': ignore poor domestic form and engineer their way to lifting the Cup? Arsenal were trying a similar stunt, and the first leg at the Bernabéu was awaited with grand anticipation.

Madrid were on good form, were scoring freely again and seemed harmonious under Lopez Caro. Then, the day before Arsenal, at a routine press conference, Ronaldo amazed all present with a quite unbelievable broadside against the Real fans. Lopez Caro must have been going ape with annoyance, as all his good work and improvements were suddenly torpedoed from left-field. Ronaldo, taking the microphone upon himself, railed against the Bernabéu faithful, saying, 'I've never felt at home in the Bernabéu; the fans have never treated me with affection. They have never accepted me. After all the efforts I made to come to this club, I don't understand why they treat me like this. I will decide my future after the World Cup.'

He continued, 'I've thought about it and spoken with hundreds of people, and I have never understood why the fans have had so little patience with me. As soon as I make an error, people jeer me.' He then showed alarming lack of tact by closing with, 'I don't know how the fans will react to this, but, to be honest, I don't care.'

Well, he didn't have long to wait, as the next evening Real put on one of the worst displays ever offered by a team of such repute. A litany of incomplete passes, inept miscues and surrender of possession wrought howls of derision and disbelief from the Madrid fans. Arsenal couldn't believe their luck. Madrid played like a Ryman League side, and Arsenal took full advantage. Only superhero Casillas, with yet more stunning saves, kept the damage down to Thierry Henry's virtuoso solo goal. The game had been billed as the battle of the strikers, namely Ronaldo and Henry. Many assumed that, after Ronaldo's unprovoked tirade against the fans and talk of a possible move, he had a blistering display up his sleeve to promote himself, ready for one last move and to thumb his nose at the Madrid fans who'd jeered him. Well, he certainly gave them plenty to jeer about, as he barely touched the ball all game and lumbered around looking sullen and sluggish. Henry completely upstaged him and rightfully took the morning headlines.

In an instant, a veil of gloom descended over Madrid once more, and Lopez Caro's mini-revival stalled. It then flatlined completely the coming Saturday when, after Madrid had taken the lead from a super Sergio Ramos header, Mallorca rallied superbly to beat them 2–1. The game was played in torrential rain, and the rain would begin to wash away all vestiges of the *galactico* project. Pérez, with whom one can sympathise to an extent, had tried to bring the greatest show on earth to his beloved club. For a while under Queiroz, he had, and this had been handsomely rewarded by umpteen lucrative sponsorship deals, which enabled Real to be labelled the wealthiest club in the world. Pérez, as he pondered things on the flight home from Mallorca, perhaps saw this as a chance to quit while could at least make reference to this accolade.

The next day, it was announced to an emergency press gathering that the architect of the flawed *galactico* regime had stood down. In his place came Fernando Martin, who wasted no time in asserting his authority and told the assembled press, 'I don't want a team of millionaires. I want a team who work 24 hours a day to achieve the best for our fans.' In a thinly veiled dig at Ronaldo and the other underperforming *galacticos*, he went on, 'Those players who think they can stay here giving only the minimum amount of effort are wrong. Those who fight and sweat for the shirt know that they will have mine and the club's full support.'

By now, it seemed that both the club and Ronaldo himself had made their own minds up: it was time for both to move on. Ronaldo was 'rested' for the next game against city rivals Atlético, and, as the crucial second leg against Arsenal approached, anticipation reached fever pitch, as the game had so much riding on it for both clubs.

I've seen many 0–0 draws in my time, and all of them have been nothing to write home about. Bar one. The 0–0 cliffhanger that Arsenal and Real slugged out on a rain-sodden Highbury pitch was an almighty game. As rain tipped down from the north-London sky, both teams went for each other's jugular, knowing that defeat was not an option. Perhaps in search of a bit of nostalgia, Lopez Caro opted for Ronaldo and Raúl up front, the pairing that had served the club so well but had been badly misfiring of late. But, as Ronaldo emerged for the pre-match warm-up, he looked alarmingly big. He looked like an ageing heavyweight who had badly underprepared for the big fight, hoping to rely on one magical counterpunch of old to floor his opponent, rather than going through the diligent preparation that he knew he should have done. As the game unfolded, he looked sluggish and disinterested, and was blowing like a veteran. He had the odd chance here and there but was of no real threat all night. It was sad to watch. Elsewhere, Zidane, despite exhibiting his magical control on the skidpan surface, was again looking past it and was upstaged by the young live wire Fabregas. Raúl and Beckham tried hard, but Arsenal and their madcap keeper Lehman contained all they had to offer.

RONALDO

As the final whistle went and Arsenal and Highbury erupted, the Spaniards Guti, Ramos and Raúl fell to their knees. In stark contrast, Ronaldo and Zidane took no time and were down the tunnel in tandem like ferrets after a rabbit. The two greatest and most-decorated players of the last ten years dissolved away from view together, and both looked like they knew time was up. Guti, Ramos and Raúl, once they had lifted themselves up, trudged disconsolately over to the pocket of Madrid fans penned in at the Clock End and threw in their shirts and received a warm round of applause. This gesture wouldn't have been lost on the fans. It was a weird sensation watching the denouement of this game. On the one hand, it was sad to see the swansong of such a set of stars and the *galactico* era to be ushered swiftly to its end; but, on the other, it was also an honour to be there and witness it – perhaps, I imagined, like being at Sinatra's last concert. But I'm sure that Old Blue Eyes wouldn't have missed so many notes as Real had that night.

For Ronaldo, he must take a long hard look at what he wants to do. Zidane is excused, to an extent, as he is 34. Ronaldo is 29 and should have a few more good years left in him at the top level, but the decision, as Roberto Baggio once advised him, 'will come from inside you'. But, at the time of writing, he would appear to be through with Real Madrid. His physical condition is a big issue in every sense, and he looks many kilos overweight, almost like a doorman. It now seems evident that, as he approaches 30, he needs to concentrate more than ever on keeping his volatile weight in check. He should have been substituted against Arsenal, but Lopez Caro kept him on, perhaps protecting Ronaldo from the indignity of it all. Caring nothing for reputations, the waggish Arsenal fans even chimed in with a hearty rendition of that English terrace classic 'You fat bastard', which I'm pretty sure is the first time Ronaldo or a World Footballer of the Year has had to suffer such indignity!

As Germany looms, he must get himself in the right frame of mind to lead Brazil's vaunted attack and, in line with that, must get himself back to the shape that Scolari's cadre of advisers got him in prior to Japan and Korea 2002. Back then, his body fat was 8 per cent. Even from the stands, it was plain to see it was nowhere near that at Highbury. If he doesn't regain his fitness, a glorious career could come to a sad premature end. He has a lot to get right before then. But don't write him off just yet. At the time of writing, Ladbrokes have him at 8–1 to be tournament top-scorer – the shortest odds of any striker. It might be worth having a punt on that; Gerry Armstrong certainly will.

LOOKING AHEAD

As the gloom descended after the Arsenal exit, Ronaldo received encouragement from a variety of well-wishers. One, understandably, was his new girlfriend, Raica de Oliveira, a rare brunette, who flew to Madrid to be with him. Messages of goodwill also came in from his ex-wife Milene, and, bizarrely, from Brazilian President Lula, who urged Ronaldo to get fit and ready for the World Cup.

As Europe's press rounded on him, even the Brazilian press were diverting from their usual course of hero-worship with some vitriolic articles about his condition and suitability to lead the line in Germany. However, on the whole, at home in Brazil he continues to be idolised and remains their top man, even with the undoubted brilliance of Ronaldinho, Adriano and Kaká vying for top-billing. Walk down any high street in Brazil and you will see his face adorning billboards, news kiosks, beer mats, fly posters – virtually everything. He remains box office. Brazil are clear favourites for Germany 2006 and will travel with a dazzling squad that, injury permitting, could contain, among others, Dida, Roberto Carlos, Cafu, Lucio, Robinho, Diego, Kaká, Ronaldinho, Cicinho, Emerson, Luis Fabiano, Adriano, and, of course, Ronaldo. Assuming Ronaldo gets his act together by then, and Parreira takes him, he will have Pelé's finals goal-scoring record firmly in his sights.

Where he goes after that has become the source of some speculation of late. Rumours have surfaced in recent weeks that Manchester United are interested in making a bid for him. The *Sunday Mirror* reported that Malcolm Glazer, the new United owner, sees Ronaldo as the man to revitalise Manchester United's stuttering global profile after some below-par seasons and dull signings in recent years. This would not only afford us the mouth-watering prospect of him pairing up with the Scouse genius Wayne Rooney, but would also tally with Ronaldo's stated desire to end his playing days in 'an English-speaking country'. With the standing ovation he received after his hat-trick at Old Trafford in 2003 still a fond memory, it is a scenario that could prove to be more than mere tabloid speculation. Both Milan clubs have also been mooted as possible destinations.

So, as a footballer, where does he now stand? This, as with all such discussions, is a matter of opinion. Ronaldinho is deservedly the incumbent World Player of the Year after a dynamic second season with Barcelona, and comparisons with Ronaldo and other Brazilian legends are justified. He is currently enjoying the form of his life at Barcelona and playing superbly in a superb side. He has rightly won many plaudits for his effervescent displays, and has recently been named FIFA World Player of the Year for the second year running. Not bad for a 25 year old, but, don't forget, Ronaldo had two on his mantelpiece by the time he was 21. Zinedine Zidane has had a quiet year by his own standards and is surely in the autumn of a wonderful, trophy-laden career. In his prime, his technique was so good and loving, he seemed to treat the ball as if it was stuffed with fifty-pound notes, but now, alas, his velvet showmanship seems to be on the wane. He too has been touched with a thick coat of genius, and, like Ronaldo, he has done it on the biggest of stages when it matters most.

For exhilaration, few can match an on-song Thierry Henry of Arsenal, who just seems to get better and better. At times, his play in the Premiership is reminiscent of Ronaldo's insultingly brilliant season at Barcelona. Henry's story is a curious one, as, unlike most other wonderful players, he seems to have acquired his magic as he's gone along. At Juventus, he was an also-ran and surplus to requirements, a peripheral figure on the left wing, only to be astutely plucked out by Arsenal coach Arséne Wenger. Since then, his career and his football have been a coruscating joy; but doubts remain as to his overall contribution at the highest level for France.

As for Ronaldo, I'll let you decide. I merely hope I have given you an accurate picture of his glittering achievements to date. For me, he stands alone. He and Zidane are perhaps the two most deeply respected footballers in the current game, and, in Ronaldo's case, Ronaldinho himself, Zlatan Ibrahimovic and Carlos Tevez are just three of a list of players who name Ronaldo as their idol. Not Cruyff or Pelé or Maradona, but Ronaldo. I think that says a lot. Ronaldinho illustrated his admiration to *World Soccer* magazine recently by saying, 'Ronaldo is the master, the eternal number one. In my opinion, he is still the best in the world.'

As Carlos Queiroz alluded to, ex-Real coach Vicente del Bosque had a marvellous description of Ronaldo that, in del Bosque's curious avuncular way, sums him up superbly. He told Spain's *AS* magazine, 'Ronaldo is different to all other footballers. Other footballers are fast without the ball but then slow when they get it. Ronaldo, he is the opposite. He is incredible.'

My favourite testimony, though, comes from Argentine superstar Gabriel 'Batigol' Batistuta. Batistuta, no slouch himself, told the Italian press what he thought of Ronaldo, saying, 'For me, Ronaldo *is* football.' I'm sure any footballer would aspire to that tribute.

LOOKING AHEAD

In conclusion, Ronaldo remains a hugely likeable, straightforward and honest chap who is blessed with fabulous footballing gifts, plus that other great human gift: humility. He doesn't refer to himself in the third person, nor does he pontificate about who his 'rightful successor' is, unlike some South American legends that spring to mind. He plays football in that joyous Brazilian way and has shown that the beautiful game is a perfume that you can't share with others without first splashing a few drops on yourself. He likes enjoying himself, but then don't we all? He's made some daft, ill-advised comments over the years, and, of late, his weight has been on the bulky side. But he has never stopped scoring goals. At Barcelona, where his play was at its most entrancing, he was the perfect footballing alloy of speed, technique and belief. He easily located the door marked greatness and walked right through it, only to later have it slammed back in his face by a uniquely awful knee injury. But he vowed to return, and he did so with his magnum opus at the pinnacle of world soccer at Japan and Korea 2002, and since then he has been irresistible at Real Madrid.

He has demonstrated that the gravity of genius cannot be defied forever.

EPILOGUE

As you will have seen, this book was written primarily from a football fan's perspective. For me, Ronaldo's play encapsulates all that is great about football and it is somehow no surprise that he is Brazilian too. The story of his recovery just adds to the lustre.

I've thoroughly enjoyed researching this book, travelling around Europe and then spending time in the marvellous city of Rio writing it. To everyone in Rio, it's been a ball. *Muito obrigado tudo mundo! Estou com saudades para vôces!*

On the whole, people have been tremendously forthcoming with their assistance and comments, and it has been fascinating to see the universal admiration for Ronaldo; I do not recall any negativity, which is surely a first for a modern footballer. My only regret through the whole experience is that, after numerous assurances from Ronaldo's press office, several scheduled meetings with Ronaldo were cancelled at the last minute and I was unable to meet Ronaldo himself. Ironically, you could say I found him as elusive as the world's best defenders have done! It would have been great to meet the phenomenon in person and thank him for all the pleasure he has given. I hereby do so.

James Mosley

APPENDICES

RONALDO'S GOAL-SCORING RECORD

Club football

Season	Team	Country	League		Cup		Europe	
			Apps	Goals	Apps	Goals	Apps	Goals
90–91	São Cristóvão*	Brazil	12	8	–	–	–	–
91–92	São Cristóvão*	Brazil	28	17	–	–	–	–
92–93	São Cristóvão*	Brazil	33	19	–	–	–	–
93–94	Cruzeiro	Brazil	54	54	6	4	–	–
94–95	PSV Eindhoven	Netherlands	33	30	3	2	2	3
95–96	PSV Eindhoven	Netherlands	13	12	1	1	5	6
96–97	Barcelona	Spain	37	34	5	9	7	5
97–98	Inter Milan	Italy	32	25	4	3	11	6
98–99	Inter Milan	Italy	19	14	2	0	6	1
99–00	Inter Milan	Italy	7	3	1	0	–	–
00–01	Inter Milan	Italy	–	–	–	–	–	–
01–02	Inter Milan	Italy	10	7	–	–	5	0
02–03	Real Madrid	Spain	31	23	1	0	10	6
03–04	Real Madrid	Spain	33	24	2	1	8	4
04–05	Real Madrid	Spain	34	20	3	1	9	3

* as an amateur

RONALDO

Brazil (source: CBF)

	Apps	Goals
1st XI (*seleçao*)	93	59
Olympic X1	9	6

HONOURS

National
2 x FIFA World Cup
2 x Copa America
1 x Confederations Cup
FIFA World Cup 2002 Golden Boot

Domestic
1 x La Liga
1 x Intercontinental Cup
1 x UEFA Cup
1 x European Cup-Winners' Cup
1 x Dutch Cup
1 x Copa Del Rey (Spain)
1 x Spanish Super Cup
2 x Pichichi Trophy (La Liga top scorer)
1 x Dutch top scorer
1 x Olympic Bronze Medal
2 x European Player of the Year
3 x FIFA World Player of the Year

BIBLIOGRAPHY

Ball, Phil, *An Englishman Abroad: Beckham's Spanish Adventure*, Ebury Press, 2004

Ball, Phil, *Morbo: The Story of Spanish Football*, WSC Books, 2003

Ball, Phil, *White Storm: 100 Years of Real Madrid*, Mainstream, 2002

Bellos, Alex, *Futebol: The Brazilian Way of Life*, Bloomsbury, 2002

Burns, Jimmy, *Barça: A People's Passion*, Bloomsbury, 1999

Burns, Jimmy, *Hand of God: The Life of Diego Maradona*, Bloomsbury, 2003

Caldera, Jorge, *Ronaldo: Gloria e Drama No Futebol Globalizado*, Editora 34, 2002

Carlin, John, *White Angels: Beckham, Real Madrid and the New Football*, Bloomsbury, 2004

Clarkson, Wensley, *Ronaldo! 21 Years of Genius and 90 Minutes that Shook the World*, Blake, 2000

Granville, Brian, *The Story of the World Cup*, Faber & Faber, 2001

Hornby, Nick, *Fever Pitch*, Indigo, 1992

King, Jeff, *Bobby Robson: High Noon – A Year at Barcelona*, Virgin, 1997

McManaman, Steve and Sarah Edworthy, *El Macca: Four Years with Real Madrid*, Simon & Schuster, 2004

Puskas, Ferenc and Karla Jamrich (ed.) and Rogan Taylor (ed.), *Puskas on Puskas: The Life and Times of a Footballing Legend*, Robson Books, 1997

Robson, Sir Bobby, *My Autobiography: An Englishman Abroad*, Pan, 1998

Periodicals consulted as references include:
AS
Champions League Magazine
Corriere della Sera
Corriere dello Sport
The Daily Telegraph
El Mundo
El Pais
Exame
Football Italia
FourFourTwo
France Football
La Gazzetta dello Sport
Marca
O Dia
O Globo
Lance! and *Lance! Revista*
The Observer
Veja
World Soccer

Websites consulted as references include:
www.as.com
http://cbfnews.uol.com.br/
www.channel4.com
www.conteudoesportivo.com.br
www.fcbarcelona.com
www.fifa.com
www.goal.com
www.inter.it
www.lfp.es
www.marca.es
www.nike.com
www.planetfootball.com
www.psv.nl
www.r9ronaldo.com
www.realmadrid.com
www.skysports.com
www.soccer-age.com
www.uefa.com

INDEX

INDEX

INDEX